I am elated to see our conservative evangelical seminaries passionately entering the worship debate with a volume of essays that is both substantial and accessible. Looking at worship with pastoral eyes, this book will surely engage not only the minds but the hearts of seminary students and pastors everywhere. Bravo!

—DR. BARRY LIESCH
author, *The New Worship*
Biola University

Exhausting battles continue to be waged over worship within our churches. Every congregation is touched by potential conflict. This scholarly work will help achieve armistice by helping educated pastors, church boards, and worship leaders think through the decisions they are being forced to make. Bateman assembles these contributions not only to help us think practically and culturally, but especially theologically. Read it carefully, thoughtfully, and with thanksgiving!

—DR. JAY A. QUINE
Dean, School of Biblical Studies,
Philadelphia Biblical University;
Senior Pastor, Calvary Bible Church,
Readington, New Jersey

Authentic Worship

To Jay!
My Friend of 20 years
and a boilder who takes
pride in his work!

Authentic Worship

Hearing Scripture's Voice,

Applying Its Truths

herbert w. bateman IV
general editor

Kregel
Academic & Professional

Authentic Worship: Hearing Scripture's Voice, Applying Its Truths

© 2002 by Herbert W. Bateman IV

Published by Kregel Publications, a division of Kregel, Inc., P.O. Box 2607, Grand Rapids, MI 49501. For more information about Kregel Publications, visit our Web site: www.kregel.com.

Scripture quotations marked NIV are from the *Holy Bible, New International Version*®. © 1973, 1978, 1984 by International Bible Society. Used by permission of Zondervan Publishing House. All rights reserved.

Scripture quotations marked KJV are from the King James version of the Holy Bible.

Scripture quotations marked RSV are from the *Revised Standard Version*. © 1946, 1952, 1971, 1973 by the Division of Christian Education of the National Council of the Churches of Christ in the United States of America.

Scripture quotations marked PHILLIPS are from *The New Testament in Modern English*. J. B. Phillips, trans. New York: Macmillan, 1958.

Unless stated otherwise by note in an essay, Scripture quotations with no version indicated are the author's translation.

Library of Congress Cataloging-in-Publication Data
Authentic worship: hearing Scripture's voice, applying its truths / Herbert W. Bateman, general editor.
        p. cm.
Includes bibliographical references and indexes.
    1. Public worship. I. Bateman, Herbert W.
BV15 .A96   2002
264—dc21   2002010414

ISBN 0-8254-2092-x

Printed in the United States of America

04 05 06 07 / 5 4 3 2

To my daughter,
Leah Marie Bateman,
who is a daily reminder
of God's grace to both
her mother and me.

Contents

Part Three: Symbols: Images of Our Worship

Conclusion

Preface

On March 23–24, 2001, Grace Theological Seminary hosted the Forty-Sixth Annual Midwest Regional Meeting of the Evangelical Theological Society on "The Worshiping Church: The Theology and Expressions of Worship for the Twenty-First Century Christian." This book, *Authentic Worship: Hearing Scripture's Voice, Applying Its Truths,* collects four plenary papers presented by two fine scholars—Richard E. Averbeck from Trinity Evangelical Divinity School and Robert E. Webber from Northern Baptist Theological Seminary. The papers have been rewritten and presented here as a unified work for worship leaders and men and women preparing for worship ministry.

Other papers, a drama, and the illustrations in this book also were presented at the meeting. Ronald E. Manahan, president of Grace College and Theological Seminary, graciously provided a rewritten copy of his opening exposition from Psalm 15. Thomas F. Atchison, pastor of Fox Valley Church, and Thomas M. Stallter, professor of intercultural studies and world missions at Grace Theological Seminary, also contributed their rewritten papers.

Finally, two students from Grace College and Seminary made contributions. Timothy D. Sprankle, a seminary student, contributed a drama he had written. Deborah Downing, a college art major, created illustrations for each plenary speaker's theme as a visual presentation. She produced three additional illustrations for use here. David P. Nelson, professor of systematic theology at Southeastern Baptist Theological Seminary, and Timothy J. Ralston, professor of pastoral ministries at Dallas Theological Seminary, also have contributed to this project.

The array of contributors captures the book's interdisciplinary spirit. Thus, worship is viewed through the eyes of a student in active pursuit of pastoral ministry, as well as from the perspectives of specialists in worship and cross-cultural value systems; theologians; and Old and New Testament scholars, all of whom have led local church worship ministries. Together they address issues of worship pertinent to worship leaders and worshipers.

I wish to thank the churches that have directly formed my appreciation for authentic worship. They served as catalysts for this book. In addition, I express gratitude to the Evangelical Theological Society. Established in 1949, the society fosters biblical scholarship among evangelicals. While denominational loyalties and doctrinal orientations are diverse, we all agree to these two doctrinal beliefs: "The Bible alone, and the Bible in its entirety, is the Word of God written and is therefore inerrant in the autographs," and "God is a Trinity, Father, Son, and Holy Spirit, each an uncreated person, one in essence, equal in power and glory."[1] I am grateful that this society provides a medium for oral exchange and written expression of thought and research in the general field of theological disciplines as centered in the Scriptures. Finally, I offer a special thanks to Kregel Publications for their willingness to publish this work and for suggestions that helped gather these presentations into a cohesive whole.

Thanks also go to participants at the conference, my fellow officers of the Midwest region (Gary Meadors and Julius Scott), the men and women who presented papers, Grace Brass, and

---

[1] Both the Purpose and Doctrinal Basis of the society are stated on the inside cover of the quarterly *JETS*.

the King's Strings (Leah Bateman, Ryan Edgington, Danielle Mowrey, and Judie Meulink). I want also to express my gratitude to the host of the conference, Grace Theological Seminary, and the many people who helped make the conference a success, specifically, Paul DeRenzo, Shirley Mackey, Skip Forbes, Vicky Decker, and Jon Varnell.

Finally, I want to thank my wife, Cindy, and, especially, my daughter Leah, who sacrificed in many ways, most significantly my presence at home during most of the 2001–2002 academic school year, so that I could take part in the University of Notre Dame's Visiting Scholar Program to complete this and other projects.

—HERBERT W. BATEMAN IV

Contributors

THOMAS F. ATCHISON is pastor of Fox Valley Church, an Evangelical Free Church in West Dundee, Illinois, and has a Ph.D. in theological studies from Trinity Evangelical Divinity School. When he arrived at Fox Valley in 1993, the church was essentially a traditional congregation of around 120 people. Today, he leads a blended worship service of some five hundred people.

RICHARD E. AVERBECK teaches Old Testament and semitic languages at Trinity Evangelical Divinity School as well as directs the Center for Personal and Relational Growth of the Bannockburn Institute, which develops spiritual formation ministries in evangelical Christian organizations. As an author, he has contributed to *Cracking Old Testament Codes, New International Dictionary of Old Testament Theology,* and *Evangelical Dictionary of Biblical Theology and Exegesis.*

HERBERT W. BATEMAN IV is professor of New Testament studies at Grace Theological Seminary. His passion for, commitment to, and leading of worship in the local church over the years has served as the catalyst for this work. He is the author of *Early Jewish Hermeneutics and Hebrews 1:5–13* and general editor and contributing author to *Three Central Issues of Contemporary Dispensationalism.*

RONALD E. MANAHAN is president and professor of Old Testament studies at Grace College and Theological Seminary. His attention to Old Testament scholarship and his heart for pastoral ministry are evident as a lecturer, author, and planter of two churches. As an author, he has contributed to *The Environment and the Christian.*

DAVID P. NELSON is assistant professor of systematic theology at Southeastern Baptist Theological Seminary. He has more than fifteen years of experience in worship leadership in local churches and also supervises music for the Southeastern Baptist Seminary Chapel. He has contributed to *Looking into the Future.*

TIMOTHY J. RALSTON is professor of pastoral ministries at Dallas Theological Seminary where he teaches courses on preaching, congregational worship, spiritual life/direction, and a Christian philosophy of art. He is a specialist in New Testament manuscripts and their textual tradition and a member of the North American Academy of Liturgy.

TIMOTHY D. SPRANKLE is a Grace Theological Seminary student preparing for pastoral ministry. As a leading member of the student-led and student-directed drama group of Grace College and Seminary, he authored, directed, and performed dramas in church and parachurch organizations. He is also the recipient of Grace College's Biblical Studies and New Testament Greek Award.

THOMAS M. STALLTER is professor of intercultural studies and world missions at Grace Theological Seminary. With seventeen years of intercultural ministry and mission work in the Central African Republic and Chad, doing social and cultural research, he actively serves as the seminar leader for Intercultural Cooperation Seminars, which offers an alternative to typical diversity training based on value systems awareness.

ROBERT E. WEBBER is the director of the Institute for Worship Studies and Myers Professor of Ministry at Northern Baptist Seminary. Although his discipline is historical theology, he conducts workshops on worship with nearly every major Christian denomination, ministry, and fellowship in North America. He is the author of more than a dozen books in the field of worship, including *Worship Old and New, Worship Is a Verb,* and editor of the eight-volume work *The Complete Library of Christian Worship.*

Abbreviations

AB	Anchor Bible
ABD	*Anchor Bible Dictionary.* Edited by D. N. Freedman. 6 vols. New York, 1992.
ANET	*Ancient Near Eastern Texts Relating to the Old Testament.* Edited by J. B. Pritchard. 3d ed. Princeton, 1969.
ANF	*Ante-Nicene Fathers*
BDAG	W. Bauer, F. Danker, W. F. Arndt, and F. W. Gingrich. *A Greek-English Lexicon of the New Testament and Other Early Christian Literature.* 3d ed. Chicago, 1999.
BHK	*Biblia Hebraica.* Edited by R. Kittel. Stuttgart, 1905–1906, 1925^2, 1937^3, 1951^4, 1973^{16}.
BHS	*Biblia Hebraica Stuttgartensia.* Edited by K. Elliger and W. Rudolph. Stuttgart, 1983.
BO	*Bibliotheca orientalis*
BSac	*Bibliotheca sacra*
CCCM	Corpus Christianorum: Continuatio mediaevalis. Turnhout, 1969–.
ChrTo	*Christianity Today*
EDNT	*Exegetical Dictionary of the New Testament.* Edited by H. Balz, G. Schneider. English Translation. Grand Rapids, 1990–1993.

EDSS	*Encyclopedia of the Dead Sea Scrolls*
ESV	The Holy Bible, English Standard Version. Copyright © 2001 by Crossway Bibles, a division of Good News Publishers. All rights reserved.
ETS	Evangelical Theological Society
EvQ	*Evangelical Quarterly*
GTJ	*Grace Theological Journal*
HTR	*Harvard Theological Review*
IBC	Interpretation: A Bible Commentary for Teaching and Preaching
JETS	*Journal of the Evangelical Theological Society*
JTS	*Journal of Theological Studies*
JW	*Jewish Wars*
KJV	King James Version
LCC	The Library of Christian Classics
LXX	Septuagint
MSJ	*The Master's Seminary Journal*
NASB	New American Standard Bible
NICOT	New International Commentary on the New Testament
NIDOTTE	*New International Dictionary of Old Testament Theology and Exegesis.* Edited by W. A. VanGemeren. 5 vols. Grand Rapids, 1997.
NIGTC	New International Greek Testament Commentary
NIV	New International Version
NLT	New Living Translation
NPNF[1]	*Nicene and Post-Nicene Fathers,* Series 1
NPNF[2]	*Nicene and Post-Nicene Fathers,* Series 2
NRSV	New Revised Standard Version
NT	New Testament
OT	Old Testament
PG	Patrologia graeca [= Patrologiae cursus completus: Series graeca]. Edited by J. P. Migne. 162 vols. Paris, 1857–1886.
PHILLIPS	*The New Testament in Modern English,* J. B. Phillips

PL	Patrologia latina [= Patrologiae cursus completus: Series latina]. Edited by J. P. Migne. 217 vols. Paris, 1844–1864.
ResQ	*Restoration Quarterly*
RSV	Revised Standard Version
TDNT	*Theological Dictionary of the New Testament.* Edited by G. Kittel and G. Friedrich. Translated by G. W. Bromiley. 10 vols. Grand Rapids, 1964–1976.
TDOT	*Theological Dictionary of the Old Testament.* Edited by G. J. Botterweck and H. Ringgren. Translated by J. T. Willis, G. W. Bromiley, and D. E. Green. 8 vols. Grand Rapids, 1974–.
TJ	*Trinity Journal*
TS	*Theological Studies*
TSR	*Trinity Seminary Review*
Vg.	Latin Vulgate Bible
VT	*Vetus Testamentum*
WBC	Word Biblical Commentary
Yhwh	*Yahweh*
ZAW	*Zeitschrift für die alttestamentliche Wissenschaft*

INTRODUCTION

CHAPTER ONE

A Call for Authentic Worship

Herbert W. Bateman IV

One of the pivotal issues around which church life moves concerns the understanding and praxis of worship. Throughout Scripture, God desires that his people worship him, celebrate him, and memorialize him. In fact, the Westminster Confession of Faith rightly acknowledges that "The First Commandment teaches us *whom* we are to worship. We are to worship the true God only." "The Third Commandment teaches us *who* they are that worship God. They are those who profess his name (take his name) with true sincerity of heart."[1]

Were we to ask any evangelical Christian today, "Is any sort of religious honor to be given to anyone besides God?" the resounding answer we would receive is, "No!" Some might even confess that the sole reason we exist, the sole function of the church, is to worship and enjoy the one true God. Yet, A. W. Tozer's extremely penetrating question continues to echo in our sanctuaries, "Whatever happened to worship?"

Prior to his death in 1963, Tozer expressed the opinion that "worship acceptable to God is the missing crown jewel in

---

[1] G. I. Williamson, *The Westminster Confession of Faith for Study Classes* (Philadelphia: Presbyterian and Reformed, 1980), 138.

evangelical Christianity."[2] Even with the increasing number of
books about worship, seminars on worship, and priority given
to worship, have we located the crown jewel? Despite the
progress that has been made since 1963, participation in worship
has been a source of strain in many established church
communities. Discontentment and disillusionment exist over
issues of worship, and thus, many would-be worshipers have
slipped away from or wandered away from worshiping God
only. For instance, as you read "The Vertical View," ask yourself,
"Does this sound like my church?"

> There once was a church upon a hill
> Where everything was fine until
> Some of the family wanted something new;
> Which made other Holy siblings mumble and stew.
>
> The pastor called a business meeting
> And after the church's traditional seating
> The deacons cried, "Come one, come all. . . .
> What style of worship should fill this hall?"
>
> Traditional, blended or contemporary,
> Each was determined and contrary.
> One lady said about the hymns, "They're so pretty.
> Good enough for Saint Peter, good enough for me."
>
> Little James he was called although he was quite old
> Said, "Aren't the hymnals getting too hard to hold?
> I visited a church within this past year.
> They projected their words on a screen in the air."

---

[2] A. W. Tozer, *Whatever Happened to Worship? A Call to True Worship,* ed. G. B.
Smith (Camp Hill, Pa.: Christian Publications, 1985), 7.

Yet another had visited a newer church plant.
And this was his view on what was their slant.
"They had a band and a neat little keyboard
That when it was played, boy did it roar.
The performances were slick,
The routines they were polished.
The drama brought the point home,
And the bulletin was abolished."

"I'll not hear the organ, I won't see the cross,
With this I am not happy," stated Miss Ross.
From that point on their voices grew stronger
Each emotional plea became longer and longer.

Then a voice of strong and stern love
Silenced the meeting as He spoke from above.

"You come to the church weekly to meet Me here
But instead of pleasing Me, you are pleasing your peers.
The music, the robes, the organ, the patter
These things, to Me, just really don't matter.

I am Who I am, and I made you like Me.
'Remember your Maker' is My worship decree.
I sacrificed My Son, I turned from Myself
So what does it matter what's on what shelf?

On Me set your mind, To Me please draw near,
Then the blessings of heaven around you'll appear.
You give many renditions of church as a game
But you fail to give water in My Holy Name.

You pray using eloquent Thee's and Thou's
And yet you forget the here's and the now's.
Your worship is not tied to a style or a post.
Heart to heart meeting is what I love most.

You struggle to have many think well of you

In so doing you forget to keep the Vertical view.[3]

If you conclude that this poem epitomizes a present conflict of worship in the church you attend or lead, restrain yourself, refrain from packing up your Bibles, and remain in your pew or position of leadership. "Conflicts over worship in general and music in particular have erupted in churches of every denomination," says Michael Hamilton. "All over North America," he continues, "worship has become contested ground." "For better or worse, the kind of music a church offers increasingly defines the kind of person who will attend, because *for this generation music is at the very center of self-understanding.*"[4] His point is this, whether boomer, preboomer (builders, ca. 1925–45), or postboomer (busters, ca. 1965–85), music has become the very center of our self-understanding. Thus, battles abound over music, which polarize many of us away from harmonious exaltations of our God.

Notably, music is a dynamic aspect of worship. Between 40 and 60 percent of any given worship service today involves music. Music, however, is not to be equated with worship. Authentic worship involves all worthy activities such as praying, reading Scripture, reciting creeds, giving gifts, listening and responding to a sermon, using symbols and drama, and, yes, listening and singing to music. Yet, due to generational self-understandings attached to music, many battle lines are being drawn over this one aspect of worship, which hinders harmonious community worship, worship that is acceptable to God. What will it take to lower defenses, create peace, and mobilize for worship acceptable to God?

---

[3] "The Vertical View," adapted from Matt Tullos, "Paint on the Wall," in *Scripts to Reach In and Out,* comp. Gail Blanton (Nashville: Convention, 1993), 141–42.
[4] Michael S. Hamilton, "The Triumph of the Praise Songs: How Guitars Beat Out the Organ in the Worship Wars," in *ChrTo* (12 July 1999): 29–35.

Authentic Worship: Hearing Scripture's Voice, Applying Its Truths takes up the gauntlet to help in reestablishing the evangelical church's crown jewel, namely, worship that is acceptable to God. First, it underscores what authentic worship is from Scripture. Second, it confronts thoughts and attitudes of a worshiper in an attempt to generate a harmonious atmosphere for cross-generational worship in established evangelical churches presently warring over various musical expressions. Finally, it calls attention to the use of three significant symbols as visual, physical, and tangible images that heighten the atmosphere for authentic worship and enhance the spiritual formation of the worshiper.

This chapter, however, not only introduces the collected contributions of the distinguished authors of this book but also contributes to the discussion by first sketching an obtrusive cultural mind-set that prevents evangelical communities from partnering in authentic worship. Second, it calls for a theologically based mind-set for community partnership *(koinonia)* in authentic worship that, if practiced, will resolve the prolonged wars that presently occur in many cross-generational evangelical churches today. The solution, however, is easier said than done. Nevertheless, it must be done if we are to reestablish our crown jewel as an evangelical church committed to worshiping God.

By way of introducing part one of this book, "God: The Object of Our Worship," I will sketch what many believe to be an obtrusive cultural mind-set that prevents evangelical communities from exercising authentic worship. I submit that authentic worship is hindered severely because more and more evangelicals have a Bob Wiley mind-set when it comes to worship.

The Mind of Bob Wiley

One of our family pastimes is collecting, watching, and rewatching video movies. As a result, we thoroughly enjoy gathering together on Friday evenings as a family, eating popcorn or pizza, and watching a movie video. One of our favorites is

What About Bob? with Bill Murray and Richard Dreyfuss. Bill
Murray plays a fellow named Bob Wiley. He is a troubled but
lovable patient who fears everything. He's afraid of leaving his
apartment. He's afraid of touching doorknobs. He's afraid of
shaking hands. He's afraid of riding in elevators. He's afraid of
riding buses. Essentially, he's afraid of everything.

After seeking help from noted psychiatrist Dr. Leo Marvin,
played by Richard Dreyfuss, Bob feels relieved. He believes
strongly that Dr. Marvin can help him. But when the good doctor attempts to take his family on a quiet vacation, Bob, afraid
of being alone, discovers where Dr. Marvin is vacationing and
follows. When Bob shows up unexpectedly at the lakeside town
of Lake Winnipesaukee, where Dr. Marvin and his family have
retreated, the doctor is appalled. Dr. Marvin tells Bob several
times to go home. The good doctor appears determined not to
allow Bob Wiley to interrupt his vacation. He tries to refuse to
succumb to Bob's selfish demand for attention.

Bob Wiley, however, is not put off. His persistence for Dr.
Marvin's attention eventually ends with—"Gimme! Gimme!
Gimme! I need! I need! I need!" At which point, Dr. Marvin
gives in to this obviously childish outbreak and selfish insistence.
He agrees to meet Bob's demand to have *his* needs met—to get
what *he* wants. Bob Wiley is a self-absorbed, self-centered, and
self-seeking character. But he is not alone. As the character of
Leo Marvin is developed, we come to realize that he suffers the
same affliction. It's a hilarious movie about two self-absorbed
individuals. Both need help, but only one of them realizes the
need for it.

Unfortunately and not so hilariously, Bob Wiley and Leo
Marvin typify the individualistic, self-engrossed, and narcissistic culture that permeates our North American society, particularly here in the United States[5] and that sadly enough has

---

[5] For a non-Christian perspective on American narcissism, see Robert N.
Bellah, *Habits of the Heart: Individualism and Commitment in American Life*
(New York: Harper and Row, 1985).

penetrated our evangelical churches. The evangelical community has not impeded its narcissistic culture; rather, our narcissistic culture has impregnated the evangelical church. Although many books on worship published during the 1990s identify this contemporary issue in various ways, I will direct attention to the infiltration and infection of narcissism in our evangelical churches on two levels.

The Infiltration of Narcissism in Marketing Worship

First, our self-engrossed culture has infiltrated the marketing of worship. One particularly alarmed author, Marva Dawn, contends that many contemporary worship services "dumb faith down" to attract the self-absorbed. "Perhaps the most dangerous of the subtle influences on contemporary worship practices," says Dawn, "is the self-centered bent of the modern world"—caused by society streams (i.e., technology, boomer, and postmodern culture) and idolatries (i.e., money, traditionalism, celebrities, numbers and success, power, etc.).[6] From Dawn's perspective, the self-centered bent of the world has infiltrated many of our evangelical communities. Much of Dawn's concern is directed at the market-driven or commodity-like contemporary worship services and the recent preoccupation to turn worship services into evangelistic growth services.[7]

C. S. Lewis expresses a similar concern. While commenting on what appeared to him as a *preoccupation* with applying novel techniques to lure people into the church, Lewis says, "'Tis mad idolatry that makes the service greater than the god."[8] Neither

---

[6] Marva J. Dawn, *Reaching Out Without Dumbing Down: A Theology of Worship for the Turn-of-the-Century Culture* (Grand Rapids: Eerdmans, 1995), 107.

[7] Marva J. Dawn develops her thoughts on worship and evangelism in: "Is There a Connection Between Worship and Evangelism?" *TSR* 22 (fall/winter 2000–2001): 97–108.

[8] Lyle W. Dorsett, *The Essential C. S. Lewis* (New York: Simon and Schuster, 1996), 407–8.

Dawn nor Lewis is suggesting, however, that we refrain from developing ways to enhance our worship of God. The problem is on *preoccupation* with a service *to lure people into the church* and the various methods employed that "dumb down" the church due to the self-centered bent of society rather than the focus on God, the one whom we have been called to worship.

Although Dawn, like Lewis, tends to favor a liturgical form of worship, she speaks directly against the infiltration of narcissism in marketing worship for the self-centered masses because it misses the point of worship. Authentic worship for Dawn must involve *encountering the subject,* namely, God in worship; it must involve *forming Christian character;* and it must involve *building Christian community.* Whether we agree entirely with Dawn's definition of authentic worship, her overall concern is worth reflection. "When we allow our society to force us to 'dumb down' the Church, we kill theological training, inhibit the forming of character, prevent appreciation for the rich gifts of the Church's past. Most of all we miss the infinitely faceted grandeur of God and destroy the awe and wonder that characterized worship before God became only a 'buddy' ill-conceived and only subjectively experienced."[9] Thus, our narcissistic manner of marketing worship as well as our egalitarian tendencies have reduced God, the Infinite-Creator-Redeemer God, to be our buddy.

Another concerned author, Sally Morgenthaler, muses, "We are not producing worshipers in this country. Rather, we are producing a generation of spectators, religious onlookers lacking, in many cases, any memory of a true encounter with God, deprived of both the tangible sense of God's presence and the supernatural relationship their inmost spirits crave."[10] Granted, Morgenthaler addresses worship issues very differently from Dawn. Morgenthaler wants pastors to reexamine, rethink, and reform worship services that involve participation of both be-

---

[9] Dawn, *Reaching Out Without Dumbing Down,* 55.
[10] Sally Morgenthaler, *Worship Evangelism: Inviting Unbelievers into the Presence of God* (1995; reprint, Grand Rapids: Zondervan, 1999), 17.

liever and nonbeliever alike in worship. Nevertheless, both women recognize the infiltration and narcissistic bent of today's evangelical worshiper. Looking at the narcissistic issue from Morgenthaler's perspective, "The sad truth is we born-again Christians [evangelicals] are an essentially insulated, narcissistic subculture, involving ourselves with very few people outside our own churches."[11]

Has North America's self-engrossed, narcissistic way of life infiltrated and stolen the crown jewel from the evangelical church we attend or lead? Regardless of whether we attend or lead a liturgical, traditional, contemporary, neocontemporary, or blended worship service, is my church market-commodity driven? When we go to our place of worship, are our thoughts and attitudes *preoccupied* with the form of worship, the style of music, or the preaching of Scripture to lure in people? Am I preoccupied with appeasing builder, boomer, or busters' likes and dislikes? These questions are not to minimize or de-emphasize helping individuals to have a personal encounter with God in a community gathering for worship. In his book *Worship Is a Verb*, Webber rightly recognizes that "worship calls for the involvement of our mind, body and soul. Worship demands nothing less than the complete, conscious, and deliberate participation of the worshiper."[12] As worship leaders, we need to create ways for the worshiper to participate in worship so that corporately we all engage and experience God.

In summary, authentic worship is not a commodity; it is not a preoccupation with luring people into our service; and it is not a preoccupation with satisfying or appeasing generational likes and dislikes. Authentic worship is first and foremost about God. So, as a pastor who wants to help individuals have a personal encounter with God, what should be my concern? To begin with,

---

[11] Ibid., 27.

[12] Robert E. Webber, *Worship Is a Verb* (Waco: Word, 1985), 12. Webber's book is organized around eight basic worship principles, with a study guide after each principle. It encourages church leaders who wish to experience worship renewal to take a second look at liturgical aspects of worship.

we need to know what a worshiper is. In other words, what does a worshiper involved in authentic worship look like? In chapter 2 of this book, "The Worshiper's Approach to God," Ronald Manahan, president of Grace College and Seminary, focuses our attention on a biblical portrayal from Psalm 15 of a worshiper who wishes to approach God in authentic worship. It confronts the thoughts, attitudes, and behaviors of a person who desires to enter into the presence of God.

The Infection of Narcissism in Preaching

Second, our self-engrossed culture also affects our approach to Scripture. Attempts to see ourselves in all of Scripture not only infects the way we study the Bible at home and teach the Bible in Sunday school, but more harmfully it infects the way the Bible is preached during worship. Walt Russell rightly recognizes that "many of us [pastors are obviously included] view the world in narcissistically wounded categories that assume every passage in the Bible is about us. Fortunately," Russell continues, "God has a grand plan that He is revealing in the Bible that encompasses insight into ourselves but that plan doesn't rotate around that knowledge. Indeed, *most passages in the Bible are about things other than us!*"[13]

Evidence of Russell's observation exists in Blount's book, *What Jesus Taught About Praise and Worship*. Though a sensitive, well intentioned, and gifted contemporary Christian artist, Ken Blount erroneously draws reasons from James 1:22–25 for seeing *ourselves* in all of Scripture. "We look into God's word," he emphasizes, *"to see who we are and what Jesus has done for us . . . to see what we need to correct."*[14] Blount obviously loves God and uses the Bible regularly to see him through difficult life situa-

---

[13] Walt Russell, *Playing with Fire: How the Bible Ignites Change in Your Soul* (Colorado Springs: NavPress, 2000), 42.

[14] Ken Blount, *What Jesus Taught About Praise and Worship: Following the Savior into the Presence of God* (Tulsa: Harrison House, 2000), 75.

tions. Nevertheless, his understanding of Scripture results in frequent misinterpretations and misapplications, two of which I will cite. First, "When we are asking God for something in line with His word," (e.g., based upon the jot and tittle of Matt. 5:18) Blount contends, "the smallest details [of our prayers] must come to pass in our lives."[15] Unfortunately, the passage has nothing to do with prayer or a believer's prayer life. Jesus' deliberate use of overstatement (hyperbole) in Matthew 5:18 declares that the law will be fully preserved as Jesus presents, interprets, and teaches it.

Second, "When a believer is filled with the Spirit," according to Blount's application of Ephesians 5:18, "he can get real answers to the challenges he faces [in life], because he is in communion and fellowship with God."[16] Within its context, however, Ephesians 5:18 *instructs* believers to live wisely, which involves yielding to the Holy Spirit. This in turn impacts our inner being in such a way that it affects how we relate with one another (v. 19). Ephesians 5:18 has absolutely nothing to do with getting answers to life.

Blount, however, is not alone in his misuse of Scripture. We all have wrongly used and abused Scripture because we have viewed it as a book about *me,* especially during tough times of life. But *the Bible is not about me.*

The realization that our narcissistic cultural orientation infects many who read, study, and teach Scripture alarms me because more and more well-intentioned students, in their genuine desire to enter teaching/preaching ministries as quickly as possible, shortcut their educational foundation. Their awareness of and knowledgeable use of equipment necessary for biblically informed learning is missing from their toolboxes for ministry. Students forge ahead in master degree programs that merely survey Jewish history, literature, and culture; minimize and possibly ignore study in biblical Hebrew, Greek, and literary genres;

---

[15] Ibid., 35.
[16] Ibid., 103–4.

and shortcut theological and intercultural study. Thus, they are not licensed builders, skilled technicians, and masters of their trade but self-taught handymen and women, who are more apt to violate codes of interpretation and thereby read, study, teach, and preach Scripture as though it is mainly about the student.

Russell points to several passages that have been preached from a culturally self-engrossed perspective, rather than from a biblically informed perspective (Deut. 28:2–14; Judg. 6:36–40; Matt. 16:24–25; 18:19–20). He rightly recognizes that God's intended truth has been delivered by various human authors through various literary packaging of God's truth, and he addresses carefully how to approach each genre in Scripture for the spiritual formation of the believer. For instance, his third point about gospel study is quite simply that, "The Focus of the Gospel is on Jesus, not us!" Russell continues to build his case when he muses,

> It is almost embarrassing to have to make this statement, but it is absolutely necessary. Why? Because the increasing tendency in our reading of the Gospels is to reduce them primarily to sources of insight about ourselves. For example, we read about Jesus calming a storm on the Sea of Galilee, and we think it is about the storms of our lives. Or read about Jesus being rejected by His friends and family in the Nazareth synagogue (Luke 4:16–30), and we think it is primarily about our possible rejection by those around us when we take a stand for Christ. Or we read in John 6:1–15 about Jesus miraculously feeding the five thousand in the wilderness with the boy's five barley loaves and two fishes, and we think it is about what we should be giving to Jesus! You get the idea.
>
> While this tendency is both a problem of our worldview glasses and a symptom of our narcissistic woundedness, its impact is still tragically the same: We end up knowing more about ourselves and less about Jesus. We become theologically impoverished in our knowledge about the only One who can really trans-

form us! We become ignorant of our Master, whom we should be seeking to please with all our being.

Perhaps a word of balance should be appropriate here. When I say that the Gospels are about Jesus, this does not mean they do not give us any insight into ourselves or have significance and application to our lives. Of course they do. However, the Gospels were primarily written to tell us about who Jesus is, what He did, and why He is the only, true object of our faith. If we change this focus, we destroy the very essence of the Gospels. By making the Gospels more about ourselves, we ironically lessen their transforming impact on our lives, because the more we learn about Jesus Christ, the more we will entrust ourselves to Him as His disciples.[17]

Russell's point is simply this: many evangelical Christians approach Scripture with self-absorbed thoughts and attitudes. As a result, Scripture reading and preaching with North American cultural self-fixations yield *me*-oriented religious expectations, namely, subjective interpretations that are then wrongly applied. *Me*-oriented fixations of interpretation are not to shape God's truth.

In my mind, preaching that causes people to focus attention on *my* needs, *my* desires, *my* troubles, and *my* wants when the text says something else reflects the infectious wounds of our narcissistic culture. It prevents the worshiper from learning to know Christ, living for Christ, and leading others to be disciples of Christ. As Webber has come to realize, "worship is a celebration of the Christ-event, his life, death, and resurrection . . . a celebration that puts me in touch with the *truth that shapes my whole life,* and I have found it to be *a necessary element for my own spiritual formation.*"[18] Thus, if the God and Christ of Scripture is not preached, it cripples the worshiper's ability from having a true

---

[17] Russell, *Playing with Fire,* 204–5.
[18] Webber, *Worship Is a Verb,* 27 (emphasis mine).

spiritual encounter with God because what we know about God affects how we worship and how we live for him. God wants worshipers who will worship him in spirit and truth (John 4:24).

In chapters 3 and 4 of this work, Richard Averbeck, associate professor of Old Testament and semitic languages at Trinity Evangelical Divinity School, presents a biblical theology of worship. His chapters provide a theological basis to help shift the evangelical worship service from a narcissistic-driven service to one driven by "Worshiping God in Spirit" and "Worshiping God in Truth." Although many books on worship talk about worshiping God "in spirit and truth," few tell us what that means biblically. Averbeck, however, demonstrates that authentic worship involves a divine/human dynamic, a spiritual exchange between God and his people, which is based upon truth in spirit, truth in action, and truth in word. Authentic worship "in spirit and truth" enables today's worshipers to know, engage, and experience God. Church communities that focus their attention on worshiping God "in spirit and truth" will not only know and experience God during a worship hour, but such attention will impact the spiritual formation of Christ Jesus' disciples in everyday life.

In conclusion, our cultural orientation tends to be *I* or *me* driven. Like our culture, many evangelicals are screaming, "Gimme! Gimme! Gimme! I need! I need! I need!" In many cases, the cries have caused (1) the infiltration of narcissism to market worship to the masses at God's expense and (2) the infection of narcissism in the self-fixatious preaching of Scripture at the worshiper's expense of knowing and engaging God. As a result, these two narcissistic preoccupations prevent today's evangelical church from repositioning its crown jewel.

Authentic worship is not about satisfying *specific generational likes* and fixations on *individualized wants*. Authentic worship is about finite beings entering into the presence of the Infinite, it is about created beings encountering their Creator-Redeemer, and it is about a *corporate community* of professing believers who participate in expressing their feelings and celebrating the triune God in both Spirit/spirit and truth regularly. Morgenthaler says it this way: "Real [authentic] worship is a lot more than this week's production. It is where we allow the supernatural God of Scripture to show up and to interact with people in the pews."[19] Thus, part one of *Authentic Worship* is devoted to focusing our attention on the object of our worship, God.

Part two, "Music: Expressions of Our Worship," addresses another contemporary issue in evangelical churches that has detracted many of us from generating worship acceptable to God. Whereas chapters 2 through 4 apply to all evangelical churches today, chapters 5 through 7 are written for cross-generational evangelical churches presently struggling with musical expressions of worship. Though not intentional, this section may reflect my preference of worship, which perhaps is the hardest form to first establish and then to retain. Admittedly, I *prefer* diverse expressions of music in worship. This section, however, is not a theological endorsement for blended worship, regardless of my preference. Rather it is a call for unity despite the cross-generational diversity of musical preferences that exist in many established evangelical churches today.

When music is at the very center of our self-understanding, how do we allow for diverse musical expressions in any given worship service? How does a community build an atmosphere for expressing authentic worship that takes into consideration the diverse musical preferences within a cross-generational community of believers? How might individuals reflect what they believe about God by participating in the variety of musical expressions chosen for any given worship gathering? In the section that follows, a theological premise is provided, oddly enough through an ancient hymn, for transforming the minds of people (1) who love the Lord, (2) who belong to an established cross-generational evangelical community where a diversity of preferences exist over musical expressions of worship, and (3) *who want to remain together.* Thus, I submit the answer lies in our developing and emulating the mind of Christ.

---

[19] Morgenthaler, *Worship Evangelism*, 25.

The Mind of Christ Jesus

The Philippians' continual participation in the gospel, God's perpetual working in their lives (past, present, and future), and their willingness to be partners in Paul's ministry and suffering for the gospel explain why he immediately expresses his gratitude and affection for them (1:5–8). Paul's letter to them, written from Rome while anticipating his release from house arrest (2:23–24), reveals that the Philippians are an extremely precious community of believers. And though Paul is desirous of death and entrance into Christ's presence, he recognizes his earthly existence as necessary to increase this particular community's confidence in the Lord Jesus (1:21–26), specifically as it concerns their stance against *aggression from without* and *division from within*.

First, Paul appeals to the community of believers to live Christ-honoring lives that will withstand *aggression from without* (1:27–30). He says to "conduct yourselves in a manner worthy of the gospel of Christ." According to Paul, a community living Christ-honoring lives portrays a confident and unified stance before those who oppose the gospel of Christ Jesus as well as signals to other believers that their salvation, which involves suffering, is from God. Whoever these opponents are, they disrupt the church with their "selfish ambition" (1:15),[20] they add to and thereby are enemies of the gospel message (3:2–3, 18), and they are condemned to eternal destruction (1:28; 3:18–19).[21] Because opponents of Christianity continue to flourish, Paul's

---

[20] Literally "self-interest" or "self-seeking." H. Giesen, "ἐριθεία, *eritheia,*" in *EDNT* (Grand Rapids: Eerdmans, 1990–93), 2:52. Friedrich Büchsel, "ἐριθεία," in *TDNT* (Grand Rapids: Eerdmans, 1964–76), 2:660–61. Unless otherwise indicated, uncited Scripture quotations from Philippians are the author's translation.

[21] Although many suggest that the opposers or Judaizers are ethnic Jews, nothing in the four contrastive statements (1:15–17; 1:27–28; 3:2–3; 3:18–21) *clearly supports* a reference to a group of ethnic Jewish opponents. See Herbert W. Bateman, "Were the Opponents at Philippi Necessarily Jewish?" *BSac* 155 (January–March 1998): 39–61.

directive remains helpful for evangelical churches today. Thus, church communities learning to live Christ-honoring lives establish confidence and unity, despite their suffering, and are thereby able to withstand aggression from without.

Second, Paul appeals for unity to thwart *division from within* (2:1–8). Paul's eventual plea to Euodia and Syntyche evidences at least one internal faction at Philippi (4:2–3). Thus, Paul's appeal for unity, which he begins in 1:27–30, continues in 2:1–4. Having already expressed his thanks to God with joy for the Philippians (1:4), Paul now says in 2:2, "fulfill my joy" or "make my joy complete that you think the same *thing*."[22] Paul's appeal to "think the same *thing*" does not mean uniformity or homogeneity but conformity.[23] Conformity expresses the community's single-minded or like-minded commitment to Christ Jesus, who is to be their standard. "Selfish ambition" (lit. "self-interest" or "self-seeking"), vain or empty conceit (lit. "vainglory"), or a total disregard of others (idiomatic, "looking at each one's own things") are divisive mind-sets, which do not promote unity (vv. 3–4). Thus, to thwart divisions from within, Paul calls for conformity *in* Christ Jesus in their mutual relations. Paul further develops the content of the call when he specifies the mind-set adopted by Christ Jesus.[24] Availing himself of a first-century hymn, Paul urges the Philippians to emulate the mind-set or attitude embraced by Christ Jesus, which is evident in his self-denying, self-giving, self-sacrificing conduct (vv. 5–8).

---

[22] Although "by being of the same mind" (NASB) or "by being like-minded" (NIV) are optional translations, the *hina* clause (ἵνα τὸ αὐτὸ φρονῆτε) clarifies the direct object, "joy," and is translated epexegetically. See Daniel Wallace, *Greek Grammar Beyond the Basics: An Exegetical Syntax of the New Testament* (Grand Rapids: Zondervan, 1996), 476. The three subsequent participles explain how the attitude of joy is to be fulfilled.

[23] H. Pausen, "φρονέω, *phroneō*," in *EDNT* (Grand Rapids: Eerdmans, 1990–93), 3:438–39. Georg Bertram, "φρονέω," in *TDNT*, 9:232–33.

[24] This "mind-set" or "frame of mind" (τοῦτο φρονεῖτε) connects with Paul's linked word and exhortation in Philippians 2:2 (ἵνα τὸ αὐτὸ φρονῆτε and ἐν φρονοῦντε"). The reuse of "humble" in 2:3 (τῇ ταπεινοφροσύνῃ) and 2:8 (ἐταπείνωσεν) reinforces the close connection between these passages.

Although we can only speculate about the nature of the divisions within the Philippian church, divisions within established evangelical churches today are not foreign to us, particularly as they pertain to divisions over musical expressions of worship. Timothy Sprankle, a student at Grace Theological Seminary, dramatizes this reality in chapter 5 of this work, "Worship: A Battle for Harmony." You are welcome to use Sprankle's drama as a way to broach the issue of authentic worship in your church.

More pointedly, however, the exposition and chapters that follow address how a cross-generational community of believers can build an atmosphere for expressing authentic worship that satisfies the diverse musical preferences that exist in most established evangelical churches today. Thus, it seems appropriate to examine and apply Christ's self-denying, self-giving, self-sacrificing mindset as a standard for us to embrace and thereby to disarm warring divisions over worship, particularly those over the diverse musical expressions that have been created for authentic worship.

Jesus Was Self-Denying

We can generate an atmosphere for diverse musical expressions of authentic worship by following Christ's self-denying mind-set or attitude. Unlike our culture, Christ Jesus was not self-absorbed but self-denying. Paul writes, *"Although* Christ Jesus existed in the form of God, he did not consider *his* equality with God *as something to be taken advantage of"* (2:6). Two details are revealed about Christ Jesus in this verse. First, he was God. Prior to his incarnation, Jesus existed *(hyparchōn)* in the form *(morphē)* of God. He did not preexist as the preincarnate Jesus; rather, he existed in a metaphysical form of God, in a manner equal to God.[25] Thus, Christ Jesus was and continues to be, in

---

[25] The two clauses "in the form of God" and "to be equal with God" contextually support the rendering "although" for the participle ὑπάρχων. For a good discussion about Christ's preexistence in Paul, see Brendan Byrne, S. J., "Christ's Pre-Existence in Pauline Soteriology," *TS* 58 (June 1997): 308–30.

his very nature and in his very character, God. He belongs to the order of the divine Creator rather than the order of a created being (cf. Heb. 1:5–13).[26]

Second is the verse's focal point, Christ Jesus' self-denying mind-set. Although God, he "did not consider *his* equality with God *as something to be used for his own advantage*" *(harpagmos)*. Unfortunately, the NIV translates *harpagmos* ambiguously. Commentators point out that "something to be grasped" (NIV, RSV) appears to be a cross between "thought it not robbery" (KJV) and "did not cling to his prerogatives" (PHILLIPS). The expression, however, seems more idiomatic and thereby suggests that, though equal with God, Jesus' attitude or conduct was such that he did not regard his divine equality as something to use for his own advantage.[27] Regardless of how we might understand this elusive term *harpagmos,* it is evident that the mind-set embraced by Christ Jesus is one of self-denial.

How might an atmosphere of self-denial impact a worshiping community in their musical expressions of authentic worship? Musical expressions of worship, created by godly musicians who lead Christ's disciples into the presence of their Infinite-Creator-Redeemer, are priceless. Yet the limitation to or favoring of one style of Christian music for worship (e.g., baroque or classical or country or gospel or . . .), to the exclusion of all others, seems to evidence our culturally self-absorbed shallowness.

For instance, one of the greatest composers and organ virtuosos

---

[26] The sentence is adopted from Gerald O'Collins's statement in *Christology: A Biblical Historical and Systematic Study of Jesus* (New York: Oxford University Press, 1995), 238. For a discussion of Hebrews 1:5–13, see Herbert W. Bateman, "Psalm 45:6–7 and Its Christological Contributions to Hebrews," *TJ* 22NS (2001): 3–21.

[27] Roy W. Hoover, "The *Harpagmos* Enigma: A Philological Solution," *HTR* 64 (1971): 95–119, esp. 117–18. For an evaluation of Hoover and others, see N. T. Wright, "Ἁρπαγμός and the Meaning of Philippians 2:5–11," *JTS* 37 (October 1986): 321–52; reproduced in Wright's *The Climax of the Covenant: Christ and the Law in Pauline Theology* (Minneapolis: Fortress, 1992), 62–98.

of the second millennium was Johann Sebastian Bach. In a recent biography on Bach, Wolff observes him to be a man "thoroughly committed to advancing 'true music,' which Bach defined as music that pursued as its 'ultimate end or final goal . . . the honor of God and the recreation of the soul.'"[28] Likewise, Stapert discovered that "writing music to the glory of God was his [Bach's] vocation, as he usually proclaimed at the end of his scores with the initials SDG—'Soli Deo Gloria.'"[29] And though Bach's sound theological understanding of the text was presented in many cutting edge musical sermons for eighteenth-century German Christians, few of us today appreciate Bach's baroque style of music. The time period, musical style, and culture separate most of us from appreciating Bach's musical contributions to the evangelical church for celebrating and adoring God. Those who do, however, continue to be led into God's presence and thereby able to celebrate God through Bach's music. "Glory to God" (from the Magnificat) and "Jesu, Joy of Man's Desiring" are two examples of Bach's music that are still enjoyed in the worship of many evangelical congregations.

Today, the evangelical church is flooded with a variety of musical expressions created to enhance a worshiper's approach to, engagement, exaltation, and adoration of, and intimacy with God.[30] Granted, our favorite style of music is likely to be the one that was part of our life during our adolescent years.[31] Perhaps our college and/or seminary experience has expanded our tastes

---

[28] Christoph Wolff, *Johann Sebastian Bach: The Learned Musician* (New York: Norton, 2000), 8.

[29] Calvin R. Stapert, *My Only Comfort: Death, Deliverance, and Discipleship in the Music of Bach* (Grand Rapids: Eerdmans, 2000), 27.

[30] The categories of worship engagement, exaltation, and adoration of/intimacy with God was adapted from Barry Liesch, *The New Worship: Straight Talk on Music and the Church,* exp. ed. (Grand Rapids: Baker, 2001), 55. Pastors and worship leaders are encouraged to look at the free or blended worship presented in this work.

[31] George H. Lewis, "Cultural Socialization and the Development of Tastes, Cultures, and Culture Classes in American Popular Music," in *Popular Music and Society* 4 (1976): 226–41.

or appreciation for other styles of music. (Unfortunately, most seminaries do little to expand or develop appreciation for the diverse styles of musical expressions that exist for worship.)

Is it possible that, with a little further music education and exercise of self-denial, we can develop a similar appreciation for the variety of today's music created for worship and thereby disarm the various divisions warring over musical preferences in today's evangelical churches? Our desire to generate a self-denying atmosphere for cross-generational worship is evident in chapter 6 of this book, "Voicing God's Praise: The Use of Music in Worship." David Nelson, assistant professor of systematic theology at Southeastern Baptist Theological Seminary, brings a historical awareness and an appreciation for the amoral variety of musical styles of celebration from a biblical, theological, and pastoral perspective. However, for a self-denying mindset to have any impact, we must also be self-giving.

Jesus Was Self-Giving

An atmosphere for expressing authentic worship through a variety of musical styles can be actualized by following Christ's self-giving mind-set or attitude. Christ Jesus was not self-centered but self-giving. Once again we read in Philippians 2, "Although Christ Jesus existed in the form of God, he did not consider his equality with God as something to be taken advantage of (v. 6), but *he made himself powerless* by taking the form of a slave, by being made in human likeness" (v. 7). As it was in verse 6, two details are once again revealed about Christ Jesus in verse 7's significantly contrastive statement. First, Christ Jesus is self-giving. In a general manner, Paul indicates "he made himself powerless" or literally "emptied himself" *(ekenōsen). Ekenōsen* speaks of Christ Jesus voluntarily "divesting himself of his prestige or privileges" associated with his existence as an equal with God the Father.[32]

---

[32] BDAG, 539.

Perhaps this divine self-abnegation refers to giving up the prestige associated with being the *sovereign Creator* over the universe,[33] namely, Jesus' living enthroned in the heavenlies, his being surrounded by cherubim, and his being worshiped by seraphim. Perhaps this divine self-abnegation refers to his divine attributes made powerless or the *inactive functioning of* (not the loss of), perhaps due to his humanity.[34] Or perhaps *ekenōsen* is merely a poetic, hymnlike phrase suggesting that Christ Jesus poured out himself, willingly putting himself at the disposal of people; this latter possibility seems best to fit the context (2:3–11) and is an exhortation for humility.[35] Since the content of what Christ Jesus voluntarily *emptied himself of* is not explicitly supplied, metaphorical translations like "he made himself nothing," "he made himself of no reputation," and "he made himself powerless" seem adequate. However we might understand this divine self-abnegation, it is obvious that, though God, Jesus embraced a self-giving frame of mind. Nevertheless, how Christ Jesus empties himself is evident in the latter part of verse 7.

The second detail of verse 7 is that Christ Jesus empties himself "by taking the form *(morphē)* of a slave *(doulou)*." To begin with, "by taking the form of a slave" and "by being

---

[33] Lightfoot speaks of his majesty. J. B. Lightfoot, *St. Paul's Epistle to the Philippians* (1953; reprint, Grand Rapids: Zondervan, 1978), 112. "Self-abnegation" was initially coined by Wright, "'Αρπαγμός" and the Meaning of Philippians 2:5–11," 321–52.

[34] Speaking metaphysically: Alva J. McClain, "The Doctrine of the Kenosis in Philippians 2:5–8," *MSJ* 9 (spring 1998): 85–96, esp. 92. Speaking metaphorically: Morna D. Hooker, "Philippians 2:6–11," in *Jesus und Paulus: Festschrift für Werner Georg Kümmel zum 79 Geburtstag*, ed. E. E. Ellis and E. Grässer (Göttingen: Banderhoeck and Rupreche, 1975), 151–64, esp. 162. Wright, "'Αρπαγμός" and the Meaning of Philippians 2:5–11," 345–47.

[35] The case is made that ἑαυτὸν ἐκένωσεν does not demand that a genitive of content be supplied from the context (e.g., Christ emptied himself *of some-thing*), but that it is enough that ἑαυτόν is the direct object of ἐκένωσεν. Gerald F. Hawthorne, *Philippians*, in WBC (Waco: Word, 1983), 85–86.

made in the likeness of men" explain how Christ Jesus "emptied himself" or "made himself powerless."[36] In addition, "taking the form of a slave" stands in contrast *(alla)* to "existed in the form of God." We might say, the divine sovereign *becomes* a human slave for others, or that the second person of the godhead, the all-powerful Creator God of the universe, *becomes* a powerless created being (except for the power or authority afforded him by the Father to carry out his ministry; John 5:19–23, 30; 14:10–12). Thus, Christ Jesus added to his deity the element of being a human slave, who in Roman society tended to have no rights and privileges. One commentary puts it this way: "[Jesus] did not consider that being equal with God was taking everything to himself, but giving everything away for the sake of others."[37] Thus, Jesus was not self-centered but self-giving.

How might an atmosphere of self-giving impact a worshiping community in their musical expressions of authentic worship? As I reflect on Christ Jesus' self-giving attitude, Ron Kenoly's "Sing Out with One Voice" comes to mind. After saying that the service he is leading will be a partial reenactment of the dedication of the temple Solomon built, a place where the presence of God rested, Kenoly acknowledges that today Christians are living stones fitted together as a temple of the Lord (1 Peter 2:5), and that they are living sacrifices to be consumed by God (Rom. 12:1). Kenoly then invites the Lord to come specifically into their living temple and ignite Christians on fire as living sacrifices in their worship of God. Thus, Kenoly begins singing the theme song for the service, "Sing Out." One verse of particular importance to our discussion speaks of worshiping together with music and singing.

---

[36] The two adverbial participles, λαβών and γενόμενος, are participles of means. See Wallace, *Greek Grammar Beyond the Basics* (628–30) for distinguishing between manner and means.

[37] Peter T. O'Brien, *Commentary on Philippians,* in NIGTC (Grand Rapids: Eerdmans, 1991), 85.

We come to worship, together as one,
With music and singing
Rejoice in all that the Father has done,
Let's lift up an offering.

Chorus
Sing out, the Lord is near
Build Him a temple here,
A palace of praise,
A throne of thanksgiving
Made for the King of kings.

Sing out a joyful song,
His love goes on and on
When praises abound,
His glory surrounds us,
Filling His temple here
Sing out, the Lord is near.[38]

After reading the lyrics to this song, the question that echoes in my mind is this, How can "we come to worship together *as one* with music and singing," if we are unwilling to be self-giving? In chapter 7 of this work, Thomas Atchison, pastor of Fox Valley Church in West Dundee, Illinois, shares his "Developing a Practice of Worship That Unites." It captures a pastor and an established cross-generational congregation coming to grips with diverse musical likes and dislikes. It promotes and offers suggestions to pastors and worship leaders that might help other established evangelical churches embrace a self-giving frame of mind whereby cross-generational disciples of Christ will be able to *worship together as one with music and singing.*

---

[38] Emphasis mine. "Sing Out" by Paul Baloche and Ed Kerr. © 1995 Integrity's Hosanna! Music/ASCAP. c/o Integrity Media, Inc., 1000 Cody Road, Mobile, AL 36695. Used by permission.

Jesus Was Self-Sacrificing

Finally, an atmosphere for expressing authentic worship in music and singing is always self-sacrificing. Christ Jesus was not self-seeking but self-sacrificing. Once again we read in Philippians 2, "Although Christ Jesus existed in the form of God, he did not consider his equality with God as something to be taken advantage of (v. 6), but he made himself powerless by taking the form of a slave, by being made in human likeness" (v. 7), being found in the appearance as a man, he humbled himself *by becoming obedient* to death—even death on a cross!" (v. 8). Building upon the fact that Jesus was a human being, Paul once again emphasizes two details about Christ Jesus in verse 8, his humility and how he humbled himself.

First, Christ Jesus humbled himself. "The real theological emphasis of the hymn," says Wright, "is not simply a new view of Jesus. *It is a new understanding of God. . . . Incarnation and even crucifixion are to be seen as appropriate vehicles for the dynamic self-revelation of God.*"[39] With this in mind, think for a moment what sort of God-*man* Jesus was. Did he strive for some pinnacle of human achievement? No! Did he seek to acquire fame and fortune? No! Self-renunciation, self-surrender, and self-sacrifice characterized this divine Creator-man, Christ Jesus. His entire divine-human existence was one of humility, which brings us to the second detail about Christ Jesus in this verse. How did he humble himself? Paul tells us, "by becoming obedient to death—even death on a cross."

Christ Jesus was obedient. Whereas the phrase "obedient to death" captures the depth of his obedience to God the Father, the magnitude of Jesus' humiliation is captured in the phrase "even death on a cross!" To the Gentile, only the lowest order of Roman society—slaves, robbers, and assassins—died by

---

[39] Wright, "Ἁρπαγμός" and the Meaning of Philippians 2:5–11," 346 (emphasis mine).

crucifixion.[40] Crucifixion was the act of binding, nailing, or impaling of a person, dead or alive, to a cross, a stake, or a tree for execution or for exposing the corpse of that individual. People who had no rights or privileges in society, people who had no claims on society, and people who had no significant worth in society experienced death by crucifixion. To the Jew, only those under divine condemnation died on a tree. Josephus, a Jewish historian of the period, calls it "the most pitiable of deaths."[41] Jewish people believed wholeheartedly that "anyone who is hung on a tree is under God's curse" (cf. Deut. 21:23 and Gal. 3:13). Thus, Christ Jesus was not self-seeking but self-sacrificing.

How might an atmosphere of self-sacrificing impact a worshiping community in their musical expressions of authentic worship? Authentic worship always involves *obedience* and *sacrifice*. It involves obedience because God desires worship from us, and such worship involves sacrifice because it is the subjective, expressive, and spiritual attitude that demonstrates our willingness to approach and encounter our Infinite-Creator-Redeemer God. In celebrating God in both *obedience* and *sacrifice*, we conform to Christ Jesus. So, when music is at the very center of our self-understanding, how do we allow for diverse musical expressions in any given worship service? It will always involve sacrifice! How does a community build an atmosphere for expressing authentic worship that takes into consideration the diverse musical preferences within a cross-generational community of believers? It will always involve sacrificing for a moment or two something of personal value and self-understanding!

Herein lies a biblical religious experience any disciple of

---

[40] For a historical discussion of crucifixion in the ancient Near East, see Gerald G. O'Collins, "Crucifixion," in *ABD* (New York: Doubleday, 1992), 1:1207–10.

[41] Josephus, *JW* 7.6.4 § 203. For a historical discussion of crucifixion in Judea, see Michael O. Wise, "Crucifixion," in *EDSS*, 2 vols. (Oxford: Oxford University Press, 2000), 1:158–59.

Christ Jesus can claim to be their own, whereby they express their love for the Lord God they worship and their love for their neighbor within their worshiping community. Evangelicals who love the Lord, who belong to an established cross-generational community of believers where a diversity of preferences exist over musical expressions of worship, and *who want to remain together* will need to sacrifice at times their preferences of musical style for the benefit of the community. Thus, worshipers become partners in their community celebration of their relationship with God and others. It takes a mature group of Christian leaders committed to authentic worship to set the tone for such a corporate worship experience. A means to enhance further this individual and corporate obedience and sacrifice is through the use of symbols.

Tangible Images of the Mind of Christ

Symbols are tangible vehicles that can enhance the atmosphere for authentic worship. A cross, a candle, a Bible, a baptismal font or pool, and a table with bread and wine on it are just a few of the most common visual pictures that convey biblical truth about the Christ event just examined in Philippians 2:5–8. Unfortunately, the use of symbols as significant expressions of authentic worship tends to be a neglected topic of discussion. With few exceptions, most worship experts have limited their attention to the object of worship, God, and music as an expression of worship, and justifiably so. Yet, the use of images is equally significant to this discussion of authentic worship because Jesus typically employed images like bread, water, shepherd, and so forth to convey truth about himself and God. Thus, visual, physical, and tangible images of obedience and sacrifice are the focus of part three of this book, "Symbols: Images of Our Worship." Chapters 8 through 10 address three significant symbols that enhance and heighten the atmosphere for authentic worship because they are a physical visual of our spiritual conformity in Christ.

Timothy Ralston, professor of pastoral ministries at Dallas Theological Seminary, begins our discussion in chapter 8 when he addresses the use of the Bible as a symbol that heightens the atmosphere for authentic worship. Since Tozer's expressed concern, some have described the past three decades of change in corporate worship as a "worship revolution" and/or "worship renewal." The overemphasis on music in worship, however, has led some worship leaders erroneously to place it at the center. Sometimes music is equated with authentic worship. Raltson, however, expresses concern over such a movement. In his chapter "Scripture in Worship: An Indispensable Symbol of Covenant," Ralston argues that the Bible is of central importance to authentic worship. The visual presence and use of a Bible symbolizes or is a visual, physical, and tangible image of God's covenant relationship with us, namely, that he has spoken in history past and is speaking today to direct and mold our spiritual formation. Ralston then explores how worship leaders can restore this dynamic symbol of God's covenant when gathering as a community in authentic worship.

Robert Webber, professor of ministry at Northern Baptist Seminary, continues our discussion of symbols when addressing the relevance of "Baptism Spirituality" and "Eucharist Spirituality" in our worship of God. He argues that these "symbols are not empty, void of meaning, and essentially useless" but that "they perform." "They speak, they act, they do." In essence, they result in our conformity to Christ Jesus and thereby affect our worshiping God and our living harmoniously with God and other disciples of Christ Jesus. Symbols during authentic worship services, like the Bible, baptism, and the Lord's Supper never end. These symbols must be lived. The images not only reflect the Christ event we read about in the Gospels but also affect our living in conformity with the Christ event spoken of in Philippians.

In conclusion, the point of Philippians 2:5–8 is that conformity to Christ Jesus promotes harmony among disciples of Christ Jesus. Embracing the biblical truth concerning renunciation of self reflects our conformity *in* Christ Jesus, which in turn results in harmonious relationships with one another. Perhaps you and your church community, like that at Philippi, are to be praised for your sacrificial partnership in your Christian faith (cf. 4:15–18). Nevertheless, like the Philippians, the call to conform all the more to the self-denying, self-giving, and self-sacrificing standard, Christ Jesus, is still in need in order to thwart divisions over worship (specifically musical) preferences. Thus, my rendering of Paul's prayer in 1:9–11 remains relevant for all evangelical churches today.

> And this I repeatedly pray. I pray that your love may overflow still more and more in your relationship with God and in your conduct with one another. I pray this for you so that you might *recognize the things that really matter*, which will enable you to be morally pure in preparation for Christ's return and thereby abound in godlike deeds through Jesus Christ. All of this is so that God might be glorified and praised.

Paul's exhortation is a sobering challenge that could help us reposition our crown jewel, namely, worship that is acceptable to God; for authentic worship is solely about obedient and self-sacrificing finite-created beings corporately approaching, engaging, and experiencing their Infinite-Creator-Redeemer.

Conclusion

Granted, a great deal of progress has been made in our worship practices over the past thirty years; but, as committed leaders of authentic worship, our narcissistic culture and subsequent struggle to conform *in* Christ Jesus are constantly before us. Yet we must be committed to authentic worship that is acceptable to God. "As a thoughtful gift is a celebration of a birthday," says Gordon Borror, "as a special evening out is a celebration of an anniversary, as a warm eulogy is a celebration of life, as a sexual embrace is a celebration of a marriage—*so worship is a celebration of God.*"[42] With the biblical mind-set or attitude of Christ Jesus, the use of songs and symbols are just some of the ways to celebrate God in authentic worship.

No book can cover everything on any given topic. *Authentic Worship: Hearing Scripture's Voice, Applying Its Truths* does not attempt to address all that could be covered concerning the various activities involved in authentic worship. Thus, the book is open-ended. The concluding chapter, "The Challenges of Multicultural Worship," notes some of the cultural barriers of multicultural worship that the evangelical church will face in the twenty-first century, especially those of us in heterogeneous communities. Thomas Stallter, professor of intercultural studies and world missions at Grace Theological Seminary, examines some of the challenges of worship faced in the United States as it becomes an ever-more-multicultural society.

Realizing that much more could be said in any given area covered in this book and that we are addressing worship leaders and students preparing for such a vocation in the local church, a bibliography has been provided for further study. As fellow lifelong learners committed to worshiping only God, I trust and I pray that we set the example and make it our objective to partner in and lead authentic worship services that are acceptable to God.

---

[42] Ronald Allen and Gordon Borror, *Worship: Rediscovering the Missing Jewel* (Portland, Ore.: Multnomah, 1982), 19.

PART ONE

GOD
The Object of Our Worship

CHAPTER TWO

The Worshiper's Approach to God

An Exposition of Psalm 15

Ronald E. Manahan

No other book in the Old Testament captures the multitude of heartfelt human responses to God as does the collection of religious lyric poems and hymns in the Psalms (*psalmoi,* Septuagint) or Book of Praises (*seper t^ehillim,* Hebrew Bible). Unlike the ancient hymns to the Egyptian sun god, the Babylonian prayers to Marduk, or the Stoics' Hymn to Zeus, Leopold Sabourin has observed that, "Israel's hymns and supplication to YHWH are still a living language of prayer, used by millions in the modern world to address the One God whom they worship."[1] Thus, it seems only right to begin this book on authentic worship with an exposition of a psalm that clearly addresses worship, namely, Psalm 15.

Psalm 15 leads its reader to the central issues of authentic worship, namely, the requirements for approaching God. A simple reading of this psalm shows that it is structured as a

---

[1] Leopold Sabourin, *The Psalms: Their Origin and Meaning* (New York: Alba House, 1970), v.

question-answer-observation sequence. The text opens with an initial question that is followed by an answer to the question plus a statement of observation. I offer this translation of the psalm.

A Reading of Psalm 15

[1]A psalm of David.
O Lord, who may sojourn in your sacred tent?
   Who may dwell on the mountain of your holiness?

[2]The one who walks with integrity
   and who practices righteousness
   and who speaks truth in his heart.

[3]He has not tripped over his tongue
   and has done no injury to his fellow citizen
   and slander has not lifted up against his neighbor.

[4]The one who despises the reprobate,
   but those fearing the Lord he honors (as with
      a banquet).

He has sworn to his own detriment and wavers not.

[5]His money he does not lend at interest
   and a bribe (intended to pervert justice) against an
      innocent person he does not accept.

The one who does these things will never be shaken.

Various Interpretations of Psalm 15

As is well known in Old Testament studies, Psalm 15; Psalm 24:3–6; Isaiah 33:14–16; and Micah 6:6–8 are linked together by vocabulary and literary form. Since the days of Gunkel[2] and Mowinckel,[3] Psalms 15 and 24 have been referred to either as "Entrance Liturgies," "Torah Liturgies," or "Confession Reflections ("Mirrors" rendering *Spiegel*)."[4] Each of these designations emphasizes a different nuance of the text. These nuances all assume that the priest is approached by the worshiper who asked the question concerning the conditions for entrance into the Lord's sanctuary and the heard reply by the priest. This exchange is followed by an observation "about how life works."[5]

However, as Willis has noted, Psalms 15 and 24 may be interpreted in light of other liturgical acts and cultic settings. He summarizes the several possibilities offered by scholars.[6]

1. We could assume the *worshipers frequent the same sanctuary* and, based upon this assumption, are expected to know and repeat the conditions for entrance. In this case the priest spoke the question, the worshipers gave the answer, and the priest bestows a blessing as evidence that entrance is acceptable.

2. On the other hand, Psalms 15 and 24 might be *Psalms of Asylum*. The question is asked by one who seeks information about the requirements for entering a city of refuge. The answer comes from those officials stationed at the entrance to the city.

---

[2] Hermann Gunkel, *Die Psalmen ubersetzt und erklart*, HKAT II/2, 4th ed. (Göttingen: Vandenhoeck und Ruprecht, 1926). See also his *Introduction to the Psalms: The Genres of the Religious Lyric of Israel*, comp. Joachim Begrich, trans. James D. Nogalski from *Einlleitung in die Psalmen: die Gattungen der religiosen Lyrik Israels*, 4th ed. (Macon, Ga.: Mercer University Press, 1998).

[3] Sigmund Mowinckel, *The Psalms in Israel's Worship*, vols. 1–2, trans. D. R. Ap-Thomas (Nashville: Abingdon, 1962).

[4] John T. Willis, "Ethics in a Cultic Setting," in *Essays in Old Testament Ethics*, ed. J. L. Crenshaw and J. T. Willis (New York: Ktav, 1974), 148.

[5] James L. Mays, *Psalms*, IBC (Louisville: John Knox, 1994), 84.

[6] Willis, "Ethics in a Cultic Setting," 154–61.

3. Or, the question-answer-observation sequence of these
    two psalms could be *antiphonal pieces,* having been writ-
    ten by priests to be sung during worship, not simply as
    preparation for it.
4. Furthermore, these psalms could have developed within
    wisdom circles by those desiring to instruct their students.
5. Perhaps Psalms 15 and 24, being devoid as they are of
    cultic or ritualistic instructions, might have developed
    out of *prophetic circles.* As such, these psalms could be
    read as a challenge to priests who were overly concerned
    about cultic and liturgical matters.
6. On the other hand, Psalm 15, because of its linkage with
    eschatological material in Psalm 24:3–6 and Isaiah 33:14–
    16, might be a *prophetic eschatological text* that pictures a
    bright future due to Yahweh's intervention.
7. Perhaps the two psalms could be understood as *choral
    pieces* emphasizing high ethical standards. As such, it
    would be presented at a king's coronation (cf. Ps. 101).
8. Or, Psalms 15 and 24 might have been developed as li-
    turgical pieces addressed to priests before they entered
    the sanctuary to remind them of the ethical requirements.
    This would seem possible because only priests were al-
    lowed to enter the Jerusalem temple proper.[7]
9. It is even possible to see Psalms 15 and 24 as *polemics
    used by the Zadokite priesthood* in Jerusalem against the
    rival Elide priesthood centered in Shiloh. The latter's
    history of evil and failure might have called for a strong
    ethical challenge as found in the two psalms.

The Nature of Psalm 15

Willis's impressive list of interpretive diversity does not obscure the fact that a priest is approached by the worshiper who

---

[7] Following the comments of H. C. Thomson, "The Right of Entry to the
Temple in the OT," *Transactions of the Glasgow University Oriental Society* 21
(1965–66): 25–34.

asks a question concerning the conditions for entrance as a guest in the Lord's sanctuary and the heard reply by the priest. Though the exact cultic setting and liturgical activities reflected in Psalm 15 remain uncertain, several factors about the psalm are widely held to be true.

Psalm 15 is structured as a question-answer-observation sequence. There is an absence of cultic and liturgical detail. The piece is instructional, giving evidence of wisdom influence. Ethical conditions for entry into the presence of the Lord in his sanctuary are clearly presented. Worship is the central focus of the psalm. *Entrance into the Lord's presence is not to be a casual matter.* The separateness of the worshiper from God is emphasized. This latter point is underscored by the psalm's opening in verse one.

The Questions of Psalm 15:1

The psalm reflects a protocol of life, if not of cultic liturgy, that one must follow in order to enter God's presence. God is unto himself and will not be rushed upon by his worshipers. They feel their distance from him. The opening lines of Psalm 15 confront the reader with these questions.

> O LORD, who may sojourn in your sacred tent?
> Who may dwell on the mountain of your holiness?

That is, "who may enter into the sacred space where the presence of the LORD especially dwells?"[8] To understand the nature of this question requires an evaluation of both the Hebrew text and the ancient Near Eastern understanding of sacred spaces. We begin by addressing the concept of sacred spaces because doing so will provide a helpful context for understanding the questions with which Psalm 15 opens.

---

[8] Mays, *Psalms,* 83.

Sacred Spaces in the Ancient World

Sacred spaces were important in the ancient world. As is well known, from Sumer to Greece, the dwellings of gods— namely, their temples—were places of fearful attraction. On the one hand, the worshipers at these ancient places were fearful and awestruck, but on the other hand drawn to them by obligation and hope. A few examples from the ancient world will suffice since the idea of the temple, as Lundquist notes, has an extraordinary continuity across societies and across time.

> In the light of the extraordinary cultural disruptions in the ancient world documented so ably by George Mendenhall, it is important to note that there were areas of equally extraordinary cultural, historical and religious continuity. I believe that the temple as an institution and the cult associated with it constitutes one of the most interesting examples of such continuity.[9]

This is not to say, however, that temples served a uniform function across the cultures of the ancient world. The following summary of Sumer, Ugarit, and Greece indicates such.

Sumer. In Sumer, Enlil's "big house," the Ekur, is depicted in Sumerian hymns as an awe-inspiring place.[10] This is not surprising because,

> While private devotion and personal piety were not unimportant, it was rite and ritual which, because of

---

[9] John M. Lundquist, "What Is a Temple? A Preliminary Typology," in *The Quest for the Kingdom of God,* ed. H. B. Huffmon, F. A. Spina, and A. R. W. Green (Winona Lake, Ind.: Eisenbrauns, 1983), 206.

[10] James B. Pritchard, ed., *ANET,* 3d ed. with supp. (Princeton, N.J.: Princeton University Press, 1969), 573–76. Both the "Hymn to Enlil, the All-Beneficent" and the "Hymn to Enlil as the Ruling Deity of the Universe" reflect this point.

the world view of the Sumerians, played the predominant role in their religion. Since man was created for no other purpose than to serve the gods, it was obviously his major duty to perform and perfect this service in a manner pleasing and satisfactory to his masters. . . . The rulers of Sumer did not weary of repeating that they had performed their cult duties in accordance with the prescribed rules and regulations.[11]

This focus on rules and regulations surely would have created a sense of awe as the worshiper approached the sacred space. Two prominent and lasting features of such temples were "a niche for the god's emblem or statue and an offering table of mud brick in front of it," constant reminders of the requirement of careful service to the gods.[12] Thus, the "Hymn to Enlil, the All-Beneficent" (lines 1–4 and 39–42) portrays the great god Enlil and his dwelling place, Ekur, in awe-inspiring terms.

> Enlil whose command is far-reaching, lofty his word (and)
>   holy,
> Whose pronouncement is unchangeable, who decrees
>   destinies unto the distant future,
> Whose lifted eye scans the land,
> Whose lifted beam searches the heart of all the land . . .
> . . . Father Enlil,
> Set up (his) dwelling on the dais of the Ekur, the lofty shrine.
> The house—its *me* (like) heaven cannot be overturned,
> Its pure rites like the earth cannot be shattered.[13]

---

[11] Samuel N. Kramer, *The Sumerians* (Chicago: University of Chicago Press, 1963), 135.

[12] Ibid.

[13] Pritchard, *ANET,* 573–74. See also the "Hymn to the Ekur" in ibid., 582–83.

On the other hand, as awe-inspiring as the Ekur was, there were times when it was ravaged, and, on one of these occasions, by one of the land's own kings, Naram-Sin. In "The Curse of Agade" (lines 102–18), Naram-Sin's activity is described.

> He put a restraining hand on the Ekur . . .
> Like a bandit who plunders a city,
> He erected large ladders against the house.
> To destroy the Ekur like a huge boat,
> To turn it into dust like a mountain mined for silver . . .
> He forged great axes,
> Sharpened double-edged "axes of destruction" . . .
> Levelled it down to the "foundation" of the land,
> Fixed axes at the top of it,
> The house lay stretched "neck to ground," like a man who had
>   been killed (in battle).[14]

Naram-Sin's purported activity suggests that, though the sacred space was awe inspiring, this fact did not keep people from approaching the Ekur! In fact, though worshipers may well have had fear in their heart as they approached the Ekur, they nonetheless were drawn to it. No doubt reasons for being drawn were varied. But worshipers were drawn. Coming to the sacred space met a part of the worshiper's need. "[T]he Sumerian priests and holy men developed a colorful and variegated complex of rites, rituals, and ceremonies which served to please and placate the gods as well as provide an emotional valve for man's love of pageantry and spectacle."[15]

Ugarit. Ugaritic temples and their uses differed, of course, from temples in Sumer. Ugaritic text 51 illustrates, however, the importance of temple-palaces among the gods. The text

---

[14] Pritchard, *ANET,* 648–49. See also Samuel N. Kramer, "The Temple in Sumerian Literature," in *Temple in Society,* ed. M. V. Fox (Winona Lake, Ind.: Eisenbrauns, 1998), 8–9.

[15] Kramer, *The Sumerians,* 112.

opens with the concern that Baal has no temple-palace. After evaluating this circumstance, Asherah, Baal, and Anath decide to seek permission from El to build such a building. The text (col. IV:49ff.) tells of Asherah's plea before El.

> There shout Asherah and her sons
>   The goddess and the band of her brood:
> "Lo there is no house unto Baal like the gods
>   Nor a court like the sons of Asherah:
> The dwelling of El
>   The shelter of his sons."[16]

El agrees to the request and Baal hurries to have a temple-palace erected for himself (col. V:114ff.). Baal's temple-palace became the center of his cult.

While there has been much discussion and debate about the exact nature and intent of the New Year festival, its activities illustrate something of the relationship that worshipers had with Baal's temple-palace. "The worshippers were active participants in the cult, weeping and lamenting when Baal descended under the earth and joining wholeheartedly in the joyful celebrations when he returned triumphantly after defeating his enemies."[17]

These two sides of the worshiper's experience, weeping and celebration, illustrate the fact that worship at Ugarit involved both fear on the one hand and attraction on the other. The fear was driven by the worshiper's realization that Baal's defeat meant loss of fertility and sufficient rainfall. His help was needed in times of distress. Sacrifice was an important aspect of the

---

[16] Translation from Cyrus H. Gordon, *Ugarit and Minoan Crete* (New York: Norton, 1966), 68.

[17] Arvid S. Kapelrud, *The Ras Shamra Discoveries and the Old Testament,* trans. G. W. Anderson (Norman, Okla.: University of Oklahoma Press, 1963), 68.

worshiper making a felt need known to the gods.[18] The triumph
of Mot meant death and aridity. However, the victory of Baal
was cause for wild celebration, a fact that attracted the worshiper
to Baal's house. To be sure, the celebration included some of
the most debased activities imaginable. The point is, however,
that fear and attraction were both present in this Ugaritic setting.
Eventually, as ritual dramas such as this one lost functional
significance, they tended to become more entertainment similar
to that seen in the "Poem of the Gracious Gods."[19]

Greece. Greek temples, though less sweeping in symbolic
meaning, were places that inspired awe.[20] However, temples in
Greece played a different role from those in Sumer and Ugarit.
Greek religion is fundamentally alien to our eyes, as Finley has
noted. He lists reasons why this is so: Greek religion had no
sacred books and revelation, there was no priesthood as that
term is commonly understood in the ancient world, the temple
was hardly ever a place for congregational worship, and yet
there was an abundance of festivals with many rituals.[21]

During the Dark Age in Greece, the period from about 1200
B.C. to the eighth century, altars were used as the center for the
cult. When temples began to flourish at the end of the Dark
Age, the altars and temples remained separate; "the open-air
altar in most places remained the focus of the cult."[22] In this

---

[18] In fact, as Andre Caquot and Maurice Sznycer say, "The most important
religious action at Ugarit was, of course, sacrifice" (*Ugaritic Religion,* Iconography of Religionsm XV, 8 [Leiden: E. J. Brill, 1980], 17).

[19] Theodor H. Gaster, *Thespis* (Harper Torchbooks; New York: Harper and
Row, 1961), 406ff.

[20] Walter Burkert, "The Meaning and Function of the Temple in Classical
Greece," *The Temple in Society,* ed. M. V. Fox (Winona Lake, Ind.: Eisenbrauns,
1988), 27–47.

[21] Moses I. Finley, foreword to *Greek Religion and Society,* ed. P. E. Easterling
and J. V. Muir (Cambridge, Mass.: Cambridge University Press, 1985), xiv–
xviii.

[22] J. N. Coldstream, "Greek Temples: Why and Where?" in *Greek Religion and
Society,* ed. P. E. Easterling and J. V. Muir (Cambridge, Mass.: Cambridge
University Press, 1985), 68.

regard the altar, though not within the temple itself, was a central aspect of the sacred space. Furthermore, as Paul Cartledge notes, "Classical Greek religion was at bottom a question of doing not of believing, of behaviour rather than faith," rather than dogmas.[23]

The doing included numerous festivals. Given the fact that the administration of public religion was in the hands of the numerous city-states,[24] the number of sacrifices and festivals was astonishing. Estimates are that "in excess of 300 public, state-run religious festivals are known to have been celebrated at over 250 places in honor of more than 400 deities."[25] Sacrifices were central to these festivals, as were hymns, dances, and processions.[26] All of these required that the worshiper pay attention to details, not wanting to offend a god. To this extent, appearance at the sacred space was fearful. On the other hand, the festivals, including competitions such as games, became occasions of celebration and attraction.

Of course, the sacred space of Yahweh in the Old Testament engendered fear and attraction on the part of his worshipers. Though more will be said later about these realities, I simply refer to Menahem Haran's work for a detailed account regarding the place and use of the temple in Israel.[27] With this summary in hand, we are ready to look at the text of Psalm 15.

The Worshipers' Attraction to Divine Presence

Clearly the opening questions of the psalm underscore the worshipers' attraction to the divine presence. They have set

---

[23] Paul Cartledge, "The Greek Religious Festivals," in *Greek Religion and Society,* ed. P. E. Easterling and J. V. Muir (Cambridge, Mass.: Cambridge University Press, 1985), 98.

[24] See on this point Burkert, "The Temple in Classical Greece," 39–40.

[25] Ibid.

[26] Finley, foreword to *Greek Religion and Society,* xviii.

[27] Menahem Haran, *Temples and Temple-Service in Ancient Israel* (Winona Lake, Ind.: Eisenbrauns, 1985).

aside other earthly duties to seek an entrance to the sanctuary. They have come and have been bold enough to ask about the requirements. To this degree they have been willing to reorder their life in order to make the journey to the sanctuary. Furthermore, they have come in the name of their covenant God, Yahweh. For these reasons we may say that their coming to the sanctuary is purposeful. Such a trip requires a certain level of orientation to Yahweh in one's life.

To be sure, Psalm 24 in its first (vv. 1–2) and third (vv. 7–10) literary units more overtly highlights this attraction to the sanctuary by highlighting the nature and works of this covenant God, Yahweh. But Psalm 15 underscores the same attraction in its opening questions. This wisdom piece mirrors the covenant relationship between God and the worshipers. That relationship is not held together by cultic rituals. No, those will not do. They are not enough. Rather, the covenant-making God holds the relationship together. In our psalm, relationship is stressed, not liturgical details. Thus, worship—authentic worship—begins with the worshipers' focus on the covenant making God and relationship with him.

The Worshipers' Fearful Approach

The questions of Psalm 15:1, however, show that the attraction to divine presence is a *fearful* one, *fearful* not in the sense that the worshipers are too terrified to seek entrance but rather in the sense that they sense their total subjection to the divine host's will and pleasure.

The first line asks, "Who may sojourn in your sacred tent?" The use of "sojourn" *(gûr)* is noteworthy. The term refers to "dwelling for a definite or indefinite period of time."[28] So, for example, the verb is used in Psalm 61:5 (MT), "I long to so-

---

[28] See the discussion in D. Kellerman, "גּוּר," in *TDOT*, ed. G. Johannes Botterweck and Helmer Ringgren, trans. J. T. Willis (Grand Rapids: Eerdmans, 1975), 2:439–49.

journ in your tent forever." The noun form is often rendered "resident alien." The designation "resident alien" refers to one who is in between a native Israelite (ʾezrāḥ) and a foreigner (nōkrî). Nor is the "resident" alien a slave (ebed). A "resident alien," as Jacob Milgrom explains,

> . . . has uprooted himself (or has been uprooted) from his homeland and has taken permanent residence in the land of Israel. . . . The ger may not own landed inheritance (subsequently reversed by the prophets, see Ezekiel 47:21–23). In an agricultural economy, such as ancient Israel's, this meant that the ger had to work for an Israelite farmer as a hired hand. Moreover, having severed his ties with his original home, he had no family to turn to for support. Thus deprived of both land and family, he was generally poor, listed together with the Levite, the fatherless and the widow among the wards of society (see Deuteronomy 26:12) and exposed to exploitation and oppression (see Ezekiel 22:7).[29]

Some "resident aliens" may have succeeded in improving their lot in life, but these are few and far between.[30]

For these reasons the status and privileges of the resident alien were "dependent on the hospitality that has played an important role in the ancient Near East ever since ancient time."[31] In a word, a resident alien was surrounded by ongoing reminders that he was in some sense a guest, at least in comparison to the native Israelites. Also, most significantly, he was a guest at risk. Zechariah 7:10 says, "Do not oppress the widow or the fatherless, the alien or the poor" (NIV). These

---

[29] Jacob Milgrom, "The Alien in Your Midst," *Bible Review* 11 (December 1995): 18.

[30] Ibid.

[31] Kellerman, "גּוּר," 443.

"categories probably had to take their seats among the blind and lame who begged at the city gates."[32]

But is it also true, according to the divine view, that Israel herself was a resident alien, as Leviticus 25:23 says (cf. Ps. 119:19). Members of the nation were tenants on God's land, guests in his world. So Soggin suggests that the root word *(gûr)* for "resident alien" could be rendered "be a guest."[33] Thus, the word "sojourn" in the leading question of Psalm 15:1 depicts the worshipers at the entrance to the sanctuary as "those who have no inherent right to be there. . . . The privilege (i.e., to enter) must be granted."[34] Hence, *the worshipers are guests.* They ask the Lord through direct address if he as host will let them enter his sanctuary, his house.

The House of God

In the ancient world, from Sumer to Greece, temples typically were the territories of the gods, the god's house as it were.[35] In the Old Testament, the temple, God's house, is given various designations such as "house of Yahweh" *(bêt Yahweh)*, "house of God" *(bêt Elohim)*, and "palace of Yahweh" *(hêkal Yahweh)*.[36] But access to God's house depends upon his hospitality. There are no other rights than those granted by the Lord. The use of "house" or "tent" *(ʾōhel)* underscores the hospitality setting ("able to enter into his house"). Thus, he "who enters the Temple becomes a guest of God and resides there in a precarious, pro-

---

[32] Mark Sneed, "Israelite Concern for the Alien, Orphan, and Widow: Altruism or Ideology," *ZAW* 111 (1999): 501.

[33] J. Alberto Soggin, *Old Testament and Oriental Studies,* in Biblical et Orientalia, 29 (Rome: Biblical Institute Press, 1975), 143.

[34] Mays, *Psalms,* 84.

[35] See Samuel N. Kramer, "The Temple in Sumerian Literature," in *Temple in Society,* ed. M. V. Fox (Winona Lake, Ind.: Eisenbrauns), 7–11; and Burkert, "The Temple in Classical Greece," 29–35.

[36] See Haran, *Temples and Temple-Service in Ancient Israel,* 13–15, for these and other designations.

visional manner without other rights than those imposed by the concept of hospitality. Otherwise, he is a guest of his Lord who generously receives him."[37] The expression in the second question in 15:1, "on the mountain of your holiness" *(bᵉhar qādšekâ),* emphasizes the exalted remoteness, otherness, of the divine host. This wording stresses again the *fearful* aspects of the worshipers' attraction to God.

The Questions Help Our Thinking About Authentic Worship

What wisdom is the text passing on to us as worshipers desiring authentic worship? More specifically, what are we to learn from the opening questions of Psalm 15? I suggest that the questions in our psalm give helpful direction for our thinking about authentic worship for the evangelical church today.

First, we are instructed that worshipers ought to sense their separation from God. They realize they gather in his presence, at his house. They understand the metaphor. They are his guests. As such, they realize that entering his presence is no casual matter. They sense their dependence. After asking as to the conditions for entrance into his presence, they must wait for his response. They are not to presume upon his presence. Mere cultic acts will not unlock the entrance to his true presence. God on his own terms will lay out the conditions for coming to him. All worshipers stand at the entrance waiting, waiting, waiting on him.

Second, we are instructed that worshipers, whatever their position or rank in life, all stand on common ground at the entrance into divine presence. No one stands above the other. This is no place for haughtiness, pride of position, or human entitlements. Worshipers are all on a common plane of

---

[37] Soggin, *Old Testament and Oriental Studies,* 148. Even the targum insertion in verse 1 (*ḥᵉmê* = "who is worthy to") characterizes this provisional nature of the temple entrance (see 143).

dependence on God. We are guests, and we know who owns the house and is our host.

Third, we are instructed that worshipers realize how deeply they depend upon the hospitality and kindness of the divine host. He has made his covenant with them and, thereby, has drawn them into relationship with him. Worshipers rest upon divine grace. They know the owner of the house is kind, and so they are attracted to his gate. They revel in him. They realize how much they need him. Though their lot in life is precarious, they count on him who is rich in mercy and grace. They long to join such a divine host. They look forward to sitting at his table. His already established relationship with the worshipers draws them on to meet him. They really do want to be with him. They really do. Thus, with those ancient worshipers of Israel, we today say, "Glory to God!"

The Answer of Psalm 15:2–5b

The psalmist now moves to answer the initial question of our psalm, namely, "Who may sojourn in your sacred tent?" There have been multiple ways of analyzing the answer. Some interpreters conclude that the *priest* asked the question in verse 1 and the worshiper gave the answer in verses 2–5b. Many others, however, believe that the *worshiper* asked the question and the priest gave the answer.[38]

A review of our findings about the psalm may be helpful at this point. There is an absence of cultic and liturgical instructions in this psalm. The psalm is cast as a wisdom piece that highlights ethical living. Most likely our psalm developed from a specific cultic setting. However, its present form suggests that it was consciously prepared as an instructional piece that draws out divine expectations about the worshiper's life. Certainly in much of the ancient world, "admission to a sanctuary," says Eaton, "was hedged about with conditions, whether ritual or moral.

---

[38] See the discussion of Soggin, *Old Testament and Oriental Studies,* 147–48.

The effect was to inspire reverence and to give priority to the requirements of the deity. Pilgrims were faced with the need to consider their ways and to undertake preparatory discipline."[39]

In Psalm 15, the ethical-moral conditions are delineated. One should not conclude from this that the psalm as it stands is a rejection of the cultic-liturgical requirements.[40] Rather, the psalm is instructing the worshiper in the importance of the ethical-moral dimensions of his life. The worshiper's character qualities are sketched out in the answer. The answer correlates the worshiper's conduct with the divine presence. According to the psalmist, conduct and temple are tied together. *Worship and life are intertwined.* This provides a general orientation to the answer. About Psalm 15, Miller rightly concludes, "The inextricable link between worship and ethics which runs throughout the Old Testament is the underlying assumption of the whole Psalm."[41] A scan of verses 2–5b suggests several details. Thus, we begin by looking at the *structure* of the answer.

The Didactic Structure of the Answer

There has been considerable discussion about the *literary* structure of the answer. Examples include the view that the proposed differing line arrangements *(BHK* and *BHS)* in verses 2–3 are both correct, highlighting a kind of purposeful ambiguity.[42] Another interpreter[43] concludes that this poetic ambiguity could be

---

[39] John H. Eaton, *Psalms,* Torch Bible Commentary Series (London: SCM, 1967), 56.

[40] As James Kugel says, "neither purely cultic, nor purely ethical matters alone constitute the standard of holiness to which Israel is to be held, but both together" ("The Holiness of Israel and the Land in Second Temple Times," *Texts, Temples, and Traditions* [Winona Lake, Ind.: Eisenbrauns, 1996], 22).

[41] Patrick D. Miller, "Poetic Ambiguity and Balance in Psalm XV," *VT* 29 (1979): 416.

[42] Ibid., 416–24.

[43] Pierre Auffret, *"Essai sur la Structure Litteraire du Psaume XV,"* VT 31 (1981): 385–99.

extended to the rest of the psalm. Furthermore, another[44] has suggested that the author of the psalm "arranged the psalm as a chiasmus." Our purpose is simply to note the variety of opinions regarding the *literary* structure of the answer. More importantly, I want to dwell on the answer's *didactic* structure.

Many have correctly observed that verse 2 identifies general moral traits, and verses 3–5b cite specific acts, both positive and negative. "It is as though the poet deliberately built up a tension wire tying in the positive and negative poles of correct conduct."[45]

James Mays points out that the general moral traits are introductory and the specific acts are illustrative.[46] Some observers have pointed to a supposed relationship between these elements of conduct and the Decalogue.[47] But such a conclusion is by no means certain.[48] Unless one of the lines (v. 3a?) is eliminated on textual grounds, we have eleven commands and prohibitions. Therefore, the decalogical approach to the didactic structure of the answer is not satisfactory.

The didactic structure of the answer purposely describes the completeness and fullness of the ethical expectations. *Entrance into God's presence is a matter that consumes all that the worshiper is and does.* It encompasses all the domains of the worshiper's life. It is as though the psalmist wants to emphasize that no aspect of a worshiper's existence is untouched by the divine answer. The covenant God takes into consideration all aspects of a worshiper's life. Thus, the answer fully extends this thought in multiple ways. Verse 2 notes the spheres of living, practicing, and speaking. Following verse 2, the author presents several

---

[44] Lloyd M. Barre, "Recovering the Literary Structure of Psalm XV," *VT* 2 (1984): 207–11.

[45] Y. Avishur, "Psalm XV—a Liturgical or Ethical Psalm?" *Dor le Dor* 5 (1977): 125.

[46] Mays, *Psalms*, 84.

[47] See the discussion on this point in Peter C. Craigie, *Psalms 1–50*, WBC, ed. D. A. Hubbard and G. W. Barker (Waco: Word, 1983), 19:150–51.

[48] Soggin, *Old Testament and Oriental Studies*, 148.

positive and negative statements in verses 3–5b. Then there is the use of opposites in the words "reprobate" and "fearing" in verse 4. Finally, there is the increasingly widening circle of the worshipers' activities, beginning with the worshipers themselves and then moving to what they do among those in their neighborhood and religious community and at last in society at large.

Taking into consideration James Mays's analysis, the following answers in verses 2–5b are framed around the worshiper's general moral traits, his life within the neighborhood, his life within the religious community, and his life within society at large.[49]

The General Moral Traits. God wants his worshipers to live with integrity, to live with a consistency that permeates one's totality (v. 2a). He also desires that his worshipers practice what is right (v. 2b) and speak truthfully what they think (v. 2c). The participles here suggest that these three activities should be an ongoing way of life. The worshipers' totality as human beings is of special interest to God. Thus, the psalmist has holistically and fully referred to the worshipers by noting their habits ("walk"), their deeds ("practices"), and their speech ("speaks"). This fullness of expression is extended by the terms "blamelessly," "righteousness," and "truth." Through use of these three parallel thoughts in verse 2, the text clearly lays stress on the worshipers' whole way of life. Thus, the general moral traits of a worshiper involve walking blamelessly, practicing righteousness, and speaking truth in his heart.

Living Within the Neighborhood. According to verse 3, the worshipers' life in their neighborhood is of interest to the covenant God. That the worshipers' nearby environs are in mind is indicated by the reference to "his fellow citizen" *(lᵉrē ᶜēhû)* and "his neighbor" *(qᵉrobô)*. In verse 3a, the one who "has not tripped over his tongue"[50] *(lōʾ rāgal ᶜal lᵉsōnô)* is one in whom

---

[49] James Mays's analysis was helpful in the development of this didactic structure (*Psalms*, 84).
[50] Mitchell Dahood, *Psalms I, 1–50*, AB (Garden City, N.Y.: Doubleday, 1965–66), 84.

there is no duplicity of heart that contributes to "stumbling speech or dubious intent."[51] This individual "does no injury" (*rā ʿāh* = "evil, misery, distress") in his neighborhood and initiates no "slander" (*ḥerpâh* = "reproach, scorn"), that is, initiates no slanderous rumor or gossip within his neighborhood.[52] Worshipers practicing these habits among their neighbors would bring well-being *(šālôm)* to the environs. Thus, living life within the neighborhood, the worshiper has not tripped over his tongue, has done no injury to his fellow citizen, and has not slandered his neighbor (i.e., the nearby one).

Living Within the Religious Community. Likewise, in verse 4, worshipers seeking entrance to divine presence are to practice certain habits within their religious community. Such a person "despises the reprobate" but "those fearing God he honors." These opposites have a theological purpose. What is at issue here is one's pattern of life in relation to Yahweh. "[I]n the psalm's theology, life either is in the right with God or it is not. No partly righteous, no a-little-bit-wicked."[53] The one seeking God's presence is committed to opposing those who perpetually undertake evil[54] and affirming those who have cast their lot with God. This individual brings *shalom* to the community of God. Thus, living life within the religious community, the worshiper despises the reprobate and honors those fearing the Lord.

Living Within Society at Large. In society at large the one who seeks God's presence ought to bring *shalom* to others by keeping his word, even when it hurts (v. 4c). This person should not lend for interest where he ought not (v. 5a), thereby avoiding the exploitation and abuse that might too easily result through such a transaction. A worshiper should reject bribes, thereby

---

[51] Craigie, *Psalms 1–50*, 151–52.

[52] Cf. ibid., 152

[53] Mays's comment is made about Psalm 1 but also applies to Psalm 15:4 (*Psalms*, 42).

[54] Craigie, *Psalms 1–50*, 152.

avoiding a perversion of justice (v. 5b). Such a person blesses society. Thus, living life within society at large, the worshiper has sworn to his own detriment and wavers not, does not lend his money at interest, and does not accept a bribe against an innocent person.

In short, the answer in these verses describes persons who bring *shalom*, not chaos, to all that they touch. Personal life is better. The neighborhood is blessed. The religious community is strengthened. The cause of good is advanced in society at large. This is the answer to the question in verse 1, "Who may sojourn in your sacred tent?"

The Answer Helps Our Thinking About Authentic Worship

Having reviewed the answer, what helpful directions for our thinking about authentic worship does the answer in verses 2–5b provide? I suggest the text's answer provides significant direction for our thinking about such worship. Several specific applications can be made to individual worshipers.

First, *all of a worshiper's life stands unfolded and open before God.* The answer presented in this psalm covers multiple dimensions of the worshiper's personal and public life. Those seeking the presence of God have heard what intimacy with him requires.

Second, *God is seeking integrity in all of a worshiper's relationships.* These relationships include one's neighbors, the worshiping community, and society at large. Compartmentalization will not do in the presence of God. All of our relationships are exposed before God, and he longs for them to have integrity. Personally I must examine my relationships with my wife, my children, my friends and neighbors, my fellow employees, my fellow church members, and other such groups.

Third, *as important as liturgy and ritual are, they cannot displace the importance of ethical and moral integrity.* Too easily the public performances of a worshiper's life become a poor substitute for inner integrity. More than one worshiper has lived the lie of a public veneer of rightness that masks deep-seated corruption.

Fourth, *as a worshiper understands what God desires, such a person cannot help but confess failure.* An individual who has heard the answer given in Psalm 15, it seems to me, cannot do anything other than confess failure and sin. Surely no worshiper, upon hearing about the pattern of life that pleases God, can conclude that God accepts moral failing.

Finally, *only by means of the Lord's mercy and grace can the worshiper enter divine presence.* The worshiper's only hope is God's extension of his mercy and grace. By God's grace and through his invitation, the worshiper comes before God. There is no other alternative. There is no source of true life. God alone is enough. And a true worshiper knows this truth as comparison is made between the way God wants life lived and the way life is actually lived.

Conclusion

We take comfort in the observation offered in the final line of Psalm 15. It says that those who do "these things will never be shaken." And why should they? They are living out the way of life that intimacy with God requires. This is really how authentic life works. Those finding their refuge in God's presence will not be moved. He protects his own. His grace draws them to himself. His power will keep them.

In real life, how might we as worship leaders pass on this type of instruction? The story of William Lane, a New Testament scholar, and contemporary musician, Michael Card, provides a good example for how to pass on a life of total worship.

While Professor Lane taught at Western Kentucky University and Michael Card was a student there, they developed a friendship that led to a discipling relationship. Their story is told in Card's book, *The Walk.*[55] The book describes the inter-

---

[55] Michael Card, *The Walk* (Nashville: Nelson, 2000).

twining of these two lives that grew out of their days together at the university. William Lane worked to live out the meaning of redeemed life to the fullest extent. But he was not content until he passed it on to others, including Michael Card. Eventually Professor Lane moved to another university. Years later through a telephone call, Card learned that Lane was dying of cancer. Eventually the Lanes moved to be near the Cards. As Card tells the story, Professor Lane had a purpose in doing this. He said to Card, "I want to come to Franklin (where the Cards lived). . . . I want to show you how a Christian man dies."[56] The Lanes made the move and many months later Card's beloved mentor died.

Lane's life mirrors the teaching of Psalm 15. Those who truly worship God do so with the totality of their being, even in the hour of dying. By life and word and death, Lane taught the psalm. He understood that God wants all that the worshiper is and does. Lane gave *full* instruction on what it means to be a worshiper. His life and teaching corresponded to the answer given in Psalm 15. He passed on the instruction of how a worshiper of God ought to live. And that is a part of our calling. Lane passed on the *full* instruction, about both living and dying, to the next generation. May God help every worshiper to do this.

Psalm 15 is intended for instruction and teaching. Those who are God's worshipers are to teach the question and the answer to others, having the deep-seated assurance that the psalm's final observation is true. The didactic nature of the psalm intends this for us today, especially for those of us who are worship leaders in the church.

---

[56] Ibid., 90–91.

CHAPTER THREE

Worshiping God in Spirit

Richard E. Averbeck

There is, in my opinion, no more important topic in Christian theology than worship, properly understood, and no more significant activity in the Christian life than worshiping God. I must confess to feeling overwhelmed by the subject, just as the object of our worship is the truly overwhelming God of the universe, who is both our Creator and our Redeemer. I take refuge in one of my favorite verses in the Psalms. Psalm 103 begins and ends with, "Praise the LORD, O my soul" (vv. 1a and 22c). It is a call to worship. Nestled within this psalm of praise is verse 14, which reminds us that God "knows how we are formed, he remembers that we are dust."[1] On one level that's what we all are. We are made of dust. Nevertheless, the fact remains that the sovereign God himself, who, in fact, created us out of the dust (Gen 2:7), has indeed called us to worship him. And what a calling it is!

The Woman at the Well

We will return to Psalms 103 and 104 in chapter 4, but first let's take a look at our call to worship from a New Testament

---

[1] Translations are from the *New International Version* (NIV) unless labeled otherwise.

point of view. The passage is John 4. Jesus responds to questions about worship from a Samaritan woman at Jacob's well near Sychar, between Mounts Ebal and Gerizim, saying:

> . . . a time is coming and has now come when the true worshipers will worship the Father in spirit and truth, for *they are the kind of worshipers the Father seeks.* God is spirit, and his worshipers must worship *in spirit and in truth.* (vv. 23–24)

It is interesting, I think, that Jesus makes this revelation to such a person, but remember that, at least on one level, we are *all* just dust. Actually, Jesus' boldness and openness toward this woman are surprising. During his ministry, Jesus himself seldom came right out and said that he was the Messiah, as he does with this woman in the following two verses. It is an amazing passage on all fronts.

First, let's not pass too quickly over the fact that, according to this passage, God actually *seeks* true worshipers.[2] This is no small matter. We worship a God who seeks us out specifically that we might become a certain kind of worshiper. The kind of worship he seeks from us is well defined in this passage, and we shall turn to that presently, but it is important to see first of all that true believers are called to be worshipers above all else. To put it another way, *worship is the most important service we could ever perform toward God.* Moreover, I will also argue here that not only is this what God seeks from us, but *this kind of worship is the most meaningful and transforming experience we can engage in as Christians precisely because it turns our heart—our human spirit—toward God.*

Second, the discussion of the biblical theology of worship I

---

[2] See, for example, the remarks in Leon Morris, *The Gospel According to John,* NICNT (Grand Rapids: Eerdmans, 1971), 271; and William Hendriksen, *Exposition of the Gospel According to John,* New Testament Commentary (Grand Rapids: Baker, 1953), 167.

am offering here divides into two parts based on the definition
Jesus offers for the kind of worship God seeks: worship in spirit
and in truth. One could treat this expression as an instance of
hendiadys, in which case "spirit and truth" would be taken as
one overall thought.[3] The preposition "in" occurs only once,
not twice, and stands for both nouns. Could it be that the combination here is like "heavens and earth" in Genesis 1:1, "brim-
stone and fire" in Genesis 19:24, or "kingdom and glory" in
1 Thessalonians 2:12? Or is this pair more like "full of grace
and truth" in John 1:17, where the distinction between the two
makes them *a powerful combination?*[4]

The correct answer, it seems to me, is the latter, as the story
itself suggests. Jesus had asked the woman to draw water for him
from the well. The ensuing discussion tells us this surprised her.
Jesus was a Jew, so why would he even engage her directly, since
she was a Samaritan, and a woman at that (v. 9).[5] Jesus' next
words to her were not only surprising but confusing: "If you
knew the gift of God and who it is that asks you for a drink, you
would have asked him and he would have given you living water"
(v. 10).[6] She was simply at a loss to understand what Jesus was
talking about. His further explanation does not help either:

> Everyone who drinks this water will be thirsty again,
> but whoever drinks the water I give him will never thirst.
> Indeed, the water I give him will become *in him* a spring
> of water welling up to eternal life. (vv. 13–14)

---

[3] For this approach see, for example, Herman N. Ridderbos, *The Gospel According to John*, trans. J. Vriend (Grand Rapids: Eerdmans, 1997), 163–64.

[4] See the brief remarks on John 1:17 and this kind of figure of speech in
Grant R. Osborne, *The Hermeneutical Spiral: A Comprehensive Introduction to
Biblical Interpretation* (Downers Grove, Ill.: InterVarsity, 1991), 106.

[5] See remarks on her status in D. A. Carson, *The Gospel According to John*
(Grand Rapids: Eerdmans, 1991), 217–18.

[6] On the expression "living water," see Carson, *The Gospel According to John*,
218–19.

It is the spring of water that wells up "in him" to eternal life that interests us here. The woman thinks Jesus is still talking about literal water (v. 15), but he is talking about something that wells up from within the person "to eternal life." In spite of her confusion, the woman becomes convinced that Jesus is a prophet because he can tell her things about her life that he should not have been able to know (vv. 16–19).

The interchange continues as the woman turns to the subject of the proper place of worship according to the tradition of the Samaritan "fathers," as opposed to the Jews. We will deal with the schism between the Samaritans and the Jews in chapter 4. The important point for our present concern is that Jesus, in turn, shifts the subject away from the "fathers" of the Samaritans to God the heavenly "Father" (vv. 20–21). Yes, "true" worship is of the Jews because salvation is of the Jews (v. 22), but there is more to it than that. The Father in heaven seeks a certain kind of worship. One of the two interdependent elements of this kind of worship is that it must be worship in "spirit"—worship that wells up from within us because we have a spring of living water there. The "spring of living water" is, of course, the Holy Spirit. We shall develop that point more later.

The second of the two elements of the kind of worship called for here is that it must be worship in "truth"—worship that is founded on the truth of the whole Word of God, not the limited and peculiar canon of the Samaritans.[7] The point is that, in John 4, spirit and truth go together in authentic worship, but they are not the same thing, and the two terms should not be treated as if they have lost their individual meanings and implications. Ultimately, of course, the "truth" Jesus is talking about here is not only the truth about the right place of worship as revealed in the *Word* of God but also refers to the truth about himself as the *Word* of God (John 1:1–5)—"the truth" incarnate (14:6).[8] That is the next point in the story:

---

[7] Morris, *The Gospel According to John,* 270–71.

[8] Ibid., 293–96.

The woman said, "I know that Messiah" (called Christ) "is coming. When he comes, he will explain everything to us." Then Jesus declared, "I who speak to you am he." (vv. 25–26)

Jesus had already said that "a time is coming and has now come" when worship in spirit and truth would be the rule of the day for all genuine worshipers. Jesus now stops and tells the woman that the Messiah she is expecting in the future is now looking her straight in the face. What a *truth* this would have been for her to take in! She could hardly believe it, but she could not ignore it either, so she brought the news to her city (vv. 28–29). The overwhelming response is testimony to the power of this "truth" in the person of Jesus the Christ (see the epilogue in vv. 39–42).

Divine Spirit and Human Spirit

In chapter 4, we will come back to the subject of worshiping in "truth." For now, let's turn our attention to a more detailed look at worship in "spirit." As Jesus put it here, "God is spirit." The point is not that the Holy Spirit, the third person of the Trinity, is God. This is true too, but Jesus is not concerned with that here. The clause "God is spirit" refers to the very nature of God *the Father* as spirit, not the Holy Spirit (v. 23). The Father is a divine spirit in his essential being.[9] Part of the point is that, since he is "spirit," the physical *place* of worship is not the real issue and it never was, even though the Jerusalem temple was the assigned place in Jesus' day, not Mount Gerizim. No place can "contain" or limit the confines of this God we are called to worship, especially since he is "spirit." Even in the Old Testament, at the dedication of the temple, Solomon included in his dedicatory prayer the following: "[W]ill God really dwell on

---

[9] Ibid., 271. For more in-depth discussion of "God is spirit," see Carson, *The Gospel According to John,* 225.

earth? The heavens, even the highest heaven, cannot contain you. How much less this temple I have built!" (1 Kgs. 8:27).

Since our worship must match the very nature of God, we need to understand what "spirit" is and how this can help us become the "true worshipers" God is seeking. God himself is "spirit" and we ourselves have a human "spirit." Unfortunately, the human spirit has been a relatively neglected subject in Christian theology, and this is perhaps why so many scholars have argued that "worship in spirit" should read "worship in Spirit," referring to the Holy Spirit.[10]

Both are involved, and later in this chapter I will emphasize the Holy Spirit in "spirit" worship in John 4 and elsewhere; but we must not lose sight of the importance of a true worshiper's "spirit" being fully engaged in worship.[11] This connection between God and us is, in fact, the most direct point of divine/human contact available to us today. Of course, the incarnation was the most direct contact in Jesus' day, but when Jesus left to be with the Father, he did not leave us without a special divine presence. This is precisely why he sent "the Spirit of truth" to be our "Counselor" (or "comforter" or "helper"; John 14:16–17) and to do the work of enlivening and transforming our human "spirit."

The existence of a human spirit in every person, and the nature of that human spirit, is clearly testified to in both the Old and New Testament. For example, Genesis 45:27 refers to the "reviving" (coming alive) of Jacob's "spirit" when he realized that Joseph was still alive. When Naboth refused to sell Ahab his vineyard, Ahab became "sullen" (NIV) or "depressed" (NRSV) so that he would not even eat (1 Kgs. 21:4–5). The actual

---

[10] See, for example, Ridderbos, *The Gospel According to John,* 163–64; Raymond E. Brown, *The Gospel According to John,* AB (New York: Doubleday, 1966), 1:167, 172, 180–81; and the helpful summary of the debate in Streeter S. Stuart, "A New Testament Perspective on Worship," *EvQ* 68 (1996): 216–17.

[11] Andrew E. Hill, *Enter His Courts with Praise! Old Testament Worship for the New Testament Church* (Grand Rapids: Baker, 1993), 25.

Hebrew expression is that "his spirit became stubborn" (perhaps meaning "resentful" or "implacable" or "illhumored"). Ahab was "spiritually dead" to be sure, but this does not mean he had no human "spirit." To be spiritually dead means that one's human spirit is not engaged with God—he or she is "dead" to God, who is "spirit." He must be "born of the Spirit," as Jesus puts it in John 3 to Nicodemus.

Elsewhere in the New Testament, 1 Corinthians 4:21 refers to Paul's gentle "spirit," and in 2 Timothy 1:7, he tells Timothy that God has given us a human "spirit" of power, love, and self-discipline" rather than "timidity." In point of fact, one can argue from the New Testament that it is precisely the presence of the immaterial "spirit" of a person that makes his or her material body alive as opposed to dead. James, for example, uses the analogy that just as "the *body* without the *spirit* is dead," so "*faith* without *works* is dead" (James 2:26 NASB; cf. also "flesh" versus "spirit" in 1 Peter 4:6).

When our human spirit leaves us, we are, by definition, physically dead. So all that one is, other than a physical body, is his or her "spirit." At the point of his physical death on the cross, Jesus echoed Psalm 31:5 when he said, "Father, into your hands I commit *my spirit*" (Luke 23:46, and parallels). Jesus is not referring to the Holy Spirit but his own human spirit. John was fully aware of this and reported Jesus' death this way: "When he had received the drink, Jesus said, 'It is finished.' With that, he bowed his head and *gave up his spirit*" (John 19:30). In other places, John also talks about Jesus being "deeply moved in (his human) *spirit* and troubled" (11:33; cf. 13:21).

The point is that the human spirit is a primary concern in authentic worship because God himself is "spirit," and true worshipers worship "in spirit." When Jesus said to the woman at the well that "a time is coming and has now come when the true worshipers will worship the Father in spirit and truth" (John 4:23), he was not saying that no one had ever done that before. These are the kind of worshipers that the Father has

always sought. Jesus' point was that the focus was going to
shift away from the legitimacy of places of worship, which was
the issue the woman had previously raised. There was a day
coming and, in fact, had come, when the *only* real issue would
be whether true worship was happening in the "spirit" of the
worshiper(s). Therefore, we need to take all that makes up
our human spirit seriously in worship, including our mind,
will, emotions, attitudes, perspectives on life, personality,
troubles, joys, and all the rest of what we know and are, other
than a physical body. In point of fact, all of these characteristics and capacities and more come through powerfully and
pervasively in the biblical songs of worship we know as the
Psalter.

The Holy Spirit and New Testament Worship

Since we each have a human "spirit" that is able to engage
with God the Father as "spirit," and it is at this level that the
Father seeks worshipers, how does the Holy "Spirit" fit into
all this as the third person of the Trinity? Earlier, in John 3,
we find the account of Nicodemus coming to Jesus at night to
try to understand him and his teaching. Here we get some
important references to the Holy Spirit. Jesus told this Phari-
see "you must be born again." In response to further inquiry,
Jesus added, "I tell you the truth, no one can enter the kingdom of God unless he is *born of water and the Spirit*" (*pneuma;*
John 3:5). There is no definite article here, so it reads literally, "born of water and Spirit," but see the definite article in
v. 8b.

Water, Spirit, and Worship in John 3–4

The close connection between the Holy Spirit and the human spirit in John 3:6 is most important for our present discussion. "Flesh gives birth to flesh, but the Spirit gives birth to
spirit." The new birth of a person in his or her spirit depends

on the work of the Spirit of God.[12] The worship "in spirit" of John 4:23–24 does, in fact, depend on the work of the Holy Spirit, according to the Gospel of John. It is the work of the Holy Spirit in our human spirit that enlivens and, therefore, enables us to worship God "in spirit" as well as "in truth."

The imagery that Jesus used with the woman at the well regarding "living water" (John 4:10) that will become in the one who drinks it "a spring of water welling up to eternal life" (v. 14) corresponds to the imagery in John 7:37–39. There, John clearly states the direct connection between this kind of water imagery and the presence of the Holy Spirit in the person. According to Jesus, "If anyone is thirsty, let him come to me and drink. Whoever believes in me, as the Scripture has said, *streams of living water will flow from within him*" (John 7:37b–38; cf. perhaps Isa. 58:11). John adds: "By this he meant *the Spirit*, whom those who believed in him were later to receive" (v. 39a; cf. John 14:16–17, 26; 15:26; 16:7, 13, and note the addition of "blood" to the mix of water and Spirit in 1 John 5:6–8).

There has been some debate about what Jesus means by needing to be born of "water" here.[13] It seems most likely that he is alluding to water baptism, specifically the baptism of John the Baptist and/or perhaps Jesus' baptizing of his own disciples (John 3:22–4:6).[14] Recall that many of the leaders of the Jews

---

[12] See the detailed, balanced discussion in R. C. H. Lenski, *The Interpretation of St. John's Gospel* (Columbus, Ohio: Wartburg, 1942), 239–40. Compare also the relatively brief remarks in B. F. Westcott, *The Gospel According to St. John* (reprint, Grand Rapids: Eerdmans, 1971), 50–51; and George Allen Turner and Julius R. Mantey, *The Gospel According to John*, The Evangelical Commentary (Grand Rapids: Eerdmans, 1964), 91–92.

[13] See helpful explanations in Hendriksen, *Exposition of the Gospel According to John*, 134; Westcott, *The Gospel According to St. John*, 49–50; Lenski, *The Interpretation of St. John's Gospel*, 237–38; and Ernst Haenchen, *A Commentary on the Gospel of John Chapters 1–6* (Philadelphia: Fortress, 1984), 200–201.

[14] For a discussion of the close bond between baptism and discipleship, see Richard E. Averbeck, "The Focus of Baptism in the New Testament," *GTJ* 2 (1981): 265–301.

had gone to John to be baptized, and he had warned them that they needed to truly repent and bring forth the appropriate fruits of repentance (Matt. 3). Personal religious piety and reputation are not sufficient. It takes an act of God—an act of the Spirit of God in particular—and for that to happen requires true repentance. In fact, Jesus is deeply disturbed by the fact that Nicodemus, a teacher of the Jews, could not seem to catch on to what he was saying (John 3:9–10).

Perhaps Jesus expected that, initially, Nicodemus might not understand the phrase "born again" (vv. 3–4). But after Jesus' explanation of what he meant by this rather surprising expression in verses 5–8, he seems to have expected Nicodemus to be able to see it, perhaps based on the substantial and sequential connection between what Jesus was saying and Ezekiel 36–37, a passage with which such a teacher as Nicodemus should be fully familiar.[15] According to Ezekiel 36:25–27:

> [25] I will sprinkle *clean water* on you, and you will be *clean;* I will *cleanse* you from all your impurities and from all your idols. [26] I will give you a new heart and put *a new spirit* in you; I will remove from you your heart of stone and give you a heart of flesh. [27] And I will put *my Spirit* in you and move you to follow my decrees and be careful to keep my laws.

Baptism is associated with Jewish water purification procedures.[16] The first point in Ezekiel 36:25–27 is that God would purify Israel from her impurities by washings with water (v. 25).

---

[15] See, for example, F. F. Bruce, *The Gospel of John* (Grand Rapids: Eerdmans, 1983), 84–85.

[16] This is evident even from John 3:22–26. Both John the Baptist and Jesus were baptizing, although not in the same location (vv. 22–23). Nevertheless, this raised the question of the relationship between the two and caused an argument between John's followers and a certain Jew "about purification" (v. 25, NRSV and NASB).

The second point is that he would put a "new spirit" within them, in fact, his divine "Spirit" (vv. 26–27). Naturally, these correspond to baptism (being "born of water) and the Spirit of God giving life to the spirit of a human person (being "born of Spirit"), respectively, in John 3.

Furthermore, Ezekiel 36 leads directly into the vision of the valley of dry bones in chapter 37. The Lord says to the dry bones, "I will make *breath* (lit. 'spirit,' Hebrew *rûaḥ*) enter you, and you will come to life" (v. 5b; cf. vv. 6–10), and later prophecies to the breath, "Come from the four *winds* (plural *rûaḥ*), O breath *(rûaḥ)*, and breathe into these slain, that they may live" (v. 9). At the end of the vision we read again, "I will put *my Spirit (rûaḥ)* in you and you will live" (v. 14a; cf. 36:27 cited earlier). As every first year Hebrew or Greek student knows, the major terms for both "spirit" (a lowercase *s*) and (Holy) "Spirit" (a capital *S*) are also the common words for "wind" or "breath" in both the Hebrew Old Testament *(rûaḥ)* and the Greek New Testament *(pneuma;* cf. the English word "pneumonia"). The connection to John 3 is unmistakable, especially the play on words with "wind" and "Spirit" in verse 8: "The *wind (pneuma)* blows wherever it pleases. You hear its sound, but you cannot tell where it comes from or where it is going. So it is with everyone *born of the Spirit' (pneuma)."* The Holy Spirit *(pneuma)* is like the wind *(pneuma)* that blows. Like wind (i.e., "spirit"), one cannot control *"the* Spirit" (again, note the definite article here).

Even earlier in John's Gospel we read that John the Baptist said, "the one who sent me to baptize with water told me, 'The man on whom you see the Spirit come down and remain is he who will *baptize with the Holy Spirit'"* (John 1:33). If John's baptism and/or the baptism of Jesus is meant in John 3:5, when he referred to being "born of water," and I think this is indeed the case, then being "born of (the) Spirit" corresponds to John's announcement that Jesus would "baptize with the Holy Spirit." Who knows? Perhaps Nicodemus was one of the Jewish leaders who had come to be baptized by John (Matt. 3:7) before Jesus himself had been baptized (vv. 13–17).

It is interesting and important that the unit of text standing between and connecting the story of Jesus' interaction with Nicodemus (John 3:1–21) and his conversation with the Samaritan woman at the well (4:7–42) is the account of the ongoing baptismal activities of both Jesus and John (3:22–4:6; note especially John 4:1b, *"Jesus* was gaining and *baptizing* more *disciples* than *John."*). John the Baptist's attitude toward the fact that Jesus was also having his own disciples baptized (4:2) was: "He must become greater; I must become less" (v. 30). After all, "the one whom God has sent speaks the words of God, for God gives *the Spirit* without limit" (v. 34; note the mention of the Holy Spirit again in a baptismal context). This combination of two baptisms resurfaces even after Pentecost in Acts 19:1–7, where water baptism in the name of Jesus, as opposed to the baptism of John, is treated as the natural lead into *the baptism of the Holy Spirit.*[17] Thus, we see the connection between water baptism and Spirit baptism from John 1 through John 3 into John 4 and beyond.

Spirit and Worship in the Epistles

It is the very "Spirit" of God that works in our human "spirit" so that we might be born again. That's what baptism of the Spirit is about. Anyone who is in Christ is thus baptized according to 1 Corinthians 12:13, "For we were all *baptized by one Spirit* into one body—whether Jews or Greeks, slave or free—and we were all given the *one Spirit to drink.*" The correspondence to John's statements about the one coming, who would baptize with the Holy Spirit, is unmistakable. It is interesting how we come back again and again to the combination of the Spirit and water: being born again by water and Spirit (John 3), the

---

[17] See, for example, the interesting remarks in Haenchen, *The Gospel of John Chapters 1–6,* 200–201. Haenchen's assumption that John 3 refers to Christian baptism is anachronistic, and there are other problems with his treatment of the verse that are beyond the scope of this volume.

woman at the well and the water of Jesus that wells up from within (chap. 4), and we all drink of one Spirit (1 Cor. 12).

First Corinthians 2:10–16 gives us more detail about the underlying realities and dynamics of this work of the Holy Spirit in the believer's spirit. Paul writes:

> The Spirit searches all things, even the deep things of God. For who among men knows the thoughts of a man except the man's spirit within him? In the same way no one knows the thoughts of God except the Spirit of God. (vv. 10b–11)[18]

So the Holy Spirit knows the very depths of God, and a person's human spirit knows the very depths of that person. Verse 12 brings this divine Holy Spirit into intimate relation with the human spirit of one who is in Christ: "We have not received the spirit of the world but the Spirit who is from God, that we may understand what God has freely given us." Recall Romans 8:16, "The *Spirit* himself (the Holy Spirit) testifies with our (human) *spirit* that we are God's children."

By the very nature of things, our knowledge of God (through his Holy Spirit) is intimately bound up with our knowledge of ourselves (that is, our human spirit), and vice versa. This is the so-called "double knowledge" that Calvin discusses in the first chapter of his *Institutes*.[19] We truly know God only when the Holy Spirit of God, who knows God deeply, is "received" into the very realm of our human spirit, which, in turn, knows us deeply. Thus, "we speak of these things in words not taught by human wisdom but taught by the Spirit, interpreting spiritual things to those who are spiritual" (1 Cor. 2:13 NRSV), for "we have the mind of Christ" (v. 16b).

---

[18] See the careful and insightful discussion of this passage in Gordon D. Fee, *God's Empowering Presence: The Holy Spirit in the Letters of Paul* (Peabody, Mass.: Hendrickson, 1994), 99–105.

[19] John Calvin, *Institutes of the Christian Religion*, 2 vols., LCC, ed. J. T. McNeil (Grand Rapids: Eerdmans, 1970), 1:37–39.

Admittedly, it is difficult to grasp the concept of "spirit." After all, it is like the "wind," and wind is not something we can lay our hands on (or even our minds) in such a way that we can control it (John 3:8; Acts 2:1). Yet wind is an important and powerful physical force in the world, and the Holy Spirit is likewise important and powerful as his work is brought to bear on a person's human spirit in ways that are deeply transforming. The same Holy Spirit who inspired the writing of Scripture through the prophets (Heb. 1:1 with 2 Peter 1:20–21; cf. also *theopneustos,* "God breathed," in 2 Tim. 3:16) brings the truths of that very same Scripture to bear upon us, especially the truths about "what God has *freely given us*" in Christ Jesus (1 Cor. 2:12b). Thus, it is the gospel that transforms us as the Holy Spirit brings its various truths to bear upon us.

Moreover, the gospel is always "good news" to everyone, non-Christian and Christian alike. Even if we are already true believers, there are always ways in which the impact and significance of the gospel still needs to be worked into our human spirit, and from there into every aspect of our lives, including our worship of God. That God himself seeks such worshipers is enough in itself, but there is also the reality of the reflexive effect this kind of worship can have back upon us. True worship, authentic worship, in spirit is one of the most powerfully transforming activities we can engage in as Christians. It has the effect of changing our whole outlook on life as we look at life from the standpoint of engagement with God in spirit. This is true not only for the individual Christian but also the community in which he lives and fellowships, and with which he worships.

This is where Ephesians 5 is most helpful. Paul writes, beginning with verse 15:

> Be very careful, then, how you live—not as unwise but as wise, **16**making the most of every opportunity, because the days are evil. **17**Therefore do not be foolish, but understand what the Lord's will is. **18**Do not get drunk on wine, which leads to debauchery. Instead, be

filled with the Spirit. **19**Speak to one another with psalms, hymns and spiritual songs. Sing and make music in your heart to the Lord, **20**always giving thanks to God the Father for everything, in the name of our Lord Jesus Christ (5:15–20; cf. also Col. 3:16).[20]

There is some debate about these verses, especially the analogy in verse 18 between being drunk with wine and being "filled with the Spirit." It seems to me that one of the most interesting background connections is to the Day of Pentecost when the onlookers were thinking that those who had been filled with the Holy Spirit were drunk. Yes, the Greek word for "being filled" is different in these two places, but Paul never anywhere uses the word used in Acts, so it is not sound method to press the distinction between them.

It is also interesting that there is no definite article with "Spirit" in Ephesians 5:18. This raises the question of whether Paul might be using the term in a more general sense, perhaps something like "God is spirit" so we must worship him "in spirit" in John 4.[21] Close attention to "filling" terminology elsewhere in Ephesians helps us here. Ephesians 1:13–14 refers to the fact that we are "marked in him (i.e., in Christ) with a seal, the promised Holy Spirit, who is a deposit guaranteeing our inheritance." Ultimately, our full inheritance is in Christ "who *fills* everything in every way" (v. 23).

In Ephesians 3:16–19, Paul speaks of his desire that we be strengthened "with power through his Spirit" in our "inner being"

---

[20] Again, see the very helpful remarks in Fee, *God's Empowering Presence*, 718–23.

[21] Carl B. Hoch Jr., *All Things New: The Significance of Newness for Biblical Theology* (Grand Rapids: Baker, 1995), 40–41, suggests that we do not necessarily need to distinguish between human and divine "spirit" here. His point is that "the human spirit energized by the divine spirit would produce the divine verbal fluidity," so that "the Christian who is full in his personal spirit expresses verbally his internal fullness by praising the Lord in psalms, hymns, and spiritual songs" (41).

(v. 16) that we "be *filled* to the measure of all the *fullness of God*" (v. 19). Similarly, in Ephesians 4, he commands us to "make every effort to keep the unity of the Spirit through the bond of peace" (v. 3). This corresponds to the fact that there is "one faith" (v. 5), and the goal is that we "reach unity in the faith and in the knowledge of the Son of God and become mature, attaining to the whole measure of the *fullness of Christ*" (v. 13). Thus, earlier in Ephesians, we hear about being "filled up" with the "fullness" of both God the *Father* and the *Son* of God.

In light of all this, perhaps the best way to understand Ephesians 5:18 is that we are to be *filled up* with the *fullness of the Spirit* of God in the "inner being." The Trinitarian pattern here is fascinating and perhaps adds helpful information for our interpretation of verse 18. However, there is also the fact that this Spirit of God fills up the "inner being" of a person in Ephesians 3:16. This is surely another way of talking about the human "spirit."

This brings us back to the connection between God as "spirit," the Holy Spirit of God, and the human "spirit." God is spirit, so we must worship him in spirit, and *this is the main concern of the Holy Spirit as he fills our spirit with his presence.* Thus, we "speak to one another with psalms, hymns and spiritual songs." We "sing and make music" in our *"heart* to the Lord, always giving thanks to God the Father for everything, in the name of our Lord Jesus Christ" (Eph. 5:19–20). Note once again the Trinitarian combination even *within* this passage. The Holy Spirit fills us so that we give thanks to the Father in the name of the Son, our Lord Jesus Christ.[22]

Worship Space and Worship Community in the Bible

There is, of course, an individual dimension to worship in the Bible. There are individual worshipers. But in Ephesians 5

---

[22] Fee, *God's Empowering Presence,* 723.

the community dimension comes through as well. The Spirit would have us "speak to *one another* with psalms, hymns and spiritual songs" (v. 19). Moreover, in this very context, we are exhorted to "Submit to *one another* out of reverence for Christ" (v. 21). In fact, the imperative "be filled with the Spirit" in verse 18 is followed by a series of participles that develop the impact such filling would have in the church: *speaking* to one another in worship, *singing* and *making music* in their heart (v. 19), always *giving thanks* to God (v. 20), and *submitting* "to one another out of reverence for Christ" (v. 21 continuing through vv. 22–23).[23] Worshiping well as a community and living well as a community go together, and both derive from "the unity of the Spirit through the bond of peace" (Eph. 4:3b).

The relationship between the community as a worshiping community and the Holy Spirit also finds its expression in another pattern that has its foundation in the Old Testament and carries profound implications in the New Testament. Earlier in Ephesians we read about the church as a holy temple. The wall of partition between Jew and Gentile has been broken down in Christ:

> [18] For through *him* (Christ) we both have access to the *Father* by one *Spirit.* [19] Consequently, you are no longer foreigners and aliens, but fellow citizens with God's people and members of *God's household,* [20] built on *the foundation* of the apostles and prophets, with Christ Jesus himself as the *chief cornerstone.* [21] In him the whole *building* is joined together and rises to become *a holy temple in the Lord.* [22] And in him you too are *being built together* to become *a dwelling in which God lives **by his Spirit*** (lit. "a dwelling place of God in Spirit"). (2:18–22)

The church is a temple of the Holy Spirit. Now, if a temple is anything, it is a place of worship, and it is a place of worship precisely because it is a place of God's presence. This brings us

---

[23] Ibid., 719, 722.

back to John 4 where the Samaritan woman turned the discussion to the subject of the proper place of worship. Jesus responded by turning the subject back again to the true worship of God in spirit, since God is by nature "spirit," and worship of him must correspond to his true nature. The temple motif, of course, has deep roots in the soil of the Old Testament and blossoms into all the glory of God in the New Testament.

The Tabernacle/Temple Presence of God in the Old Testament

Let's look at the Old Testament roots first. In a sense, it all begins with the tabernacle back in Exodus through Numbers. The ratification of the Mosaic covenant took place in the shadow of Mount Sinai, the mountain of God (Exod. 18:5; 24:13; cf. 19:2, "in the desert in front of *the* mountain"). This was the mountain where Moses first encountered Yahweh at the burning bush (3:1; cf. 4:27). At the burning bush, God promised Moses that his presence would be with him in bringing Israel out of Egypt back to this very place of divine presence (3:12–15) on their way to the Promised Land. Part of God's plan and purpose for building the tabernacle was to provide a place or "sacred space" for the Lord to "dwell among them" even after they left Sinai (25:8).[24] In essence, the tabernacle was to be a moveable Sinai. It was a place of worship and a place of God's continued presence. It was also a symbol. Wherever the tabernacle was the Lord would be present in all his glory just as he had been at Sinai.

This worship of God in his very presence is the perspective that surrounds and pervades the book of Leviticus. Exodus 40:17–33 recounts the erection of the tabernacle in the second year on the first day of the first month. Exodus 40:34–35 describes the Lord's immediate and glorious habitation of the tabernacle:

---

[24] Ron Manahan introduced the ancient Near Eastern concept of sacred space in Chapter 1, pp. 60–65.

Then the cloud covered the Tent of Meeting, and the glory of the LORD filled the tabernacle. Moses could not enter the Tent of Meeting because the cloud had settled upon it, and the glory of the LORD filled the tabernacle.

Moses could not enter the tabernacle because of the intensity of the Lord's manifest presence there, so the book of Leviticus begins, "The LORD *called to* Moses and spoke to him *from* the Tent of Meeting" (Lev. 1:1).

The last three verses of Exodus anticipate the Lord's guidance of Israel through the wilderness from Sinai to the Promised Land:

. . . whenever the cloud lifted from above the tabernacle, they would set out; but if the cloud did not lift, they did not set out. . . . So the cloud of the LORD was over the tabernacle by day, and fire was in the cloud by night, in the sight of all the house of Israel during all their travels (40:36–38).

This, of course, is a continuation of the Lord's guidance and presence with the people previously, even before the construction and erection of the tabernacle, from Egypt to Sinai (Exod. 13:21–22). The same point is repeated over and over again as instruction for the journey from Sinai to the Promised Land in Numbers 9:15–23, just before their departure from Sinai in Numbers 10:11–12, 33–34.

Leviticus 1 through Numbers 9:14, therefore, are encased between these two tabernacle presence and guidance passages (Exod. 40:34–38; Num. 9:15–23), and the regulations contained therein focus especially upon the need to "practice" that presence on various levels (i.e., in the tabernacle as well as in the community at large) and in multiple ways: in worship, through maintaining the purity and holiness of God's presence, in relationships within the community, and separation from corrupting influences of the surrounding nations, etc. Even the main narrative section within the book of Leviticus focuses on the consecration of the tabernacle and the priesthood, and the inauguration of tabernacle worship in Israel (Lev. 8–9). Moreover, it was on the inauguration day that:

> Fire came out *from the presence of* (lit. "from to the faces of") the LORD and consumed the burnt offering and the fat portions on the altar. And when all the people saw it, they shouted for joy and fell facedown (9:24).

Sometime soon thereafter, on the same day (note the reference back to the inaugural sin offering of 9:15 in 10:16–20), Aaron's two oldest sons, Nadab and Abihu, violated the sanctity of the Lord's presence (10:1), "So fire came out *from the presence of* (lit. 'from to the faces of') the LORD and consumed them, and they died before the LORD" (10:2; cf. 9:24). The Lord had already made it clear that "Among *those who approach me* (i.e., the priests) I will show myself *holy;* in the sight of all the people I will be *honored*" (10:3).[25]

The same glory cloud and divine consuming of sacrifices by fire recurred at the dedication of Solomon's temple, when the Lord took up residence there (1 Kgs. 8:10–11; 2 Chron. 5:13–14; 7:1–3). As we have already observed, like Jesus in John 4, Solomon recognized the limitations of the temple even at the dedication of the temple: "The heavens, even the highest heaven, cannot contain you. How much less this temple I have built!" (1 Kgs. 8:27b). Nevertheless, there was a visible physical manifestation of the Lord's presence in the tabernacle (and later the temple), centered in the most holy place, the "holy of holies" (Lev. 16:2, "I appear in the cloud over the atonement cover"). Unfortunately, by the time of the Babylonian captivity in 586/7 B.C., the Israelites had so desecrated and defiled the temple that the glory

---

[25] For more on this incident, see Richard E. Averbeck, "Clean and Unclean," in *NIDOTTE,* ed. W. A. VanGemeren (Grand Rapids: Zondervan, 1997), 4:478–81.

cloud presence of the Lord departed from the temple, abandoning it to destruction (Ezek. 8:4; 10:3–4, 18–19; 11:22–25). Even then, however, there was the promise of the Lord's return (Ezek. 43), which brings us to the New Testament.

The Tabernacle/Temple Presence of God in the New Testament

The whole tabernacle/temple system of the Old Testament comes through into the New Testament in explicit and authoritative ways, albeit with transformations that correspond to the fact that Jesus has "opened" for us "a new and living way" to God "through the curtain, that is, his body" (Heb. 10:20). There is a new kind of sacrifice for this new covenant community, so these are two different kinds of communities: one of Jew only and one of mixed Jew and Gentile with the wall of partition broken down between them (cf. Eph. 2:14–16); one constituting a political national entity and the other permeating the world across political and national boundaries; one with a physical temple and one actually constituting the *temple of God in the Spirit* and, therefore, *the manifestation of his glory in this age.*

As far as we know, the cloud of God's glorious presence never returned to the rebuilt Jerusalem temple in the same way after it departed in the days of Ezekiel. Perhaps there will be a millennial restoration of the temple, perhaps not. The eternal state and new Jerusalem are still another matter, which we will introduce later. But for the moment we are not concerned with these. Instead, as John 1:14 puts it, "The Word became flesh and *made his dwelling* ('tabernacled') among us. We have seen *his glory, the glory of the One and Only,* who came from the Father, full of grace and truth" (cf. 2:11; 7:18; 17:24). Later, in his "high priestly prayer" on behalf of those who would believe in him (John 17:20), Jesus said to the Father, "I have given them *the glory* that you gave me, that they may be one as we are one: I in them and you in me" (vv. 22–23a).

This glory comes from the Holy Spirit of God who indwells

us (2 Cor. 3:17–18; 4:4, 6; cf. John 14:16–17). The church is "a *holy temple* in the Lord . . . *a dwelling* in which *God lives by his Spirit*" (Eph. 2:21–22; cf. 1 Cor. 3:16–17; 1 Peter 2:4–5). According to 2 Corinthians 3:18, we are actually the reflection of God's glory in the world: "And we, who with unveiled faces all reflect the Lord's glory, are being transformed into his likeness with ever-increasing glory, which comes from the Lord, who is the Spirit." As in the Old Testament, the sanctuary presence of God is nothing to trifle with. The corporate body of believers is sacred to him, and God takes violation of that sacred domain seriously. First Corinthians 3:17 says, "If anyone destroys God's temple, God will destroy him; for God's temple is *sacred*, and you are that temple." Similarly, the individual believer is "*a temple of the Holy Spirit*," so we must not defile ourselves through immorality (1 Cor. 6:18–19) but instead "honor (lit. 'glorify,' Gk. *doxazō*) God" with our bodies (v. 20; cf. Lev. 10:3 cited earlier). Thus, the presence of God is the key to tracing the theology of sacred worship *place* in the Old Testament into the New Testament in terms of the theology of sacred worship *community*.

Finally, we need to say something about the new heaven and earth in Revelation 21–22. Once again we clearly have "sacred space" terminology. There is, for example, "*the Holy City*, the new Jerusalem, coming down out of heaven from God. . . . And . . . a loud voice from the throne saying, 'Now *the dwelling of God is with men*, and he *will live with* them (cf. the same terminology in John 1:14). They will be his people, and God himself will be with them and be their God" (Rev. 21:2–3; cf. 21:10; 22:19). This city "shone with *the glory of God*" and, in fact, there was *no* "*temple* in the city, because *the Lord God Almighty and the Lamb are its temple*," and there was no need for sun and moon "for *the glory of God* gives it light, and the Lamb is its lamp" (21:22–23; cf. 22:5). Accordingly, "*Nothing impure* will ever enter it, nor will anyone who does *what is shameful or deceitful*, but only those whose names are written in the Lamb's book of life" (21:27).

Ultimately, therefore, we will end up in the ultimate temple that is not a temple but the very presence of God himself. This actually reflects back on the first heaven and earth, in which we now live, for Revelation 21–22 not only draws on concepts of sacred space but is replete with references back to the Garden of Eden in Genesis 2–3. In the new heaven and earth, for example, the waters that flow out from the throne of God (Rev. 22:1), the precious stones (21:11–21), and especially "the tree of life" (22:2, 14, 19) all call to mind the original Garden. Moreover, in that place the Lord himself "will *wipe every tear* from their eyes. There will be *no more death or mourning or crying or pain,* for the *old order* of things has passed away" (21:4), and "No longer will there be any *curse*" (22:3). In essence, we are heading back to where we came from—even better.

In recent years, scholars have recognized that there is "sanctuary symbolism in the garden of Eden story."[26] In essence, the Garden of Eden is "an archetypal sanctuary." There are various kinds of seeming correspondences between the Garden of Eden account and the tabernacle and temple texts later in the canon. Some of these correspondences are less convincing than others, and there is no explicit statement in Genesis 2–3 that this was a "sacred place." To my way of thinking, however, it certainly was a place of worship. God was manifestly present there. So, when all is said and done, from the very beginning we have been called to be worshipers (Gen. 2–3), and that, above all, is what we will be for all eternity (Rev. 21–22).

First of all, above all, and throughout, we are to become the kind of worshipers that God seeks: "[W]hether you eat or drink or whatever you do, do it all for the glory of God" (1 Cor. 10:31). The theology of authentic worship permeates Scripture

---

[26] See Gordon J. Wenham, "Sanctuary Symbolism in the Garden of Eden Story," in *Proceedings of the Ninth World Congress of Jewish Studies* (Jerusalem: World Union of Jewish Studies, 1986), 19–25.

from beginning to end, and it stands at the heart of God's creative and redemptive work. Think of it! As a worshiping community we get to be the very manifestation of the "glory" of God's presence in this world. This underlies the words of Jesus when he said to the Samaritan woman at the well:

> . . . a time is coming and has now come when the true worshipers will worship the Father in spirit and truth, for they are the kind of worshipers the Father seeks. God is spirit, and his worshipers must worship in spirit and in truth. (John 4:23–24)

Conclusion

Before moving on to "worship in truth," let me make a few final points based on the substance of this chapter. The principle of worship in "spirit" has two sides: the human side (the human spirit) and the divine side (the nature of God as "spirit" and the Holy Spirit). The Holy Spirit gives us new birth in our human spirit and from that point forward stimulates us to worship God in spirit, since God is spirit. The direct correspondence and functional connection between the divine Spirit and the human spirit is of the utmost importance in worship.

There are, of course, any number of things that could squelch the divine/human spiritual dynamic of worship in our lives and communities. But let me suggest two that come directly out of the way we approach Scripture as pastors, teachers, or students. We are each called to engage in serious study of God's Word as "a workman who does not need to be ashamed and who correctly handles the word of truth" (2 Tim. 2:15b). This is important, but I fear that we sometimes teach and practice *a way* of studying God's Word that, in fact, diminishes its effect in our lives and ministries by undermining our worship as his children and our ministries as his servants. Let me explain.

Since the Scriptures are God's Word, *we need to take God*

seriously in our study of the Bible by making our study above all else
an encounter with him. Too many of us frequently approach the
Bible in our study as an object of research in preparation for
some occasion of preaching or teaching rather than as a means
of encountering God himself in a personal and transforming
way. We are more concerned about gaining a right and profound understanding than living a holy life. I am not arguing
that we should not be concerned about getting it right. No, we
need to handle the Word of truth "correctly," but that does not
mean just getting it right. It also involves engaging with it in a
way that gets *us* right even as we study. Recall, for example,
Joshua 1:8, "Do not let this Book of the Law depart from your
mouth; meditate on it day and night, so that you may be careful to do everything written in it. Then you will be prosperous
and successful" (see also Pss. 1:1–3; 25:4–5; 119:14–16, 33–36,
etc.).

If it is true, and I think it is, that the most personally transforming activity we can engage in is worship, then we need to
be worshipers even in the study. We ourselves need to be impacted and transformed by an encounter with God in the study
before we attempt to bring it to other people from behind the
pulpit or the lectern, or even in personal one-on-one or small
group ministry contexts. Our study needs to be a time and
place where we "practice God's presence" while we are attend-
ing to his holy Word. We need to experience our study of God's
Word as an encounter with God himself, worshiping him "in
spirit and in truth" as we study. If we do this, then application
will not be a last step artificial add-on to our preaching or teaching but will, instead, be woven into the warp and woof of our
ministry of the Word.

On the human spirit side of this divine/human dynamic, *we*
need to take our human nature and experience seriously by function-
ing as a fully human person in the study. Our mind, will, emotions, attitudes, perspectives on life, personality, personal and
interpersonal problems, background, and all the rest of what
we are as a living breathing person need to be fully engaged as

we study. When it comes right down to it, the most important exegetical and theological "tool" we have is our own "heart" as it has been shaped by our life experiences and especially by personal and communal encounter with God himself. We have all sorts of tools to use in our study of the Bible: biblical languages and language resources, various kinds of reference books, and so on. Our human "spirit," our "heart," is the most important of all because we are not just a brain to be filled with data to manipulate, even biblical data. God did not write the Bible to computers.

By encountering God in all our humanness, we present our whole person to him for change as we study. There is no place here for a coldly objective purely cognitive rational study that tries to get a right understanding of the text while shutting out whole parts of one's life and person. Doing that amounts to shutting those parts of oneself or one's life off from God in the midst of encountering him in his Word. As we have already observed, our knowledge of God through his Holy Spirit is intimately bound up with our knowledge of ourselves, that is, our human spirit, and vice versa.

Finally, assuming that one has made his or her own study of God's Word an encounter with God, with the human spirit fully engaged, we still need to reckon with the fact that none of us can make change happen in the heart/spirit of another person. Change does not come easy. None of us has a small problem with sin. We all have a *big* problem with sin, and that's true even of a man or woman who truly has a heart for God (see, e.g., David in 1 Sam. 13:14 and 16:7, and yet his serious problems with sin, e.g., in 2 Sam. 11–12 with Ps. 51). Only the Holy Spirit can change a heart, and only the Holy Spirit can change a church or Christian school community. It is the Holy Spirit's work to sanctify us as individuals and communities of believers, and we have been arguing here that one of the most powerfully transforming processes through which he does this is worship. In fact, it all really starts and ends with worship. Worship shapes and motivates the whole sanctification process through the divine/human "spirit" dynamic that is of the essence of worship "in spirit."[27]

One of the basic elements of this dynamic of worship in spirit is seeing God with the "eyes" of our "heart," as Paul puts it in Ephesians 1:18. One thing is for sure, if we do indeed see God, like Isaiah, we will most certainly be impressed (6:1–4). That, in turn, will put the issues of our own lives and ministries in proper perspective (vv. 5–8). One of our main problems in life and ministry as preachers, teachers, students, scholars, and simply as Christians is that we are often impressed with the wrong things, something other than God himself. We can know a lot and learn more without being transformed. Biblical transformation of the heart takes place when we become so deeply impressed with God and his purposes in and through our lives that our will, our volition, becomes engaged in the ongoing process of change and growth. When that which we are impressed with changes, then what we desire changes along with it. Worship, authentic worship, is about God and about desiring him above all else. Deep and meaningful change takes place when the things that matter to us change; and when God matters most, then worship has had its true intended effect in spirit and in truth.

---

[27] This is the burden and passion of Stuart's treatment of John 4 in "A New Testament Perspective on Worship," esp. 217–21. "One worships God by entering into his presence, by establishing a spiritual relationship with him. It is not physical acts done in physical places which define worship. We worship God by participating in the life that is spiritually defined and by living in the truth. It is life on a new spiritual level and life that acknowledges truth which is worship" (218).

CHAPTER FOUR

Worshiping God in Truth

Richard E. Averbeck

In the previous chapter we looked at John 4 from the perspective of "worship in spirit." Now we turn to "worship in truth." Although the present discussion is split along these lines, it is important to keep in mind that the two, spirit and truth, are inextricably bound together. They work in combination with one another. They do not actually function independently in the grammar of the passage or in the act of worship itself. The preposition "in" occurs only once in the Greek text of John 4:24b: God's "worshipers must worship in spirit and truth" (not "in spirit and in truth").

Jesus encountered the Samaritan woman at a well, "Jacob's well" (v. 6), which became an occasion for introducing the Holy Spirit as water that becomes "a spring of water welling up to eternal life" (v. 14; cf. John 7:37–39).[1] This water wells up "in" anyone to whom Jesus gives it. This, in turn, leads to the subsequent focus on "spirit" (human) and "Spirit" (divine) in genuine worship, as discussed earlier in chapter 3. The first part of the encounter, therefore, turned on the issue of water, the Holy Spirit, and the (human) spirit of the worshiper.

As Jesus and the woman continue, there is a subtle shift to issues of truth along with spirit. It begins with the woman's

---

[1] Translations are from the *New International Version* (NIV) unless indicated otherwise.

admission of her questionable marital status and Jesus' response to it: "What you have just said is quite *true*" (John 4:16–18). Eventually we find out that this was a turning point for the woman (v. 39). Since Jesus knew things about her that there was no way for him to know, humanly speaking, she became convinced that this man knew the truth about other things as well. The woman immediately turns to the question of the right place of worship, a major point of contention between Jews and Samaritans, and, like the water at the well, Jesus turns that into an opportunity to go beyond the woman's current conception of what mattered to make the point that "the *true* worshipers will worship the Father in spirit and *truth*" (v. 23). Later, the Samaritans end their confession with this: "we know that this is *truly* the Savior of the world" (v. 42b).

Truth and the Woman at the Well

The meaning of "truth" in John's writings has been a subject of interest to all who have done serious work in this Gospel.[2] In John 4, the truth that Jerusalem was the acceptable place of worship, not Mount Gerizim (v. 22), provided the background for the emphasis Jesus placed on truth in worship. This is not the place to go into a full treatment of the history of the Samaritans and their relations with the Jews. Just a few of the major points will serve our purposes here.[3]

---

[2] See especially the helpful discussion of "truth" in John in Dennis R. Lindsay, "What Is Truth? Ἀλήθεια in the Gospel of John," *ResQ* 35 (1993): 129–45, along with the brief excursus in Leon Morris, *The Gospel According to John,* NICOT (Grand Rapids: Eerdmans, 1971), 293–96.

[3] See the helpful brief summary of Samaritan history, their relationship with the Jews, and their theology in J. Julius Scott Jr., *Customs and Controversies: Intertestamental Jewish Backgrounds of the New Testament* (Grand Rapids: Baker, 1995), 196–200. Robert T. Anderson, "Samaritans," in *The Anchor Bible Dictionary,* vol. 5, ed. D. N. Freedman (New York: Doubleday, 1992), 940–47, discusses conflicting views of history and theology between Jews and Samaritans, with good bibliography.

First, the history of the Samaritans goes back to the days when the Assyrians took the northern kingdom of Israel into captivity, around 722 B.C. The northern kingdom had fallen and much of its population had been taken into captivity into Assyria because of its sin against the Lord described in 2 Kings 17. The Assyrians, however, not only deported Israelites but also brought people from Babylonia and Syria to settle them in Samaria (v. 24). At first, they worshiped only their former deities, but then they also adopted what they called the "god" of the land and created a syncretistic form of worship (vv. 25–40). In the meantime, it appears that the remaining Israelites (see 2 Chron. 30:1–2) intermarried with the new inhabitants of the land. The chapter ends: "Even while these people were *worshiping the Lord*, they were *serving their idols. To this day* their children and grandchildren *continue to do as their fathers did*" (2 Kgs. 17:41). So in the day of the writer of this section of 2 Kings, they were engaging in syncretistic worship of Yahweh.

Second, when the Jews who were exiled into Babylonia returned from that exile over a century later, they encountered the descendants of this people. They had been sent back specifically to rebuild the Jerusalem temple as a place of pure worship of Yahweh. Moreover, they were especially concerned about the purity of the Jewish race. These two factors and caution about political and religious maneuvering caused the leaders of the restored Jews to reject the help of the Samaritans in rebuilding the temple. As a result, increased enmity developed between the Jews and the Samaritans (Ezra 4:1–4).

Third, around 400 B.C., the Samaritans built a temple on Mount Gerizim, which was destroyed by the Hasmonean leaders of the Jewish Maccabean revolt in 128 B.C. This, of course, further strained relations between the Jews and the Samaritans. The ongoing enmity is reflected in John 4:9, when the Samaritan woman said to Jesus, "You are a Jew and I am a Samaritan woman. How can you ask me for a drink?" The apostle John adds the remark, "For Jews do not associate with Samaritans." The woman eventually brings the subject of their conversation around to one of the major points of contention between the Jews and the Samaritans—the proper place of worship. As she puts it: "Our fathers worshiped on this mountain, but you Jews claim that the place where we must worship is in Jerusalem" (v. 20).

Jesus affirmed the fact that the Jews were right about it being Jerusalem, not Mount Gerizim—the mountain next to which they were standing (note the woman says, "Our fathers worshiped on *this* mountain," v. 20), but he did it indirectly.[4] To begin with, Jesus turned the focus away from the place of worship: "a time is coming when you will worship the Father neither on this mountain nor in Jerusalem" (v. 21). Then, and more to the point of the issue as the woman has raised it, Jesus said, "*You* Samaritans worship what you do not know; *we* worship what we do know, for salvation is from the Jews" (v. 22; both the "you" at the beginning of the verse and the "we" in the middle of the verse are emphatic in Greek). The implications are clear regarding the proper place of worship, but there is much more to it than that. Not only are the Jews right about the proper place of worship, but they are also, in fact, the ones through whom salvation comes.

In comparison to that, the place of worship is relatively insignificant, especially in light of the fact that, "a time is coming when you will worship the Father neither on this mountain nor in Jerusalem" (v. 21), and "a time is coming *and has now come* when the true worshipers will worship the Father in spirit and truth, for they are the kind of worshipers the Father seeks" (v. 23). Here Jesus takes his point further. Not only is a time of this kind of worship coming, but it "has" already "come." This sets the background for Jesus' response to the woman's next assertion: "'I know that Messiah' (called Christ) 'is coming. When he comes, he will explain everything to us'" (v. 25). Jesus responded by proclaiming to her, "I who speak to you am he" (v.

---

[4] D. A. Carson, *The Gospel According to John* (Grand Rapids: Eerdmans, 1991), 223–24.

26). There is a truth here that is bigger than the woman could have imagined at the beginning of this conversation. But she became convinced, and so did many others of the Samaritans (v. 41), that this "Jesus" (the Greek form of the Hebrew name *yehoshuah*, "Joshua," which means "Yahweh is salvation") was indeed the Messiah and the "*Savior* of the world" (v. 42).

Salvation really is of the Jews, but to worship the Savior does not require any particular place of worship, so Samaritans are not required to go to Jerusalem to worship. What it does require is worship that wells up from within the worshiper's human spirit through the regenerating and sanctifying work of the Holy Spirit (see chap. 3 earlier). By its very nature, this kind of worship is characterized by truth as well. As remarked at the beginning of this chapter, spirit and truth go together in genuine worship, and that's the only kind of worship that is acceptable to the Father.

Ultimately, the "truth" Jesus is talking about here is the truth about himself as the *Word* of God (John 1:1–5)—"the truth" incarnate: "I am the way and *the truth* and the life. No one comes to the Father except through me" (John 14:6).[5] So *worship that is acceptable to God* the Father (4:21–24), as opposed to the teachings of the "fathers" of the Samaritans (v. 20), *begins with accepting Jesus as the Messiah.* Jesus is the one who explains "everything" (v. 25). Here stands truth, staring the woman directly in the face. God's "truth" comes to concrete expression in Jesus the Messiah. On one level, therefore, his point is that if we are going to worship God the Father, we will need to accept his expression of "truth" in his Son.

Interestingly enough, later in his Gospel, John refers to the Holy Spirit as "the Spirit of truth" (John 14:17; 15:26; esp. 16:13, "when he, the Spirit of *truth,* comes, he will guide you into all *truth*"). So, in a sense, for John spirit and truth eventually come together in the testimony that "the *Spirit* of truth" gives to Jesus, the *Son* of God, as the Messiah, which comes to expression in

---

[5] Morris, *The Gospel According to John,* 293–96.

the worshiper's life when he or she worships the *Father* acceptably, "in spirit and truth." Perhaps we can say it this way: the
Trinity is fully occupied with truth, and the only kind of worship that is acceptable to the Trinitarian God is the kind where
truth wells up within our human *spirit.*

Truth in John

Unfortunately, like Pilate, in our North American culture,
we tend to think of "truth" as an abstract concept ("What is
truth?" John 18:38); and/or knowing "truth" is to know about
something or someone. Sometimes this is indeed what "truth"
means in John. For example, Jesus refers to himself as "a man
who has told you the truth that I heard from God" (John 8:40),
as opposed to the devil who does not hold "to the truth, for
there is no truth in him. When he lies, he speaks his native
language, for he is a liar and the father of lies" (v. 44).

However, there are times in the biblical world, Old Testament and New, when "truth" has a more full and active meaning. We have it in English too. For example, we can sometimes
refer to a person as a "*true* friend." This usually does not just
mean that it is correct to say that this or that person is my
"friend." It means that this is a loyal friend, who has shown
that he or she is my friend in various meaningful ways. The
biblical foundation for this understanding of truth in the Bible
is the Old Testament Hebrew root *ʾmn,* from which derive the
following words. First, there is *ʾamen,* from which we get our
English word "Amen" (used to end prayers, and often an essential element of doxologies and benedictions). It means literally
"truly" or "surely," affirming the reliability of what has just been
said, whether in oaths (e.g., Num. 5:22; Deut. 27:15–26), pro-
nouncements (e.g., 1 Kgs. 1:36; Jer. 28:6), or doxologies (e.g.,
Neh. 8:6; Pss. 41:13[14]; 72:19; 89:53; 106:48, which are the
points of division between the books of the five books of the
Psalter). It is sometimes transliterated into Greek in the New
Testament word *amen* (e.g., Rom. 1:25 in affirming the blessed-

ness of the Creator God; 1 Cor. 14:16 for saying amen when one gives thanks to God).

Second, "faithfulness, steadfastness, fidelity" *(ʾᵉmûnâ)* in the Old Testament comes from the same root in Hebrew *(ʾmn)*. It is used of people who are faithful (e.g., 1 Sam. 26:23 and Ps. 119:29–30, where the "faithful way" of life is contrasted with the "false way"), the faithfulness of the coming Messiah, the branch of David (Isa. 11:5, parallel with "righteousness"), and of the faithfulness and reliability of God and whatever he says (e.g., Deut. 32:4; Isa. 25:1 with another form of the root, meaning literally "trustworthy faithfulness"). In the LXX, this word is most often translated with the New Testament Greek word *pistos,* "faithful, trustworthy, reliable," or *pistis,* which often means "faith, trust, confidence" but can also mean "faithfulness, fidelity."

Third, "true" or "genuine" *(ʾᵉmet)* also comes from the same Hebrew root *(ʾmn)* and is paralleled in the New Testament with "truth, truthfulness, integrity" *(alēthinos* or *alētheia).* The latter is the word used in John 4:24 for worship "in spirit and *truth.*" In the Hebrew Old Testament, *ʾᵉmet* can signify the "truth" of a fact or statement (e.g., 1 Kgs. 17:24; Eccl. 12:10; 2 Chron. 15:3, "the true God" is lit. "the God of truth") as well as the "trustworthiness" or "dependability" of people (e.g., Exod. 18:21, lit. "men of truth"; Neh. 7:2 NIV, "a man of integrity") and of God (e.g., Ps. 30:9[10]; Isa. 38:18–19). Most importantly, the same word occurs numerous times in a pair with the well-known Hebrew word *ḥesed* "kindness, (covenant) loyalty, steadfast faithfulness." This pair is often used to refer to the relational commitment and loyalty of people (e.g., Gen. 24:49, "if you will show [lit. 'do'] kindness *[ḥesed]* and faithfulness *[ʾᵉmet]* to my master"; cf. Gen. 47:29; Josh. 2:14; 2 Sam. 15:20; Prov. 3:3; 14:22; 16:6; 20:28) or the lack thereof (Hos. 4:1).

The same pair also characterizes God's way of relating to his people. Note especially Exodus 34:6, where it refers to Yahweh as "the compassionate and gracious God, slow to anger, abounding in love *(ḥesed)* and faithfulness *(ʾᵉmet).*" This is part of the character of God that causes him to forgive even the sin of the golden calf in his covenant relationship with his people (Exod. 32–34). In fact, this description of God becomes Israel's 1 John 1:9, so to speak. It is repeated in the context of God's willingness to forgive sin. See especially Psalms 86:15 and 103:8 (the latter leaves off "and faithfulness," perhaps for metrical reasons; cf. Neh. 9:17; Joel 2:13; Jonah 4:2). The word pair itself occurs many times in various kinds of contexts (e.g., Pss. 25:10; 26:3; 40:10–11; 54:3, 10; 61:7; 89:14; 108:4; 115:1; 117:2; 138:2; Mic. 7:20).

All three of the Old Testament words referred to above and their meanings come through in John. Note especially his combination of all these terms in Revelation 3:14, "These are the words of the Amen (Greek *amen* = Hebrew *ʾamen*), the faithful (Greek *pistos* = Hebrew *ʾᵉmûnâ*) and true (Greek *alēthinos* = Hebrew *ʾᵉmet*) witness, the ruler of God's creation." As Dennis Lindsay puts it, "The meaning of *alētheia* (ἀλήθεια) in John cannot be fully appreciated apart from the meaning of the Hebrew substantive *ʾemeth.*"[6] It begins in John 1:14 and 17, where we have the word pair "grace" *(charis)* and "truth" *(alētheia),* which he suggests calls to mind the Hebrew word pair "love *[hesed]* and faithfulness *[ʾᵉmet]*" treated earlier. He refers specifically to Exodus 34:6 and points out the manifold parallels between John 1 and Exodus 33–34. For example, in both places God's glory is associated with a tent in the midst of his people (Exod. 33:7–11; John 1:14), there is the issue of seeing God (Exod. 33:20–23; John 1:18), and the giving of the law through Moses (Exod. 34; John 1:17).[7] In this and some other passages, therefore, "truth" in John is about actions that are truthful.

In John 3:20–21, Jesus says,

> Everyone who does evil hates the light, and will not come into the light for fear that his deeds will be exposed. But whoever *lives by the truth* (lit. "does the truth")

---

[6] Lindsay, "What Is Truth?" 130.

[7] Ibid., 131–32.

comes into the light, so that it may be seen plainly that what he has done has been done through God.

The expression "does the truth" also has background in the Old Testament (see, e.g., Gen. 24:49 cited earlier). It is about acting faithfully in relationship toward God and man. Living this way can only happen if the truth of God is woven into the warp and woof of one's life. This, it seems to me, is what Jesus means when he says to the Samaritan woman, "true worshipers will worship the Father in spirit and truth, for they are the kind of worshipers the Father seeks. God is spirit, and his worshipers must worship in spirit and in truth" (John 4:23b–24).

Yes, Jesus is the truth, and those who worship the Father must not only believe he is the truth, but they must live according to the standards of the truth manifest in him. Just like "spirit" in worship requires the welling up of the Holy Spirit in the human spirit, "truth" in authentic worship requires both the acceptance of Jesus as the truth and weaving him and the truth he proclaims into all aspects of our lives. As David put in Psalm 51:6, "Surely you desire *truth in the inner parts;* you teach me wisdom in the inmost place." There is a "spirit of truth" just as there is the divine "Spirit of truth" who works in those who worship "in spirit and truth."

Truth in the encounter in John 4 begins with biblical truth about the place of worship and ends up at truth about the very nature of God ("God is spirit") and the incarnate presence of the Son of God (Jesus the "Messiah"). Whatever is true about God, people, and the relationship between the two is important in authentic worship. Truth is true to life, and worship "in truth" will only arise out of a faithful life. Truth permeates the life of the one who worships "in spirit and truth."

Truth in Authentic Worship

In the remainder of this chapter, I will argue that such *worship is, in fact, one of the most important principles, if not the most*

important all-organizing principle of the faithful Christian life. Worship "in spirit and truth" is the presentation of the kind of life
to the Father that brings the work of the Holy Spirit in the
human spirit and the impact of the truth embodied and made
manifest in the Son to full effect in the practicing of God's
presence in all walks of life. The whole of the Christian life can
be understood in these terms, as is clear, for example, from
Romans 12:1, "Therefore, I urge you, brothers, in view of God's
mercy, to offer your bodies as living sacrifices, holy and pleasing to God—this is your spiritual act of worship."

It is well known that many of Paul's epistles have two main
parts: the doctrinal foundation followed by the application of
that foundation to the lives of those to whom the letters are
addressed. Romans 12:1 is at this turning point in the book.
Paul concluded chapter 11 with a magnificent doxology (11:33–
36) that ends with "Amen" (v. 36b; see the remarks on this
term earlier). Then he turns to the implications of all he has
said by exhorting the Roman Christians to live as sacrifices.
This, of course, is an oxymoron. Live as a sacrifice? But it is the
only reasonable ("spiritual," *logiken*) way for us to perform acts
of worship *(latreian)* toward the God about whom it can be
said, "For from him and through him and to him are all things"
(11:36a).[8]

Paul begins 12:1 by recalling God's mercy (lit. "mercies")
toward us and moves immediately to the sacrificial metaphor
as the only proper response of those who are the objects of
that mercy. All of us belong to God, so the only thing that
makes sense is to live a life of "holy and pleasing" sacrifice to
God. In point of fact, since Jesus came to become a sacrifice on
our behalf (e.g., Mark 10:45; Phil. 2:8, etc.), the only way we
can become like Christ is if we too give ourselves as sacrifices
to God. This indeed is worship "in truth." Thus, there are three

---

[8] For a well-balanced discussion of the meanings of these terms and this
phrase overall, see James D. G. Dunn, *Romans 9–16,* Word Biblical Commentary, vol. 38 (Dallas: Word, 1988), 711–12.

basic concerns that I would like to treat under the topic of "truth in authentic worship": truth in the spirit of worship, truth in the action of worship, and truth in the word of worship. All three have their roots set deep in the Old Testament and their branches extend into the New Testament. We will focus first on what it means to have a spirit of truth in our lives as worshipers.

Truth and Purity in the Spirit of Worship

Holiness and purity are of primary concern here (cf. Rom. 12:1, "living sacrifices, holy and pleasing to God"). The holy nature of God the Father as "spirit" comes to prominence. This is the main point the Seraphs proclaimed in the hearing of Isaiah in the *heavenly temple:* "Holy, holy, holy is the LORD Almighty; the whole earth is full of his glory" (Isa. 6:3). Some people seem to think that the closer we get to God, the more holy we will feel. Clearly, that was *not* Isaiah's experience. Seeing God made him overwhelmingly aware of how defiled he really was (v. 5), and this, in turn, made him ready to feel the full force of God's forgiving and purifying grace (vv. 6–7). The closer he came to God, the more impressed he was with the holiness of God. Any degree of personal holiness Isaiah may have experienced in his life faded into impurity in the presence of the Most Holy One. This, I expect, would be the experience of anyone who truly draws close to God—one who worships God in truth.

The Old Testament foundation for this finds its starting point in Exodus 3:5, which is the first canonical occurrence of the term "holy" in reference to a "sacred *place*." It is the story of Moses at the burning bush. God says, "Do not come any closer, . . . Take off your sandals, for the place where you are standing is *holy ground*." This was, as the text puts, "the mountain of God." The Lord went on in verse 12 to promise that he would be present with Moses in bringing Israel out of Egypt and, in fact, they would all come back here together to "worship God on *this mountain.*" This comes to pass in Exodus 19:2 when "Israel camped there in the desert in front of *the mountain.*"

It was there that the whole nation would experience the theophanic presence of God in an awe-inspiring and even terrifying way. In preparation for the theophany, which would take place on the third day, Moses was told to "Go to the people and *consecrate* (i.e., sanctify) them today and tomorrow" (v. 10a). They were to "wash their clothes" (v. 10b) and "abstain from sexual relations" (v. 15b). When the third day arrived, the Lord descended on the mountain in fire and smoke and with great thunder and lightning. Moses brought the people out to the mountain to hear the word of the Lord. There are some difficulties in sorting out the text here, but it appears that Moses then ascended the mountain to meet with God separately. As Moses came down the mountain again, the Lord descended farther down as well, drawing closer to the people.

In the meantime, the people were trembling in fear and "stayed at a distance" (Exod. 20:18). They were afraid that if God continued to speak with them in such a manner and in such close proximity to them, they would die (v. 19). Of course, the Lord had no intention of breaking out against them and had taken precautions to see that they would do nothing to bring that to pass. In the parallel passage in Deuteronomy 5:28, Moses recounts that, "The LORD heard you when you spoke to me and the LORD said to me, 'I have heard what this people said to you. *Everything they said was good.*'" According to Exodus 19:9, the Lord had intended from the start to make Moses the mediator, and they were to trust him for that: "The LORD said to Moses, 'I am going to come to you in a dense cloud, so that the people will hear me speaking with you and will always put their trust in you (Moses).'"

The Lord, therefore, responded positively to both the people's standing at a distance and their request for a mediator and expanded upon it even further in this way in Deuteronomy 5:29: "Oh, that their hearts would be inclined to *fear* me and keep all my commands *always,* so that it might go well with them and their children forever!" After the ratification of the covenant in Exodus 24:1–11, Moses once again ascended the mountain. There he received the actual tablets of the ten words along with the instructions for building the Lord's "sanctuary," his "sacred" tent. The tabernacle was to be the place where the Lord would actually "dwell among them" (Exod. 25:8) as they traveled from Sinai to the Promised Land. It was a moveable Sinai.

In the previous chapter, I discussed the movement from Old Testament theology of sacred space to the New Testament theology of worship community. The church (Eph. 2:18–22; 1 Cor. 3:16–17), and even the individual Christian (1 Cor. 6:18–20), is now the "temple," so to speak. Along with this comes principles and regulations for holiness and purity based in the Old Testament but with correspondences in the New Testament. The basic Old Testament principle is that the physical ritual nature of the holiness and purity laws of Leviticus 8–16, for example, corresponds to the visible physical presence of the Lord in the tabernacle and later in the temple. This concept even comes through in the Gospels in certain instances.

For example, Leviticus 12:6–8 requires that a woman bring a "sin (i.e., purification) offering" to purify herself from her flow of blood during the birth of a child. As part of her purification for bearing Jesus, Mary went to the temple in Jerusalem "to offer a sacrifice in keeping with what is said in the Law of the Lord: 'a pair of doves or two young pigeons'" (Luke 2:22–24). Mary certainly did not "sin" morally in bearing Jesus, but her blood flow did make her physically impure according to the Levitical system. Physical purity was important because God was physically present in the tabernacle and temple. One of the purposes of the "sin (i.e., purification) offering" was to ritually purify from physical impurities.

In the New Testament world of the church, we think in terms of moral, spiritual (or heart), and relational purity, rather than physical ritual purity, because the presence of God in our midst is a spiritual presence (a presence of the Holy Spirit) that inhabits and manifests itself in our hearts and communities on the moral, spiritual, and relational levels. This corresponds directly to the truth of our theme verse: "God is spirit, and his worshipers must worship in spirit and in truth" (John 4:24). We have no tented tabernacle or stone temple that we can look at from our doorways or go visit on a pilgrimage. Our kingdom is of a different kind—"the kingdom of heaven" as it is called in Matthew (3:2; 4:17; 5:3, etc.). God's form of presence with us today matches that kingdom difference, and we are to live in the light of that presence in a way that corresponds to the very nature of it.[9]

Of course, where God is physically present in the Old Testament, he is also spiritually present; so, for example, David was also concerned about having a "pure heart" in Psalm 51 (v. 10), not just maintaining ritual physical purity. This psalm is, in fact, a good place to see the truth in worship as it relates to the spirit in worship. One cannot have true worship without truth in heart and life. This is where David found himself in trouble because of his sin involving Bathsheba and Uriah (see the psalm title). A few observations will be sufficient here.

Note the build up of words for washing and purification from sin in verses 1–2, 7, 9, and the explicit concern for David's "inner parts" and "inmost place" in verse 6:

> 1Have mercy on me, O God,
>   according to your unfailing love;
> according to your great compassion
>   *blot out* my transgressions.
> 2*Wash away* all my iniquity
>   and cleanse me from my sin.

---

[9] For a more detailed treatment of purity and impurity in the OT and its relationship to the NT, see Richard E. Averbeck, "Clean and Unclean," in *New International Dictionary of Old Testament Theology and Exegesis,* ed. Willem A. VanGemeren (Grand Rapids: Zondervan, 1997), 477–86, and the literature cited there. See also idem, *"khattā᾽t,* 'sin, sin offering,'" in *New International Dictionary of Old Testament Theology and Exegesis,* vol. 2, ed. Willem A. VanGemeren (Grand Rapids: Zondervan, 1997), esp. 100–103.

> **6**Surely you desire truth in the *inner parts;*
>   you teach me wisdom in the *inmost place.*
>
> **7**Cleanse me with hyssop, and I will be clean;
>   *wash* me, and I will be *whiter than snow.*
> **9**Hide your face from my sins
>   and *blot out* all my iniquity.

The hyssop in verse 7 refers to a kind of plant that was used to sprinkle the water of cleansing for the leper in Leviticus 14. David was not a leper. He was using all these terms for washing metaphorically, the point being that he needed washing in his inner being, in his spirit.

Verses 10–12 once again focus on David's "heart," his "spirit," and even the "Holy Spirit," which is one of only three occurrences of the term "Holy Spirit" in the Old Testament, although there are many other references to "the Spirit (of God or the LORD)."[10] David writes:

> **10**Create in me a *pure heart,* O God,
>   and renew a steadfast *spirit within me.*
> **11**Do not cast me from your presence
>   or take your *Holy Spirit* from me.
> **12**Restore to me the *joy* of your salvation
>   and grant me *a willing spirit,* to sustain me.

---

[10] The other two occurrences are in Isaiah 63:10–11. The expression in these three passages is literally "the Spirit of Holiness." The LXX renders it "Holy Spirit," using the same Greek words as in the NT. Isaiah 63:9–10 refers to Israel's grieving of the Holy Spirit that the Lord had put in their midst in the days of Moses. Isaiah 63:14 identifies this "Holy Spirit" with "the Spirit of the LORD." The latter expression and its interchangeable counterpart "the Spirit of God" (cf. 1 Sam. 10:6 with 10:10) occur ninety-four times in the Hebrew Bible if one includes instances where "the Spirit" in context clearly refers to "the Spirit of the LORD/God."

David's fear that the Lord might take the Holy Spirit from him probably relates to David's experience with Saul. When Samuel anointed David in 1 Samuel 16, "from that day on the Spirit of the LORD came upon David in power" (v. 13). The next verse says, "Now *the Spirit of the Lord* had *departed* from Saul, and *an evil spirit from the Lord* tormented him" (10:14).[11] This is not the place to discuss the "evil spirit from the LORD," but David himself became Saul's minstrel to calm Saul's troubled spirit. David knew firsthand what a disaster it could be if the Lord took the Holy Spirit from him.

Again, in Psalm 51:17, we read of David's description of the kind of "spirit" and "heart" the Lord wants from his worshipers: "The sacrifices of God are *a broken spirit; a broken and contrite heart,* O God, you will not despise." It is this kind of worship in spirit that the Father seeks, and only with that will the physical actions of Old Testament temple worship be pleasing in God's sight (vv. 18–19). Until the inner reality is dealt with, the external actions are of no benefit, according to verse 16: "You do not delight in sacrifice, or I would bring it; you do not take pleasure in burnt offerings." David's penitence here and other penitential psalms provide a link between the temple sacrificial worship system of the Old Testament and truth in the spirit of worship in the New Testament.

The movement from Old Testament to New in this regard begins in earnest with John the Baptist's baptism with water, which most certainly had its background in Jewish physical ritual purifications attested to in the Old Testament, on through the intertestamental period, and in the many *miqvot* (ritual baths) found in archaeological excavations. But John himself looked forward to the coming of the one who would "baptize with the Holy Spirit and with fire" (Matt. 3; Luke 4, etc.).

Therefore, except for instances where the Old Testament context of the Gospels is being reflected as, for example, in the

---

[11] See the remarks in Robert P. Gordon, *I and II Samuel: A Commentary* (Grand Rapids: Zondervan, 1986), 152.

cleansing of the leper in Matthew 8 (vv. 3–4) and in Mary's purification offering in Luke 2 explained earlier (vv. 22–24), the concern for holiness and purity in the New Testament is oriented
toward the spiritual presence of God in the individual believer
and amid the collective body of believers, the church. Before the
inception of the church, Jesus said, "God is spirit, and his worshipers must worship in spirit and in truth" (John 4:24). Elsewhere he says, "nothing that enters a man from the outside can
make him *'unclean'*" because it goes "into his stomach, and then
out of his body" not "into his heart" (Mark 7:18–19). Jesus is
concerned with the fact that "from within, out of men's hearts,
come evil thoughts, sexual immorality, theft, . . . All these evils
come from inside and make a man *'unclean'*" (vv. 21–23).

Ritual physical purity concerns are ever present throughout
Leviticus, even in 17–27. But purity of the heart is by no means
ignored. In fact, according to Jesus, if one misses this he or she
has missed one of the two greatest commandments of the law
(Matt. 22:40; cf. 5:20–48, etc.). Leviticus 19:17–18 says, "Do not
hate your brother *in your heart*. Rebuke your neighbor frankly
so you will not share in his guilt. Do not seek revenge or *bear a
grudge* against one of your people, but *love* your neighbor as
yourself. I am the LORD."

In the context of making remarks on teaching the Old
Testament law in the church, Paul writes in 1 Timothy 1:5, "the
goal of our instruction is love from *a pure heart* and a good
conscience and a sincere faith" (NASB). Peter uses the Levitical
holiness formula ("Be holy, because I am holy," 1 Peter 1:16,
from Lev. 11:44–45; 19:2, etc.) to exhort us to "not conform to
the evil desires you had when you lived in ignorance. But just
as he who called you is holy, *so be holy* in all you do" (1 Peter
1:14–15). Moreover, as verse 22 puts it, "Now that you have
purified yourselves (lit. 'your souls') by obeying the truth so that
you have sincere love for your brothers, *love* one another deeply,
from the heart." True love for God and people comes only from
a pure heart that motivates holy living. All the holiness and
purity concerns of Leviticus come into the New Testament for

application to the Christian life in this way, and they have a profound effect on our worship. After all, one cannot worship God in spirit if one's spirit is not pure, since God himself is absolutely pure as "spirit."

I am suggesting that *true love for God and people comes only from a pure heart that motivates holy living, and this is the basic starting point and priority of authentic worship,* according to Jesus. It can be helpful to consider the physical place of worship to the degree that it can help us with worshiping God in spirit. But if we become obsessed on place or aesthetics, we will tend to lose the focus on spirit, *in which case we are no longer worshiping in truth, either.* This is, in fact, Jesus' reaction to the woman when she brings up the issue of place. He turns the subject back again to what he had talked about earlier in the form of another motif—water that could well up from within the woman.

A person's spirit is with that person no matter where he or she is and no matter what kind of place or situation he or she finds himself or herself in. In spirit there is never any good reason to be out of God's presence because he is by nature spirit. What we need is a "practicing of his presence" in all the venues of our lives. *Authentic worship, namely, a conscious practicing of God's presence, is the most transforming experience available to the Christian, because it is the main way our heart gets turned around to go in a different direction.* We are told in Proverbs 4:23, "Watch over your heart with all diligence, for from it *flow* the springs of life" (NASB). The heart in Hebrew includes intellect as well as attitudes, volition, and the inner life overall. One mode and effect of worship is what we might call "getting impressed with God." Putting it in those terms, one of our main problems in life is that we are often impressed with the wrong things, something other than God himself.

We can know a lot and learn even more without being transformed. Transformation takes place when we become so deeply impressed with God and his purposes in our lives and the lives of others that it gets our will engaged for change and growth. *What we want changes when we get impressed.* Deep change takes place when the things that matter to us change, and that is what authentic worship can do in us. We need to see God! *If we see God, we will most surely be impressed!* Isaiah certainly was. The effect is the same if we see God with the eyes of our heart (Eph. 1:18).

Truth and Sincerity in the Actions of Worship

The actions of worship in the Old Testament are closely bound to altar, tabernacle, and worship in the temple. I do not have time or space here to set forth the details of this system of worship. It goes way back to the Cain and Abel incident in Genesis 4, forms the substance of the first part of the book of Leviticus, and is reflected upon in the Psalter and much of the rest of the Old Testament in one way or another. Although it is true that Leviticus is one of the books most likely to be ignored by readers and preachers of the Bible, the plain truth is that it is one of the most theological books in the canon, and some of the most important principles of worshiping God in truth arise from it.

But there is a problem. One can compromise his worship actions by not doing them in truth, whether it be in the manner of worship or the attitude (i.e., "spirit") of worship, or both. This is what happened with Cain right at the beginning of the recorded history of sacrificial worship. Genesis 4:3–5 says:

> In the course of time Cain brought *some of the fruits of the soil* as an offering to the LORD. But Abel brought *fat portions from some of the firstborn* of his flock. The LORD looked with favor on Abel and his offering, but on Cain and his offering he did not look with favor. So Cain was very angry, and his face was downcast.

There has been no end of speculation why God favored Abel and his offering over that of Cain. The only clear indicator we have as far as I can tell is the discrepancy between the two descriptions of the offerings. "*First* fruits" of the soil is conspicuous for its absence in the description of Cain's offering in light of Abel's "fat portions" and "firstborn." Hebrews 11:4 tells us that, "By faith Abel offered God a better sacrifice than Cain did." The point is that there was something about Cain's offering that reflected a lack of the kind of faith that Abel's offering expressed.

This problem also stands out in Psalm 51:16–19 (the conclusion to this psalm). It comes down to this:

> **16***You do not delight in sacrifice,* or I would bring it;
> you do not take pleasure in burnt offerings.
> **17**The *sacrifices of God* are a broken spirit;
> a broken and contrite heart,
> O God, you will not despise.
>
> **18**In your good pleasure make Zion prosper;
> build up the walls of Jerusalem.
> **19***Then* there will be *righteous sacrifices,*
> whole burnt offerings to delight you;
> then bulls will be offered on your altar.

The sacrificial actions that were called for in the Old Testament would make no sense without the underlying truth and purity in the spirit of David's worship. This was his first concern, and it meets with the very heart of God.

Psalm 50 is particularly interesting in this regard. In fact, one wonders if this is not part of the reason that Psalms 50 and 51 are paired together in the book. Psalm 50 is a prophetic psalm, reflecting something of the same critique of the cult that we find in certain places in the prophets (e.g., Isa. 1:4–17; Jer. 7:21–26; Hos. 6:6; Amos 5:21–24; and the well-known Mic. 6:1–8). At the beginning of the psalm, God presents himself as a coming judge and a plaintiff at the same time, storming forth to declare and judge the injustice done to him (vv. 1–6). The indictment reads as follows:

8I do not rebuke you for your sacrifices
  or your burnt offerings, which are ever before me.
9I have no need of a bull from your stall
  or of goats from your pens,
10for every animal of the forest is mine,
  and the cattle on a thousand hills.
11I know every bird in the mountains,
  and the creatures of the field are mine.
12If I were hungry I would not tell you,
  for the world is mine, and all that is in it.
13Do I eat the flesh of bulls
  or drink the blood of goats?
14*Sacrifice thank offerings* to God,
  fulfill your vows to the Most High,
15and *call upon me* in the day of trouble;
  I will deliver you, and *you will honor me.*

God's primary concern was not the sacrifices the people offered. Even if God were hungry—which he never is, but if he was—he certainly would not tell them about it. He owns the cattle on a thousand hills, as the hymn goes. His rebuke had nothing to do with that. What he wants is worshipers that worship in true sincerity, bringing expressions of thankfulness, the kind that come from being delivered in the day of trouble. Thank and votive offerings come out of a sincere response to God in life. This is worship in truth and sincerity. It truly honors God.

Of course, in many places the New Testament uses the background of the Old Testament offerings and sacrifices as a way to help understand more fully what Christ has done as the sacrifice on our behalf. Romans 3:25 refers to Jesus as God's "sacrifice of atonement, through faith in his blood." According to Hebrews 9–10, the sacrificial blood of Christ cleansed our *conscience* (9:14), as opposed to the blood of the Old Testament sacrifices, which cleansed only the *flesh*, outwardly (v. 13). Moreover, Jesus' blood purified the *heavenly tabernacle permanently,* once and for all, as opposed to the Old Testament Day of Atonement sin offerings that purified the *earthly tabernacle* and that only for *one year* (9:11-12, 23-25; 10:1-4).

According to the book of Hebrews, Jesus was both a better *priest* and a better *sacrifice* than those that are found in the Old Testament. In the Old Testament, a particular animal could serve as only one kind of sacrifice (e.g., a burnt offering, peace offering, sin offering, etc.), but the New Testament refers to Jesus, for example, as our Passover sacrifice (1 Cor. 5:7), our peace offering covenant ratification sacrifice (Luke 22:19-20; cf. Exod. 24:3-8), and our sin offering in Romans 8:3. The latter reads literally, "The one who knew no sin he made sin on our behalf in order that we might become the righteousness of God in him," which one translation renders, "For God made Christ, who never sinned, to be the offering for our sin" (NLT). (See also 2 Cor. 5:21: "God made him who had no sin to be [a] sin [offering?] for us.") We are delivered, forgiven, cleansed, and have communion with God through the blood of Christ.

But the New Testament does not stop there. Peter writes about us *as Christians,* that we "are being built into a spiritual house to be a holy *priesthood, offering spiritual sacrifices* acceptable to God through Jesus Christ" (1 Peter 2:4-5). In verse 9, Peter quotes Exodus 19:6 in application to the church. Israel was to be a kingdom of priests—so is the church. Peter goes on to exhort us to be willing to suffer for our faith just as Jesus gave himself as a suffering servant on our behalf (see 1 Peter 2:21-25, where the apostle refers explicitly to Isa. 53; cf. Acts 8:26-36). If we are to become like Jesus, we must be willing to suffer sacrificially (Rom. 12:1; Eph. 5:1-2; Phil. 2:1-11). Paul "poured" himself "out like a drink offering on the sacrifice and service" of promoting faith in the Philippians (2:17; cf. 2 Tim. 4:6). He viewed his ministry to the Gentiles as "an offering acceptable to God, sanctified by the Holy Spirit" (Rom. 15:16).

The author of Hebrews reminds his readers that "since we are receiving a kingdom that cannot be shaken, let us be thankful, and so worship God acceptably with reverence and awe, for our 'God is a consuming fire'" (12:28–29). He goes on to exhort his readers to "continually offer to God a sacrifice of praise—the fruit of lips that confess his name," and "to do good and to share with others, for with such sacrifices God is pleased" (13:15–16). The point is this: *authentic worship in spirit leads to action in life, and this life action in turn becomes worship.* In a sense, all that we do with and for God is worship, if it honors him. We could easily get the wrong idea about all this, as the ancient Israelites often did. We could overestimate our own importance and by doing that underestimate God. There is humility and dependence in true worship. Our view of our actions shows whether we are truly impressed with God.

Truth and Authenticity in the Words of Worship

Like actions in worship, the use of words in worship finds its origin in Genesis 4. At the end of the chapter we read:

> Adam lay with his wife again, and she gave birth to a son and named him Seth, saying, "God has granted me another child in place of Abel, since Cain killed him." Seth also had a son, and he named him Enosh. At that time *men began to call on the name of the Lord.* (vv. 25–26)

This is the first occurrence of this well-known clause in the Bible, and its importance in its context cannot be overestimated. Just before these final verses, Lamech in the line of Cain boasted:

> Adah and Zillah, listen to me; wives of Lamech, hear my words. I have killed a man for wounding me, a young man for injuring me. If Cain is avenged seven times, then Lamech seventy-seven times. (vv. 23–24)

Lamech's response to the struggles of life was the very opposite of "calling on the name of the LORD" that follows (v. 26). He would depend on no one else to handle the things he faced.

He would handle it all himself, and he would do it with a vengeance unmatched by anyone in his day and time.

The expression "call on the name of the Lord" is seeded throughout the Old Testament and on into the New Testament, often as the *words* of worship in the context of worship *actions*. It signals the words of authentic worship, for example, in Genesis 12:8, where we are told that, after Abram entered Canaan: "he went on toward the hills east of Bethel and pitched his tent, with Bethel on the west and Ai on the east. There he *built an altar* to the LORD and *called on the name of the Lord*." The building of the altar is the worship action, and it probably included making offerings, although they are not mentioned explicitly. Calling on the name of the Lord was the invocation, that is, the call to God to meet Abram in his need right there in the context of his actions of authentic worship. The same thing occurs in multiple places throughout the Old Testament. For example, Isaac did the same thing in Genesis 26:25; Elijah did it on Mount Carmel in his confrontation with the prophets of Baal (1 Kgs. 18:24); and it is held forth as an ideal of authentic worship in Psalm 116:17 and Zephaniah 3:9–10 (cf. also Ps. 50:15).

We need to pause here for a moment to return to the issue of Samaritan worship at Mount Gerizim. Just before he moved on to Bethel and built the altar in Genesis 12, Abram built an altar at Shechem, where Mounts Ebal and Gerizim are located. Much later, when the Israelites entered the land to conquer and occupy it, they worshiped back at Shechem as Moses had instructed them (cp. Deut. 27 with Josh. 8). It was at Shechem that God originally told Abram, "To your descendants I will give this land" (Gen. 12:7), and it was there that this promise was declared as fulfilled (Josh. 8:30–35). Thus, Mount Gerizim was no mean place in the history of Israel. The problem was that the Samaritans only accepted the Pentateuch as Scripture (i.e., their own peculiar version of it), which left them with no Jerusalem.

Returning now to our main point, the expression "call on the name of the LORD" occurs in Joel 2:32 as the only proper response to the coming great and terrible Day of the Lord. From there it is taken into the book of Acts as the last line quoted by Peter in his quotation of Joel 2 in Acts 2. It launches him into his sermon on the Day of Pentecost, the main point being that the Day of the Lord is coming so "call on the name of the Lord." In Romans 10, Paul emphasizes the faith basis of relationship to God by quoting the same line, "Everyone who calls on the name of the Lord will be saved" (v. 13). Then, in 1 Corinthians 1:2, he addresses the believers at Corinth "together with all those everywhere who call on the name of our Lord Jesus Christ."

Calling on the name of the Lord is at the core of authentic worship. It is the essence of what we do when we go to God in the midst of life circumstances, whether it be for eternal salvation or for help in the life of the believer. Here is where there is a serious problem with what we sometimes ask people to do in worship. We have a tendency to think that people need to leave off their life concerns when they come to worship so they can concentrate on God. This is not really what appears to be the case in the Psalms, which are above all words of worship. On the contrary, the Psalter is heavily weighted with the concerns of life and life situations. They are anything but an escape from life. In fact, the main point here is that the heart of authentic worship is the bringing of one's life and concerns to God, that they might be set before him and worked through in his presence. One "calls on the name of the Lord" in the midst of it all. In a sense, *authentic worship is seeing God while looking life squarely in the face.*

We have already observed this in Psalm 51. An extreme case on the negative side of life is Psalm 88, the bleakest of the lament psalms in which there is hardly a stitch of anything positive to say about life or even God. What do we do with such things? Well, at least the writer is bringing it to God. It is a word of authentic worship, even though there is not a single expression of trust or praise in the whole song. It is an authentic call to God. Sometimes in life there is virtually nothing positive to say, and to try to say something positive anyway is to compromise the very authenticity of the worship experience. Lament is as much a part of the Psalter as praise. We should not underestimate its power.

On the other hand, the last five psalms in the Psalter constitute an explosion of praise. We have much to praise God about. Perhaps one of the best ways to summarize it is by reference to the pairing of Psalms 103 and 104. They are bound together by their common beginning and ending: "Praise (lit. 'bless') the LORD, O my soul" with an additional "Praise the LORD" appended to Psalm 104. Psalm 103 is about God's redemptive work and Psalm 104 is about his creative work. There is no time left to develop them here, but in my opinion these are the two major poles around which all biblical theology revolves. The Bible starts with God as our Creator and it is not long before he also becomes our Redeemer. Those who know him in truth, know him as both.

Conclusion

So we end up back at Psalm 103 from which we began our discussion. Recall Psalm 103:14, which says that God "knows how we are formed, he remembers that we are dust." After all, he is the one who formed us from the dust (cp. Gen. 2:7 with 3:19). From the point of view of the overall scheme of things, the struggles that we face, whether individual or corporate, get folded back into God as our Redeemer, even when deliverance seems far away and hard to believe in. We are but grass that withers, but God endures forever and so do his promises to those who fear him (Ps. 103:11, 13, 17). That is the point of Psalm 103. Psalm 104 takes us back to the Creation itself and displays the wonder of God's creation. This too is a primary stimulus to worship in the Psalms. We stand in awe of him because of who he is *and* because of what he has done in both creation and redemption.

Authentic worship of God in truth entails worshiping him in

spirit. And worshiping him in spirit naturally leads us to worship with true faithful actions and with words that speak the truth about God, the world, and our experience of both in real life. *So authentic worship is made up of truth in spirit, truth in action, and truth in word.* Worshiping in truth is about a genuine pursuit of God. Worshiping God in truth is about being impressed with our overwhelming God in the midst of life. Worshiping God is about seeing him while looking life squarely in the face.

Contrary to our narcissistic North American culture, a good Christian will live a life of sacrifice (Rom. 12:1), just as Jesus did. It really is possible to organize one's whole life around the worship of God, understanding and articulating everything in terms of worship. *Authentic worship is a place of purity, a place of praise, and a place of passion in the very presence of God.* This is not a particular physical place but a place where the human spirit can soar with the God of heaven, who is by nature spirit and, therefore, must be worshiped in spirit and in truth.

PART TWO

MUSIC
Expressions of Our Worship

CHAPTER FIVE

Worship

A Battle for Harmony (Drama Presentation)

Timothy D. Sprankle

This skit is intended to be done as a Reader's Theater piece; however, it can easily be modified.[1] *The nature of the skit deals with the problem of finding a balanced musical selection in Sunday church worship when dealing with three different generations of Christian worshipers. Taken to its satirical extreme, this skit uncovers impure motives of worship leaders and the leaders' concurrent acts of sabotage to become the predominate style of worship for the church.*

PASTOR: I am one confused pastor. I memorized the King James Bible. I study the New American Standard (NASB). And I teach from the NIV. There are so many choices. And I don't know whether to preach exegetically, topically, or do different character sketches from the Bible. There are too many choices. And

---

[1] The skit was prepared and performed for the Midwest Region ETS Conference (23–24 March 2001), hosted by Grace Theological Seminary. Remnant, a student-led and directed drama group of Grace College, performed the skit.

choices are the very things that are becoming the bane of evangelical worship. Our church is no different. Each week our members are given the choice between three services to attend: Traditional, Contemporary, and Progressive. The only difference, though, is the style of music that is played and what people wear. The service is really only named by its worship style and dress, because I've been preaching the same sermon in every service. The question isn't what will I preach, but what will I wear when I preach it, and what style of musical worship will lead into the message? And in our church these battle lines are clearly drawn.

TRADITIONAL: Hymns are the original language of worship. If the lyrics aren't theologically rich, they sound worshipfully poor to God.

CONTEMPORARY: We need to be in the world but not of it. Our music is simple and catchy, so you don't get caught up on the verbiage, but you can actually hear yourself over the instruments.

PROGRESSIVE: Worship is a time to experience God with excitement and joy. You need a worship band to give passion to the people.

PASTOR: I fear these lines. Instead of creating diversity within our church, they've created three different churches. Basically, old, young, and middle-aged. We used to have one service, and we'd ask a series of questions: Do we dust off the hymnals and crank up the organ? Do we light up the projector and hit the keys for some choruses? Or do we pound the drums and shout to the Lord? Now we just save the varieties for their respective services. Three choices. Three

	churches. One body. It's a mathematical paradox, our church's own little Trinity, only it's not a holy union. Anyway, I decided to call the three worship leaders together to discuss the problem.
PROGRESSIVE:	So, Pastor, why exactly have you called us here? Did we do something wrong?
CONTEMPORARY:	No, this probably concerns the Easter cantata. You wanted to stick with the arrangement that I composed last year?
PASTOR:	That is for a different discussion. I actually was wondering what you thought of worship last week.
	[At first they respond to Pastor.]
TRADITIONAL:	The organ seemed a little clogged, but we still sang some classics. We had about two hundred at the service.
CONTEMPORARY:	There were 248 in attendance, and . . .
PROGRESSIVE:	322. 322 at our service. We even played an extra song because people were so into it. Sorry if we cut into your time, Pastor.
PASTOR:	Well, you are all awfully excited about the numbers, but I was wondering about worship. How do you think worship helps the unity of our church?
ALL:	Everyone gets what they need.
TRADITIONAL:	We have the words.
PROGRESSIVE:	We have the energy.
CONTEMPORARY:	We have simplicity.
ALL:	And what we have is the best.
PASTOR:	I hadn't known what to expect, but I quickly found that worship was not about God. It was about what style was truer, purer, or louder, and who could have the greatest attendance while doing it. So I bluntly asked: Do you worship in spirit and truth?

TRADITIONAL: Do you think that our worship has gone sour? Hymns are timelessly true and spiritual.

PROGRESSIVE: What are you talking about? I've never felt anything more spiritual or true than our worship. Just take last week. I don't think I've ever heard it that loud in our auditorium. The claps. The drums. Man that was an awesome experience.

CONTEMPORARY: Pastor, you make it sound like we have a large problem. Our songs were spiritual and true a couple years ago. Why should we modify our selection now? The key is our worship isn't complicated. That's why every week we sing "Majesty" and "As the Deer." No one gets confused.

PASTOR: Then the battle began.

[Now they respond to each other.]

PROGRESSIVE: Yeah, but no one gets excited about *your* worship, either. The same songs, every week, every month, every year in the past decade— the songs get drained of their meaning.

TRADITIONAL: As though you can speak of meaning. You may play different songs each week, but how many times are you going to repeat the same line within one song? Are you trying to prove it when you say that you could sing of his love forever?

PROGRESSIVE: The only proof I have is that, when I lead worship, people are up, out of their seats, clapping their hands, and singing with some energy. When you lead worship though, people are busy staring at a hymnal and trying to sing loud enough to drone out the organ. *[Make whining noises.]*

TRADITIONAL: Well, I think you are just as close to dron-

| | ing out the Holy Spirit with that devil music of yours. The pounding drum. The electric guitar. It's the devil's symphony. |

CONTEMPORARY: You two are both so extreme. The key is that we are all getting people involved.

TRADITIONAL: We all know how he does. He just puts more people on stage. You have more people on stage and less in the pews and thus you think your worship is better.

PROGRESSIVE: Wrong. We just try to create an environment where people feel alive. No offense, but putting one older man, constrained by his three-piece suit, with only his finger *[mocks a conductor]* to excite the audience, you don't have a very good show. And anyway, isn't pointing wrong? I mean, it's rude to point, isn't it? Because when you just stand up there waving your finger at the whole congregation *[mimics Hymnal]*, I can't help but feel singled out. *[Waving finger and using an old British accent]* "Thou shalt sing louder!"

CONTEMPORARY: Com'on now. Don't you think that you take things to a different extreme? Maybe James looks a bit like a dictator up there, doing the solo show, but you and your band don't quite balance the scales either. You have twelve different instruments, each with their own solos, and six different singers hitting every harmony. What is there left for the congregation to do? That's why everyone claps. It's like we're at a concert, not a worship session.

PASTOR: Worship was a great problem in our church. It was not just that we had too many choices, it was that in the midst of the choices, of the various styles, worship had become a battleground of competition. Who could sing louder? Who could sound better? Who had the best words? And just when I thought the discussion couldn't get any worse, it did.

PROGRESSIVE: *[Nodding]* "The glory of the youth is his strength." That's what the Proverbs state. You two are afraid of my youth, my strength, aren't you? The drums are of the devil, you always say. That's not because you have a problem with the drums. You have a problem with change.

TRADITIONAL: And you have a problem with tradition. With things that are tried and true. Well, I'll have you know that I do not doubt—you are the one who glued all the hymnbooks shut a few weeks ago.

CONTEMPORARY: That was you?

PROGRESSIVE: Like you can play innocent. You were the one who recently changed all our slides on PowerPoint during last week's service. I know it wasn't James. I don't even think he knows how to use the computer. That was real cute, by the way, putting pictures of _____ *[i.e., President Clinton]* on all the slides, instead of words. That'll really get the congregation turned against us.

TRADITIONAL: I know how to use a computer . . .

PROGRESSIVE: The organ is not a computer and neither is your hearing aid. I don't doubt you do know how to use a saw, though. That's how the number of drumsticks magically doubled while the size of each split in half. We'd have an easier time playing with our thumbs.

CONTEMPORARY: Now, Matt, let me ask you . . . did you really think that my transparencies were pagans?

PROGRESSIVE: Pagans? What are you talking about?

CONTEMPORARY:	Pagans—apparently you must have felt the need to purify them, because I found them in the baptismal.
TRADITIONAL:	No offense, Sue, but it's not like we really needed the overheads. We sing those songs every week. I think we know the words by now.
CONTEMPORARY:	So you put it in there?
TRADITIONAL:	Well, it was a test.
CONTEMPORARY:	A test?
TRADITIONAL:	To see if we would still sing the song anyway . . . and we did.
PROGRESSIVE:	Surprise. Not really.
CONTEMPORARY:	What's wrong with repetition?
PROGRESSIVE:	What's wrong with repetition?
TRADITIONAL:	What's wrong with repetition?
CONTEMPORARY:	OK. I get the point.
PASTOR:	No, you haven't. None of you have.
ALL:	[POINTING TO THE OTHERS. FREEZE.] The point is they do worship wrong.
PASTOR:	As the shepherd of the church, I felt sad, sick, sorry, and frustrated all at the same time. Corporate worship had grown to mean louder noise and higher attendance. Spirit and truth had grown to mean experiential and theological. And my worship leaders had submitted themselves to competition and sabotage. I felt like Israel, bringing her sacrifice before the Lord focused on the form but forgetting the heart. And I knew this problem couldn't be quickly resolved, but I had nothing to say to them. So I figured I would just let them stand there, pointing, looking foolish. I would just let them stand there until they realize they're pointing in the wrong direction. Worship is about God.

CHAPTER SIX

Voicing God's Praise

The Use of Music in Worship

David P. Nelson

Discussions about the use of music in Christian worship may be a bit like, to adapt the old saying attributed to von Bismark, the making of sausage and the making of laws. It is often a messy business and people tend to leave the process dissatisfied. Yet questions about the use of music in worship are important ones, not simply because they are the source of much controversy but because worship is a matter of such importance to the Christian faith. My purpose in this chapter is to explore the use of music in worship by raising three questions about the subject and then to suggest answers to those questions from a biblical, theological, and pastoral perspective. These questions will serve as a point of departure for a discussion of some central issues related to the use of music in Christian worship.

The Primary Question: What Is the Purpose of Music in Worship?

This question leads us to explore how the Bible instructs the church about music and worship. This is the fundamental question of the three considered in this essay. Other issues surrounding the purpose and use of music in worship should be based on what the Bible has to say about this primary question. I intend to answer this question using a framework of three dimensions of worship drawn from the Scriptures. We will then consider how these liturgical dimensions inform our use of music in worship.

The Popular Question: What About Musical Style?

This is not a new question for the church. Unfortunately, we tend to be ignorant of the history of music in the life of the church. The church has often struggled with which kinds of music are appropriate for worship and which musical instruments, if any, are appropriate for worship. For instance, there was a clear sentiment against the use of musical instruments in worship during the Patristic period (second–fourth century). Clement of Alexandria, for example, considered the employment of various instruments, along with hand clapping, to be a dangerous prospect, declaring instruments other than the human voice (which is "a peaceful instrument") "to be warlike, inflaming to lusts, or kindling up amours, or rousing wrath," and in general to be associated with the corruption of morals and licentiousness.[1] He and other Church Fathers, including Tertullian, Basil, Chrysostom, and Augustine, express reservations about the use of music. All were troubled about the association of church music with the music of the theater and the pagan culture of the day.

During the time of the Reformation, Erasmus criticized the use of theater music in the church, along with musical instruments that "vie and sound along constantly with the voices. Amorous and lascivious melodies are heard such as elsewhere accompany only the dances of courtesans and clowns. The

---

[1] Clement of Alexandria, *Paedagogus* 2.4 (*ANF* 2:248; PG 8:441c, 444c).

people run into the churches as if they were theatres, for the sake of the sensuous charm of the ear."[2]

Various tensions related to musical style existed in New England during the eighteenth and nineteenth centuries. Westermeyer notes several examples, three of which are presented here. First, the use of instruments in some churches, called "Catgut churches" due to their use of bass viols, was a source of controversy. Second, Charles Chauncy, pastor at First Church in Boston, "opposed the excesses" of the singing associated with the Great Awakening (ca. 1735–43), an American awakening that was greatly shaped by the Presbyterian Gilbert Tennent, the Congregationalist Jonathan Edwards, and the itinerant Anglican preacher George Whitefield. Finally, "the Presbyterians engaged in the fiercest strife about hymns;" "nasty conflicts and divisions" occurred among them over the use of the hymns of Isaac Watts and others.[3]

While I do not believe the question about musical style to be the most important question, it is likely the one most often asked about music and worship today. That is to say, I do not believe that the issue of musical style is the fundamental issue related to worship in the church today. The fundamental issue, which will surface in our discussion of the first question and reappear in the discussion of the third question, has to do with the church's understanding of the primacy of the glory of the triune God and the unity of the Holy Spirit manifested in the church. Nevertheless, while "worship wars" and rumors of worship wars abound, we cannot neglect the question of musical style. I do hope, however, that we can put the issue in proper perspective.

---

[2] Quoted in Paul Westermeyer, *Te Deum: The Church and Music* (Minneapolis: Fortress, 1998), 163.

[3] Ibid., 251–53. Westermeyer's text is an excellent resource for understanding the general contours of the use of music in Christian worship.

The Pastoral Question:
How Should We Handle Problems Related
to the Use of Music in the Church?

With this question, we inquire about how to handle issues related to the use of music in congregational worship so as to foster a vital, growing ministry of worship in the local church. We will especially concentrate on advice about how to make transitions associated with music in worship. While methodological matters are vitally important, theology must precede methodology in shaping our thinking about ministry. In fact, I would suggest that the failure to recognize this axiom is at the root of much of the contemporary struggle related to authenticity in worship. Therefore, we will begin by observing some fundamental biblical and theological considerations related to the use of music in Christian worship and then proceed to see how those considerations help to answer our three questions.

The Use of Music in Worship

Although the use of music in worship is a given for most modern Christians, this has not always been the case. Opposition to the use of music altogether is attributed to the Egyptian abbot Pambo (4th c.)[4] and is also seen in Zwingli, the Swiss reformer.[5] The opposition to singing among some seventeenth-century Baptists is highlighted by the attempts of Benjamin Keach, a Particular Baptist pastor, in London. He wanted to institute the singing of psalms and hymns at Horsley Down Church, a case he argues in the tract *The Breach Repaired in God's Worship, or Singing of Psalms, Hymns and Spiritual Songs*

---

[4] See Johannes Quasten, *Music and Worship in Pagan and Christian Antiquity*, trans. B. Ramsey (Washington, D.C.: National Association of Pastoral Musicians, 1973), 94–95.

[5] Westermeyer, *Te Deum*, 149–53. Cf. Charles Garside, *Zwingli and the Arts* (New Haven: Yale University Press, 1966).

proved to be an Holy Ordinance of Jesus Christ, published in 1691. The church slowly adopted hymn singing, beginning with a single hymn after observance of the Lord's Supper in 1673. It was twenty years later that the congregation accepted regular hymn singing, at which time a number of people withdrew membership from the church.[6]

The pressing question today, though, is usually not *whether* we should use music in Christian worship but *how* we should use it, *what kind* of music we should use, and for *what purpose* we should employ music in worship. In order to understand the use and purpose of music in worship, we need to ask an even more fundamental question regarding the purpose of worship itself. Since music is one of several biblical elements of worship in the Scriptures, a basic definition of worship will inform us about how music fits in the context of congregational worship.

There are different ways to define worship, including the distinction between worship as a way of life and worship in the congregation. I offer a provisional definition of worship that includes both a "way of life" worship and congregational worship, which should provide context for the rest of the chapter:

> Worship is the human response to the self-revelation of the triune God, which involves: (1) divine initiation in which God graciously reveals himself, his purposes, and his will; (2) a spiritual and personal relationship with God through Jesus Christ enabled by the ministry of the Holy Spirit; and (3) a response by the worshiper of joyful adoration, reverence, humility, submission, and obedience.

The Primary Question

Our understanding of the use of music in worship must be informed by the purpose of worship in the church. Therefore,

---

[6] See H. Leon McBeth, *The Baptist Heritage* (Nashville: Broadman, 1987), 94–95.

we will proceed to look at some basic biblical concepts that describe the ministry of worship in the local church and then consider the implications for the use of music in worship.

I would like to frame the discussion that follows in the context of three liturgical dimensions: doxology ministry to God, edification ministry to the church, and proclamation ministry to the world.[7] It is important to keep in mind the definition of worship previously offered in order to appreciate the liturgical dimensions, since, at first glance, two of the three dimensions may seem to be focused on man, rather than God. It will become clear that, quite to the contrary, recognition of these dimensions will keep the church properly focused on the glory of God in worship and will give us direction on understanding the biblical purpose of music in worship.

Music and Doxology: Ministry to God

Doxology is a "word of glory" or a "word of praise." Worship is doxological in that it is supremely concerned with ascribing glory to God. The Bible is replete with references to the glory of God and commands for man to give glory to God (e.g., Pss. 29:2; 105:3; 115:1), some that specifically refer to the use of music (e.g., Pss. 66:2; 96:1–3).

Doxology is clearly in view when Paul instructs the Ephesian and the Colossian Christians to employ "psalms, hymns and spiritual songs" in the congregation (Eph. 5:19; Col. 3:16). This is the language of praise. Further, both passages instruct the church to give thanks to God. The book of Revelation informs us that this doxological ministry to God will be an eternal occupation (Rev. 5:13). That music should be employed for

---

[7] Here I draw from the work of A. M. Triacca, "Le sens théologique de la liturgie et/ou le sens liturgique de la théologie: Esquisse initiale pour une synthèse," in *La liturgie, son sens, son esprit, sa méthode: Liturgie et théologie*, ed. A. Pistoia and A. M. Triacca (Rome: CLV Edizzioni liturgiche, 1982), 329–36; and David B. Pass, *Music and the Church* (Nashville: Broadman, 1989).

doxological purposes is no surprise. But a careful look at certain biblical texts inform us that the doxological ministry of the worshiping church extends into other liturgical dimensions and that each of these ministries may employ music.

Music and Edification: Ministry to the Church

While some may suggest that edification has nothing to do with worship, there are biblical passages that indicate otherwise. By "edification" I mean the biblical concept of "building up," "encouraging," or "exhorting" someone. We will call this the hortatory function of music, referring to that which exhorts. We learn in 1 Corinthians 14 that edifying the body of Christ in the public assembly is critically important. The doxological dimension of the liturgical assembly is noted in this passage, with references to prayer and praise (vv. 14–15, 26), thanksgiving (vv. 16–17), and the hope that the unbeliever will come to worship God (v. 25). Yet Paul insists that giving thanks to God is not enough if "the other person is not being built up *(oikodomēn)*."

This is a continuation of Paul's teaching about life in the congregation in chapters 11–14 of 1 Corinthians, where he instructs them about how to conduct the Lord's Supper (chap. 11), the purpose of spiritual gifts (chap. 12), and the primacy of love (chap. 13). This concern for building up the body is also seen in Paul's call for intelligibility in public worship throughout 1 Corinthians 14. It is not enough to build up oneself in worship. We must always ask whether our doxological actions encourage the edification of the whole church (vv. 4, 13–17, 26). A comparable problem arose during the Counter-Reformation due to the use of polyphony in choral music,[8] which obscured the meaning of the text for the listeners. The Council of Trent modified the use of polyphony in order to make texts more understandable to the congregation.[9]

---

[8] Polyphony is the simultaneous combination of two or more independent melodic parts.

[9] Westermeyer, *Te Deum*, 163–64.

Instructions in Ephesians 5:19 and Colossians 3:16 echo some of the themes of 1 Corinthians 14. As previously noted by Richard Averbeck in chapter 3,[10] the Ephesians 5 instruction about worship and singing is given in the context of an instruction for believers to live wisely and to be filled with the fullness of God by the Holy Spirit. Five participles related to life in the congregation hang on the command to "be filled" in Ephesians 5:18. It is striking to me that the first of these participles involves the instruction to "speak *to one another* in psalms, hymns and spiritual songs (5:19)."

That these liturgical actions are doxological is clear, by the very nature of the terms "psalms" and "hymns." Yet, there is also an emphasis here on "edification, instruction, and exhortation."[11] The nature of this edification is more explicit in Colossians 3:16. There Paul specifically encourages the church to "teach" *(didaskō)* and "admonish" *(noutheteō)* one another with its music in congregational worship. Worship, then, while doxological, may also serve to build up the congregation by both instruction and correction. The medium of this edification, in this instance, is psalms, hymns, and spiritual songs.

It seems clear enough that these passages indicate the relationship between doxological and hortatory dimensions of worship. I think there are a number of ways in which attention to the hortatory dimension may benefit our understanding of the use of music in worship. First, passages like 1 Corinthians 14; Ephesians 5:19; and Colossians 3:16 indicate that music is one medium through which the congregation may be taught the truths of the Christian faith. As was noted in the comments on Colossians 3:16, this may be prescriptive ("teaching") or corrective ("admonishing"). One should note, also, that the Psalms, composed for Israel's worship of God, are filled with hortatory and didactic elements. Doxology and edification are integrated in the Psalms as in the Pauline passages we have examined.

---

[10] Ibid., 93–94.

[11] Andrew Lincoln, *Ephesians*, WBC (Dallas: Word, 1990), 42:345.

Second, music does affect those who sing, play, and listen to music. The extent of such influence is a matter of some debate, along with whether the affects are psychological or physiological, or some combination of the two. John Calvin noted the positive possibilities of music in his instructions about prayer and singing. For Calvin, since "singing is a strong force and vigorously moves and enflames the hearts of men," it should be employed in the praise of God.[12] We may note the healing, soothing effect music has on people, as with Saul in 1 Samuel 16:23.[13] Augustine, in *Confessions,* struggles with the effects of music upon man and the appropriate use of music in the liturgical context. At times he thinks it may be best to dispense with the use of music in the church altogether or at least to use it minimally. Then he recalls how the "cantus Ecclesiae," the songs of the church, were instrumental in his return to faith, and he is inclined to believe that the church should keep singing so as to strengthen the faith of the weak. Nevertheless, he admits that there are times that he is more "moved by the singing than by what is sung," which is sinful.[14] There are legitimate concerns on this point, which we will address later in the chapter.

Third, attention to the hortatory dimension of worship promotes Christian unity. This is a primary consideration for Paul in 1 Corinthians. The use of music in worship should never be an issue that divides; rather, its use presents each member of the congregation continuous opportunity to "look not only to [his] own interests, but also to the interests of others" (Phil. 2:4). The notion of worship that fosters unity in the congregation is a

---

[12] John Calvin, "La Forme Des Prieres et Chantz Ecclesiastiques," in *Opera Selecta* 2:15 (translation mine).

[13] The passage also indicates that music has something to do with spiritual warfare, though we should be careful to observe the emphasis of the Holy Spirit in the text. The text contrasts the departure of the Spirit of the Lord from Saul with the arrival of the evil spirit in him and notes that David's ministry to Saul occurs after "the Spirit of the Lord rushed upon David from that day forward" (1 Sam. 16:13 ESV).

[14] Augustine, *Confessions* 10.33 (*NPNF1* 1:156; PL 32:799–80c).

central concern for church fathers like Clement of Rome, Ignatius, and Clement of Alexandria, among others.[15]

Music and Proclamation: Ministry to the World

This third liturgical dimension emerges in a number of biblical passages. It is the kerygmatic dimension, from the Greek kerygma, meaning "message" or "proclamation." The association of God's glory and proclamation to the world about his glory is seen in Psalm 96:1–3 (ESV):

> Oh sing to the LORD a new song;
>   sing to the LORD, all the earth!
> Sing to the LORD, bless his name;
>   tell of his salvation from day to day.
> Declare his glory among the nations;
>   his marvelous works among all the peoples!

In Solomon's prayer of dedication for the temple in 1 Kings 8, there is an interesting passage that demonstrates this connection between proclamation of the glory and power of God and the worship of God. Solomon prays to the Lord:

> Likewise, when a *foreigner*, who is *not of your people Israel*, comes from *a far country* for your name's sake (for they shall hear of your great name and your mighty hand, and of your outstretched arm), when he comes and prays toward this house, hear in heaven your dwelling place and do according to all for which the *foreigner* calls to you, in order that *all the peoples of the earth* may know your name and fear you, as do your people Israel, and that they may know that this house that I have built is called by your name. (vv. 41–43 ESV, emphasis added)

---

[15] Westermeyer, *Te Deum*, 62–63.

The "outstretched arm" of verse 42 recalls God's creative power (Jer. 27:5; 32:17) and his power to save (Deut. 7:19; 9:29; 11:2), along with his power to judge (Isa. 14:26–27; "outstretched hand"). Here, God's desire to save the nations is set in the context of worship, as it is in Psalm 96.

A similar link between proclamation and worship is seen in the writings of the apostle Paul. In Romans 15:16, Paul states his intent "to be a minister *(leitourgon)* of Christ Jesus to the Gentiles in the priestly service *(hierourgounta)* of the gospel of God, so that the offering *(prosphora)* of the Gentiles may be acccptable *(euprosdektos),* sanctified *(hēgiasmenē)* by the Holy Spirit." Paul employs common liturgical language from the LXX not to refer to congregational worship but to the proclamation of the gospel and the conversion of the Gentiles to faith in Jesus Christ. It is difficult not to conclude that Paul sees evangelism in some sense as an act of worship itself. That he does so becomes clear in 1 Corinthians 14. There, Paul's demand for intelligibility in public worship which includes singing (vv. 15, 26), is not limited to the need to build up the body, but it also applies to the proclamation of the gospel (vv. 23–25).

While it is impossible for an unbeliever to authentically worship God, Paul assumes that unbelievers will be present during times of congregational worship and indicates that worship has a genuinely evangelistic purpose. This reality should cause us to consider how well the content, clarity, and intelligibility of the music we use in worship communicates the truth of the gospel and the glory of God to the unbeliever. This is not to say that the liturgical agenda should be *driven* by such concerns, but the church must certainly be *sensitive* to them.

The Popular Question

We now turn to the second query, the popular question, *What about musical style?* We have already mentioned the tensions resident during the Patristic period concerning the use of musical instruments in worship. Controversy emerged during the Medieval period as well. The Cistercian abbot, Aelred (twelfth c.), comments on the new music of his day:

> In the meantime the people stand in fear and astonishment listening to the sound of the bellows, the crash of cymbals, and the tuning of flutes; but when they see the lascivious gesticulations of the singers, and hear the meretricious alternations and shakings of the voices, they cannot restrain their laughter, and you would think they had not come to prayer, but to a spectacle, not to an oratory, but to a theater. There is no fear for that fearful Majesty in Whose presence they stand.[16]

This is not altogether unlike certain criticisms of contemporary music today. We should note that Aelred's concern is not to forbid music but to ensure that the weak in faith are moved to genuine piety instead of "illicit pleasure," and that "sound [music] is not preferred to sense, but sound with sense may arouse and more often allow greater affection."[17]

In his letter to the clergy of Neocaesarea in 375, Basil the Great[18] wrote to defend himself against criticisms about, among other things, psalm singing and music that vary from the customs held by his opponents. He replies to his critics, "it is alleged [that] these practices were not observed in the time of

---

[16] Quoted in Westermeyer, *Te Deum*, 125. See Aelred, *De Speculo Caritas* 2:23 (CCCM 1:97–99).

[17] Aelred, *De Speculo* 2:23 (CCCM 1:98). Translation mine.

[18] Basil the Great (c. 330–79) served as bishop of Caesarea and archbishop of Cappadocia. He was a leading theologian and defender of orthodox Christology. Basil contributed to the development of Eastern monasticism and was noted for founding hospitals and hostels to provide for the sick and the poor. See F. L. Cross and E. A. Livingstone, eds., *The Oxford Dictionary of the Christian Church*, 3d ed. (Oxford: Oxford University Press, 1997), 166.

the great Gregory.[19] My rejoinder is that even the Litanies which you now use were not used in his time. . . . You have kept none of his customs up to the present time."[20] For Basil, it is not so important that they maintain the practices of Gregory as it is that they worship out of a motivation to serve and love the Lord, and that their practice finds acceptance among a broad spectrum of churches. Again, these tensions have a tone not unfamiliar in our day. In order to approach the question of musical style, I want to suggest three proposals concerning the use of music in worship drawn from two Christian doctrines: the doctrine of creation and the doctrine of the church.

The Doctrine of Creation

God created the world and he called it good, indeed, very good (Gen. 1:31). The world and all that is in it are to give glory to God (Ps. 148). So, if I may be permitted to state the obvious, man should give glory to God and man's music should be employed for the glory of God. I am not suggesting, however, that all music must be composed for use in Christian liturgy or that music presently in use in Christian liturgy was composed to glorify God. We sometimes forget that, like the Israelites, the church has borrowed poetry and styles of music from their cultural settings.

Old Testament scholars readily acknowledge that Israeli psalmists adapt Egyptian and Mesopotamian hymns to declare Yahweh's superiority over creation (Pss. 29; 104).[21] Likewise, in 1907, the

---

[19] The "great Gregory" to whom Basil refers is Gregory Thaumaturgus (c. 213–c. 270). He was a student of Origen and the bishop of Neocaesarea, known for "his uncommon strength of character [and] his popularity." See Cross and Livingstone, *Oxford Dictionary of the Christian Church*, 713.

[20] Basil, *Letter CCVII* (*NPNF2* 8:246; PG 32:760–61c; 764–65c).

[21] See, for example, P. C. Craigie, "The Comparison of Hebrew Poetry: Psalm 104 in the Light of Egyptian and Ugaritic Poetry," *Semitics* 4 (1974):10–24.

New England Presbyterian pastor Henry van Dyke composed
the following poem and set it to the last movement of Ludwig
van Beethoven's 1824 Symphony No. 9, "Ode to Joy."

> Joyful, joyful, we adore Thee,
> God of glory, Lord of love;
> Hearts unfold like flowers before Thee,
> Opening to the sun above.
> Melt the clouds of sin and sadness,
> Drive the dark of doubt away;
> Giver of immortal gladness,
> Fill us with the light of day.[22]

Other examples may also come to mind. Israel and the church
have always borrowed hymns and music styles from their respective cultures. Nevertheless, we should constantly affirm that
the "chief end of man," as the old confession puts it, is to glorify God forever. Therefore, the primacy of God's glory should
motivate worship leaders in their composition, borrowing, and
use of music. Any discussion of musical style that fails to recognize this point is off to a false start.

Not only should we consider that all of creation, including
man and music, exists for the glory of the Creator, but our
inquiry about musical style should involve the recognition of
the amazing diversity and quality of the world that God created and sustains by his providence. Whether we think of the
variety of plants, animals, topography of the earth, the expanse
of the cosmos, or the uniqueness of each man, woman, and
child, the immensity of God's creativity is stunning. Additionally, we should be astonished that, amidst the diversity and excellence of God's good creation, God created man in his own
image and, as the psalmist recites, sets his attention and affec-

---

[22] Donald P. Hustad, *Dictionary-Handbook to Hymns for the Living Church* (Carol
Stream, Ill.: Hope, 1978), 29–30.

tion upon us (Ps. 8). We can note, then, a few important truths related to the doctrine of creation that should inform our thinking about music and worship.

First, man was created to bring glory to God and to reflect his glory continually (Isa. 43:7). As a part of the created order, we are to join in praising God and this includes our music making, whether composing, playing, or singing. Second, because man is created in the image of God, all mankind must be treated with equal dignity. Third, I believe that the diversity of God's creation should lead us to appreciate a diversity of musical styles.

The Doctrine of the Church

I want to focus here on the concept of the church as a fellowship or community of the Holy Spirit. Identification of the church with the Holy Spirit is a recurring New Testament theme. The church owes its existence to the ministry of the Spirit (Acts 2; 1 Cor. 12:13), is gifted for ministry by the Spirit (1 Cor. 12), grows and matures by the ministry of the Spirit (Eph. 2:21–22), has fellowship with the Spirit (2 Cor. 13:13 [14]), and enjoys the unity of the Spirit (Eph. 4:3).

To point out that the church exists, as a community, is to point out what should be obvious. Yet, in the church, it is too often the case that the idea of genuine Christian community is secondary to the variety of individual tastes and competing preferences. Such an environment, which neglects the reality of the church as community, is fertile soil for controversy over musical style.

As the community of the Spirit, the church should exhibit a healthy unity with diversity. In Acts 2, the work of the Holy Spirit includes drawing diverse peoples into the church. The ethnic diversity of the crowd is recounted in verses 5–11. The implication of Acts 2:45 is that these were people from diverse economic strata. These diverse peoples are found worshiping together following the Spirit's work at Pentecost. In 1 Corinthians, we note similar themes. Paul corrects the Corinthians concerning their failure to recognize their unity in the Spirit, even though the one body (the church) is made up of many members (1 Cor. 12:13). Paul heralds the diversity of the congregation. They possess varieties of gifts, ministries, and engage in diverse activities, but they do so by the power of the one triune God (vv. 4–6); and this is so for the common good of the body of Christ as determined by the Holy Spirit (v. 7).

There are two important conclusions I would like to draw at this point. First, the church should be the one place in the world where ethnic, sociological, class, and generational diversity exists in unity. Second, if such diversity properly belongs within the church, and since God's creation exhibits such wonderful diversity, then it seems logical to conclude that the music of the church's worship would reflect diversity as well. The extent of that diversity is a matter that cannot be explored adequately within the current essay. But I hope that we can admit that diversity should in fact exist.

This is, to me, the reason that we should answer the question about musical styles by asking congregations to consider the possibility of a diversity of musical styles, rather than settling on one style or another. This approach offers at least two advantages to the church. First, a commitment to diverse musical styles should protect the church from becoming "time bound" in its worship. When a congregation adopts a single musical style, which is inevitably associated with a certain period in history and culture, it may become unduly bound to that musical style. Then, when certain groups within the congregation seek to introduce different musical styles, there is often tension. A commitment to a diversity of styles that is not bound to the music of a single era may avoid, or at least lessen, such tensions. Then, when changes begin to occur in a congregation, transitions are less difficult and the church is better poised to minister to diverse peoples.[23]

Second, if this approach is taken, the rationale for using various styles is no longer rooted simply in personal musical tastes but in the diversity of God's good creation and the diversity of the people whom the Holy Spirit births into the church. Thus, the focus is taken off the individual and returned to God and the community of faith. One implication of adopting such a vision is to admit the beauty of seeing people of diverse ages, diverse social classes, and diverse ethnicities worshiping together. Too often our strategy for ministering to diverse peoples is to build separate churches for them, or at least to develop different services based, usually, on differing musical styles within a local church. I think we should consider that this actually may be antithetical to the nature of the gospel and the reality of the church as the community of the Spirit. In fact, with so much talk about the Spirit's work in worship these days, it occurs to me that at least one aspect of the Holy Spirit working freely and powerfully in the church should be some evidence of diversity, rather than homogeneity, whether ethnic, social, class, generational, or musical.

Three Proposals Concerning the Use of Music in Worship

Drawing from our brief survey of the doctrines of creation and the church, I now want to offer three general proposals to guide the church in its use of music that arise from our previous doctrinal considerations: (1) we must properly account for

---

[23] I have suggested elsewhere that such a commitment to diversity in musical style is the product of a proper eschatological vision that the church should possess and that reduces the likelihood that the church will lose a distinctive voice in its culture. See my "Messianic Intermezzo: Eschatology, Spirit, and Worship in the Church," in *Looking into the Future,* ed. D. W. Baker (Grand Rapids: Baker, 2001), 315–24.

the glory of God; (2) we must properly account for the nature of God's creation; and (3) we must properly account for the nature of God's church.

We must properly account for the glory of God. I suggest that a proper view of the glory of God will lead the church to a commitment to excellence with respect to its worship, including its use of music. Such a commitment should involve an understanding of the distinction between moral excellence and artistic (aesthetic) excellence in the use of music in worship.

To understand the importance of moral excellence in relation to our use of music in the church, we must make another distinction, between the music we use and our use of music. That is to say, we have to distinguish properly the music itself from our music making. While some will surely disagree, I do not believe that music itself has the capacity to be immoral. I have yet to encounter an argument, ancient or modern, that adequately demonstrates how musical notes, rhythms, timbres, and such are immoral or evil.

While music itself cannot be immoral, it is true that music may be used for immoral purposes. In this sense, however, music is not immoral any more than I believe an automobile, gun, or camera to be immoral when employed for immoral purposes. That being said, there are moral considerations for our thinking about our use of music, and these considerations are directly related to the glory of God. These moral considerations have to do primarily with our morality as music makers.

Christian musicians and the entire worshiping community have an obligation to make music with moral excellence. That is, the church should appear before the Lord with clean hands and a pure heart (Ps. 24; Jas. 4:7–10). The congregation's worship of God should flow from a lifestyle of worship that is marked by personal purity and obedience to God. This is not simply a matter of individual purity and piety. It also involves the church's response to issues of social justice (Amos 5:18–24). While we must not neglect the reality that God is a God of grace, and that we are only able to worship because of the perfect worship of our Lord Jesus Christ, we also must not forget that God is holy and requires that his people lead holy lives (1 Peter 1:16) and worship him in holiness (Ps. 96:9; 1 Peter 2:5).

Not only is it important to approach our use of music in worship with moral excellence, but it is also important to make music before God with artistic excellence. Artistic excellence is important not because, as trained musicians, we have certain musical standards but because Scripture demands it. It is interesting to note how skillful craftsmen, led by the Holy Spirit, were involved in the construction of the tabernacle and the implements made for the worship of God (e.g., Exod. 26:31; 28:15; 35:35). Other passages in the Old Testament demonstrate the importance of skill in the use of music in the worship of God (1 Chron. 15:22; Pss. 33:3; 47:7).

There are two things I should clarify at this point. First, the issue of skill is not related directly to God's acceptance of our worship. Scripture indicates that moral excellence is prior to artistic excellence on this point. Artistic excellence, however, is important in that it is associated with the glory of God. If we properly account for his glory, we will want to reflect, as those made in his image, his glory in our worship, in our music, and in our music making.

Second, when speaking of "excellence," I borrow from Harold Best, who says, that *"excellence is the process—*note that word *process—of becoming better than I once was."*[24] Music of poor quality exists within every musical style or genre, and latitude on the issue of musical quality may be allowed, but we should admit that some music is simply bad and thereby not suitable for worship. In this way, the church makes a commitment to a lifelong pursuit of excellence, not for the purpose of impressing other people but for bringing glory to God and making his name great. This means we should use music of excellent quality,

---

[24] Harold M. Best, *Music Through the Eyes of Faith* (San Francisco: HarperSanFrancisco, 1993), 108. This is one of the most useful resources for thinking through the use of music in Christian worship.

which exists within a wide variety of musical styles, and that the congregation (not just trained musicians) should make music with excellence.

We must properly account for the nature of God's creation. I wish to make two points here, involving the diversity of God's creation and the dignity of man as created in the image of God. As I argued earlier, a proper view of creation will lead us to appreciate both the diversity of people (e.g., ethnic, social, generational) and the diversity of musical styles that exist in God's world. The extent of that diversity will likely vary from congregation to congregation, sometimes based on a simple factor like the location of a certain church. Nevertheless, each congregation should be aware of and open to the diversity that exists not only in creation but also within the larger new creation of the church community (2 Cor. 5:17).

The doctrine of creation demands that Christian musicians take into account the equal dignity of all humans when planning and presenting music for worship. So, following Eric Routley, I will always ask of my music making, "Whom is this leaving out?"[25] This does not mean that a church must have complete unanimity of musical taste before one chooses a certain piece of music. But it does mean that we should have such a question in mind as we plan music for congregational worship.

Attention to human dignity should also make the church sensitive to the fact that our music making, if we are not careful, may result in manipulation. This is a matter of moral excellence and human dignity. The line between using music to encourage the congregation to worship and using it to manipulate human affections is sometimes difficult to discern (and sometimes not so difficult!). But worship leaders must at least be aware of the possibility that music may be used to manipulate people, whether intentionally or unintentionally. This is

---

[25] Eric Routley, *Church Music and the Christian Faith* (Carol Stream, Ill.: Agape, 1978), 135.

when, to borrow a phrase from Hugo Cole, good may be bad.[26] That is, one may use good music, presented excellently, for bad purposes. This is to forsake moral excellence and to refuse the reality of human dignity, and it is to sin in our music making.

We must properly account for the nature of God's church. First, not only should we recognize the diversity of God's creation, but we should also recognize that, in the church, diversity exists within the unity of the Holy Spirit. Therefore, diversity is not a cause for division but is, rather, an opportunity for the congregation to submit to the leadership of the Holy Spirit and to see the diversity of God's good creation abound to his glory. With respect to our use of music in worship, we should celebrate the use of diverse styles, even those we don't prefer, as they reflect the glory of God and his world.

Second, music and musicians must be servants of the triune God and his church. Christians, as members of the body of Christ, are servants of God and his church. Service is the essence of ministry and worship. If it means anything to do music *ministry,* then, when we think about the use of music in worship, we must also think about ourselves as servants. Herb Bateman, in the introduction, has well articulated that our thinking about worship should reflect the mind of Christ in that we lay aside all self-interest and assume the cloak of self-giving, self-denial, and self-sacrifice as faithful disciples of Jesus Christ. To glory only in the Cross of our Lord Jesus Christ can mean nothing less (Gal. 6:14). This is true for the entire worship community, and it is true for all who provide musical leadership in the local church. To exercise such a servant mentality is at the root of liturgical and musical ministry to God, his church, and his world.

---

[26] Quoted in Andrew-Wilson Dickson, *The Story of Christian Music* (Oxford: Lion, 1992), 243. See Hugo Cole, *The Changing Face of Music* (London: Oxford University Press, 1978), 91.

The Pastoral Question

We now take up the third question posed at the beginning of the essay, *How should we handle issues related to music in the church?* The following suggestions, in a summary fashion, address how to manage issues related to music in worship. They include some foundations that emerge from our previous biblical and theological inquiry, some advice about pastoral leadership, and several ideas about how to handle the changes and transitions that congregations inevitably face with respect to music in worship.

Two Foundational Issues in Trinitarian Context

Very simply, I want to reemphasize (1) the priority of the glory of God and Christ and (2) the reality of the unity of the Spirit in the church. If a congregation is experiencing tensions about changes in musical styles, the best way to put things in proper perspective is for the church to affirm that they exist to give glory to God and to make his name great before the nations. The congregation facing worship transitions must also affirm that it is their responsibility to make every effort to preserve the unity of the Spirit in the church (Eph. 4:3), and to do so means that each member of the body of Christ should lay aside self-interest in interest of what is best for the well-being and growth of the entire body of Christ.

Three Keys for Pastoral Leadership

First, we must *know the people truly*. If you are to perceive accurately the strengths, weaknesses, needs, and desires of a congregation, you must know the people; and to know them, you will have to be among them, spending time with them, praying with them, listening to them, ministering to them, and serving them.

Second, we must *love the people sincerely*. Demonstrate love, not to achieve your goals but because you genuinely care for the people and desire to see them grow in their devotion and service to Christ. When they know you love them, they will more readily accept change, even if they do not like it.

Finally, we must *communicate with the people clearly.* Simply let them know about how you believe God is directing the church. Communicate to leaders and communicate to the whole congregation. Communicate in advance, communicate clearly and honestly, and communicate repeatedly. Communicate, communicate, communicate!

Ten Tips for Transitions

Every congregation faces the need for transitions at some point. The question is whether the transition will be handled well and whether it will be a time of healthy growth or a time of destructive controversy. As any congregation faces transition, the obvious sometimes eludes us. The following are tips for transitions, which include some suggestions and reminders about previous points in our discussion.

1. *Develop a loving servant mentality throughout the congregation.*
2. *Foster a healthy respect for diversity: ethnic, sociological/class, generational, and musical.*
3. *Develop a clear rationale for change, rooted in biblical principles, and inform the congregation accordingly.*
4. *Develop an appreciation in the congregation for both the traditional and the contemporary that is rooted in an appreciation for God's people.*
5. *Don't make it all about musical style.* Showing people how transitions in worship have more to do with the purpose of worship, the various liturgical dimensions, God's work among the congregation, and the opportunity to exhibit Christlike selflessness and servanthood should put the musical style issue in proper perspective.
6. *Carefully evaluate the singability of new music.* If you

introduce new music that is difficult to sing, you will
face greater resistance to change. When introducing a
new style, be certain that you begin music that is
accessible to the majority of the congregation.

7. *Don't let the medium crowd out the message.* If you are introducing changes such as the addition of various instruments, be certain that the changes are introduced
appropriately. For example, if the transition involves the
addition of a trap set, it will not be wise to allow the
drummer to play so loud that the congregation is dis-
tracted (whether because they like or dislike the drums).
Instead, musicians who are sensitive to the Spirit of God
and sensitive to others should hope to play in such a way
as to harmoniously contribute to the overall texture of
the ensemble and assist the congregation to more ably
worship God.

8. *When making changes in musical repertoire and style, be certain
that the church musicians are adequately prepared.* This will
prevent frustration on the part of the musicians, most
of whom prefer to be well prepared before they enter a
worship service. It will also prevent sloppiness in the
worship service itself, which is often a distraction for the
congregation and another potential cause for criticism.

9. *Recognize that transitions often involve changes in form as
well as changes in style.* Transitions may involve adjust-
ments in the order of service, or additions or deletions
to the order. Either way, this is sometimes as difficult for
people to accept as changing musical styles.

10. *Don't introduce too much change too quickly* (unless you can!).
In most congregations change must be introduced in-
crementally. On some occasions the congregation will
move more quickly. Leaders who know and love their
congregation will know the difference between the two.

Conclusion

I do not think it incidental that the end of the Hebrew Bible concludes with the book of Chronicles. There the Scriptures record the ebb and flow of good and bad kings among God's people. Two of the kings, Hezekiah and Josiah, were careful to encourage authentic worship according to the instructions of the Lord. Chronicles details the sad account of other Davidic kings who failed to lead the people to worship God. The temple, a sanctuary built out of God's desire to dwell with his people (Exod. 25:8), was desecrated by the priests and the people of Judah: "And they polluted the house of the LORD that he had made holy in Jerusalem" (2 Chron. 36:14b). The Bible records that God continued to extend compassion toward his people and his dwelling place, yet the people rejected God's message, "despising his words and scoffing at his prophets until the wrath of the Lord rose against his people, until there was no remedy" (v. 16). Chronicles then notes the eventual possession of the land by foreigners and the destruction of the temple. Created for God's glory, God's people fell mute and the house of God silent. One must wonder if we, by ignoring biblical instructions and principles about the use of music in worship, might, even in making much music, likewise render silent the genuine praise of God.

In the final verses of 2 Chronicles, Cyrus, King of Persia, was charged by God to "build him a house at Jerusalem" so his people might worship him once again (36:23). Such is God's desire for authentic worship. God desired authentic worship then, and he desires authentic worship now. The renewal of authentic worship must include the proper use of diverse music, based upon the principles of God's Word. Then, the diverse peoples of God's creation will have opportunity to voice God's praise in the congregation and to witness God's temple, the body of Christ, filled with his glory.

CHAPTER SEVEN

Developing a Practice of Worship That Unites

Thomas F. Atchison

"Where there is no vision, the people are unrestrained, but happy is he who keeps the law" (Prov. 29:18). Rightly understood, these words of wisdom strike at the core of the issues that often divide the unity of a congregation over styles of worship. In other words, the biblical writer asserts that, without divine counsel or communication, the people lack restraint, if not order and direction.

A good measure of the confusion and division in our churches exists because pastors do not bring God's Word to bear on theological issues of worship for purposes of order and direction; for, indeed, happy are those who order their lives by God's instruction. Rather, all too often choices are made and direction is set for worship based upon taste, issues of church growth, tradition, trends, and the like. Therefore, it follows that tensions develop when the congregant approaches his or her pastor with the following. God deserves the best! Or, why don't we sing more hymns? Or, why don't we sing more contemporary music that is far more engaging? This contemporary music is too self-centered! And the drone lists on. The spiritual leader must lead with a clear, biblical understanding of worship or the people will lack restraint in their confusion.

The purpose of this chapter is to address some biblical, theological, and historical concerns in worship toward the outcome of developing a practice of worship that *unites* a congregation. The heart of God's instruction, summed by Jesus, is as follows: "Love the Lord your God with all of your heart and with all of your soul and with all of your strength and with all your mind . . . love your neighbor as yourself" (cf. Matt. 22:37–40). Therefore, the main thrust in what follows focuses on the *moral excellence* of loving God and loving people, not external excellence expressed in forms and style (as important as these are or may be for a particular church context). This chapter seeks to help establish a church in blended worship. In order to do this, the chapter will, first, develop *three observations* concerning worship; second, consider *two shaping questions* necessary for leadership to move forward in unity; and third, express *a single, direct conclusion.*

Before launching into this discussion any further, some context for how these thoughts and practices emerged may be helpful. When I came to Fox Valley Church, one might say there was a gentle breeze. The worship service was essentially traditional with some entrenched practices, yet there was a growing interest on the part of some to contemporize. However the winds developed in this new direction of using contemporary music, the *how* and *why* and *what* was not yet being considered. To my own foolishness, I stumbled forward with a practice of blended worship in mind. A misguided understanding of what it means to worship in S/spirit and truth as well as a weak knowledge of how to lead a body into authentic worship advanced into more confusion. Rather quickly, the winds grew to gale force. I wasn't sure what to do, so I started to pray, to talk to all the various people involved, to study the Word, and to read everything and anything on worship. This produced only more confusion in my heart and mind. In addition to my own morass, God was pleased to bless this body (of approximately 120 at this time) with many "artsy" types. As in most cases, the convictions ran strong and the opinions easily expressed. I was living Proverbs 29:18.

The questions and issues listed above intimate the general direction of the forces confronting me. I lacked a biblical perspective. Intuitively knowing this was entering storm stage winds with the potential of even a hurricane, I asked the elders if we could put this discussion on hold and return to earlier practices. I needed time to absorb the developments so that I could lead with biblical authority and conviction in loving servanthood. In addition, I readily confessed to all those involved that I was unprepared to lead and to seek forgiveness where I offended others in the matter.

All this said, I am grateful to the people of Fox Valley Church and I love them. It was my lack of leadership that brought the difficulties to a stage of increased tension. In impressive earnestness, they sought to follow, but I failed to lead in love, in an understanding of the Word on worship, and in an appreciation for *every* individual in the body. An important distinctive of our body emerged with fresh vigor: *we genuinely appreciate diversity while championing unity.* All is to be done in love, in *moral excellence,* to the glory of God (1 Cor. 10:31).

What follows was hammered out in personal study, a task force of very gifted people from Fox Valley Church, and numerous discussions with others who are far more godly. I will be forever grateful to all those that demonstrated such patience and understanding as I sought to get the proverbial horse before the cart in matters of worship. In all matters, God graciously led his people into deeper discoveries of his matchless worth.

Three Observations Concerning Worship

Many recognize today that authentic worship is simply "to ascribe worth to the God of the Bible with all of one's heart, soul, mind, and strength." Somehow it does not stay that simple when it comes to working it out in a church. As the definition suggests, a dynamic exists between God and his people. Yet in this mix, first things must remain first things. Three of the most often *forsaken first things* follow from this definition.

We Gather to Worship God

Much ink has been spilled pointing to this forsaken first thing—God is the most important focus of the worshiping dynamic. Ascribing worth to God arises from how he has revealed himself in Scripture and how he has acted in history, not least in his redemptive work. With respect to the former, God's self-disclosure includes revelation of his holiness, justness, goodness, wisdom, power, and the like. Or, as the Israelites sang to Yahweh, "Who among the gods is like you, O LORD? Who is like you—majestic in holiness, awesome in glory, working wonders?" (Exod. 15:11).

With respect to the latter, God reveals and explains such things as his acts of creation, covenants with people and the nation of Israel, and dealings with sin (creation *by his Word,* expulsion from the Garden, a catastrophic flood, Tower of Babel, etc.). Indeed, "He established a testimony in Jacob . . . that they should put their trust in God and would not forget the works of God, but keep His commands" (Ps. 78:5, 7 NASB). His Word alone narrates a true story (or worldview) that provides a basis for deep, authentic worship. In this postmodern age and the related issues, the importance of the Bible as the authoritative source of revealing God as he truly is must not be minimized. If this focus on God and his engagement in human history is maintained in worship, a step away from the trivialization of God may be taken. Certainly the God of the Bible is One with whom a true believer dares not trifle; he is a consuming fire (Heb. 12:29).

Since the object of the believer's worship is a person, the encounter involves individual intimacy. As in all personal relationships, dangers exist that can potentially distort the closeness. A husband can love his wife for her bodily beauty, what she does for him, how she makes him feel, etc. This can be fine until they are made central in the relationship. A mature and abiding love focuses on who an individual is (i.e., one made in the image and likeness of God). Likewise, in a relationship with

God, our love and worship entails a true understanding of who God is. We seek, first and foremost, to worship God. As Carson writes,

> We do not meet to worship (i.e., to experience worship); we aim to worship *God*. "Worship the Lord your God, and serve him only": there is the heart of the matter. In this area, as in so many others, one must not confuse what is central with by-products. If you seek peace, you will not find it; if you seek Christ, you will find peace. If you seek joy, you will not find it; if you seek Christ, you will find joy. If you seek holiness, you will not find it; if you seek Christ, you will find holiness. If you seek experience of worship, you will not find them; if you worship the living God, you will experience something of what is reflected in the Psalms. Worship is a transitive verb, and the most important thing about it is the direct object.[1]

In other words, while all of these by-products (peace, joy, holiness, and experience) are in themselves good, they are not the very first thing. God is. Certainly our greatest joy, our most abiding peace, our deepest satisfaction flow from God and are found only in him, but perhaps a tendency of today's worship patterns is to confuse what is central with by-products. So, for example, in worship, where the music (contemporary or traditional) is so engaging, the worshiper's elation may rise from the tune *and not God*. Or, where the music is so poor, the worshiper's disengagement may reveal a heart set on the need for a certain music style *and not God*. Music often engages the soul and thereby can aid in worship, or it can lead astray from the main purpose in a variety of ways. Of course, this is the rub

---

[1] D. A. Carson, "'Worship the Lord Your God': The Perennial Challenge," in *Worship: Adoration and Action,* ed. D. A. Carson (Grand Rapids: Baker, 1993), 15.

and why discerning leadership is necessary. We want to be engaged with God, which attractively enlivens deep and real emotion. We desire to escape the hurt and pain caused by sin. We long to know God more intimately and appreciate his goodness in our lives. So, while the defining of worship proves simple, developing the practice that keeps God first can be elusive.

We Gather to Worship God as He Directs

An important observation is that the people of God respond in patterns of worship that change over time as God reveals them. Hattori notes,

> At any given point there are at least two axes to observe: the redemptive-historical axis (and therefore what God required of his people at this point), and the historical-cultural context (and therefore what forms of corporate worship were judged admissible, appropriate, not improperly syncretistic and so forth).[2]

His point is appreciated: issues of God's redemptive plan and one's culture (today as always) shape worship practices. Appropriate and authentic worship is sensitive to the pull of these two axes. As God progressively revealed himself, patterns of acceptable worship changed for his people. This is an important observation about worship because, while the praxis of worship changes, some underlying elements remain the same.[3]

With respect to the *historical-cultural context*, it is helpful to understand that bowing or prostrating oneself in the ancient Near East is a physical expression or response (often to a supe-

---

[2] Yoshiaki Hattori, "Theology of Worship in the Old Testament," in *Worship: Adoration and Action*, ed. D. A. Carson (Grand Rapids: Baker, 1993), 49.

[3] It is outside the scope of this chapter to trace the redemptive-historical practices of worship in the Old Testament. However, two treatments worth investigation include Hattori, "Theology of Worship in the Old Testament"; and David Peterson, *Engaging with God* (Leicester, England: Apollos, 1992).

rior) *reflecting an inward heart attitude of humility and submission.* A key Old Testament word for worship is "to bow down" or "to prostrate oneself" *(šāḥāh).* Because of the significance of bowing in the Israelite culture, the term adopts the notion of reverence, thus worship.

An example of this is seen in Moses. After Israel's episode with the golden calf, Moses encounters God on Mount Sinai "as he called upon the name of the LORD" (perhaps an expression for prayer); and when the Lord revealed himself, "Moses made haste to bow low (from the Hebrew root *qdd*—which is always translated 'bow, bend, or stoop') toward the earth and worship" (from *šāḥāh*—which is sometimes translated as bow down or worship, depending on the context). With Moses in Exodus 34:8, "to bow down" seems best to understand as a natural, if not uncontrollable, reverential response to one being in the presence of the Lord God. There is in Moses a recognition of God's supremacy as well as Moses' own inferiority. Though the text makes clear he expressed himself physically, it equally conveys Moses' heart of reverence; or said differently, the Bible reflects Moses' attitude of submission and humility.

In the final analysis, cultures often have physical expressions that intimate the inward heart attitude (e.g., bowing, prostrating, lifting the hands, clapping, etc.). Of course, there can be the external expression that is vacated of a true, internal reality. Although Thomas Stallter will address multicultural expressions of worship in the concluding chapter of this book, the point to be made here is that the heart attitudes, regardless of culture, are supremely important to God.

With respect to the *redemptive-historical aspects* of worship, God required different practices at various times. While the Old Testament spans many centuries with varying forms of worship, the temple certainly punctuates the most important development of worship in Israel. The requirements were a significant part of the worship experience. For example, the unfolding drama of bleeding sheep being sacrificed with all the accompanying smells intensified the experience. That, accompanied with prayers, song, and the priest, serves to draw the worshiper into the larger drama of an encounter with God.

The relational heart element between God and his people, however, even in the midst of prescribed forms of worship, proves vitally important. Isaiah 1 reveals a nation that practiced the externals as the prophet writes, "What are your multiplied sacrifices to Me? says the LORD. I have had enough of burnt offerings of rams and the fat of fed cattle; And I take no pleasure in the blood of bulls, lambs, or goats" (1:11). Yahweh rejects the prescribed forms of worship because of the incongruity of the appropriate corresponding heart attitude. As Isaiah continues, "this people draw near with their words and honor Me with their lip service, but they remove their hearts far from Me" (29:13). *How* one worships (not only in external form but also in internal attitudes) further determines its acceptability and appropriateness as genuine worship to God. An underlying indifference or apathy may signify pride, the very opposite of submission and humility.

The redemptive-historical aspects greatly shift with the arrival of the perfect temple. Jesus Christ arrested all when he pointed to himself as the place to find God (cf. John 2:18–22). In short, he replaced the temple and its accompanying practices. The implications for worship are legion (as will be seen shortly).

The New Testament uses two main words to express worship. The first is "to prostrate or bow down" *(proskuneō)*. (The Septuagint generally uses *proskuneō* for the Hebrew word *šāḥāh*.) Like its Old Testament counterpart, the semantic range is very similar; it is difficult to escape attitudes of submission and humility.

As Richard Averbeck has already developed in chapter 3, a key passage for worship is John 4:7–26. For purposes here, however, a focus will be on verses 23–24: "But an hour is coming, and now is, when the true worshipers *(proskunētai)* will worship *(proskunēsousin)* the Father in spirit and truth; for such people the Father seeks to be His worshipers *(proskunountas)*. God is spirit, and those who worship *(proskunountas)* Him must worship *(proskunein)* in spirit and truth." It is important to reemphasize the point that Jesus himself makes this possible. Without denying the difficulty of the debate on whether Jesus is referring specifically to the Holy Spirit, Jesus' driving point is not only that the place is insignificant (Jerusalem with the temple or Mount Gerizim) but also that *he is the object of such worship,* though this latter point is not explicit in this passage.

As it has been said, "There are two kinds of idolatry: to worship a false God, or to worship the true God falsely." To worship "in truth" minimally means to worship the true God; to worship "in spirit" minimally means to worship the true God appropriately (i.e., properly relating to God through the Holy Spirit and in the sphere of the Spirit).

The second key word in the New Testament is *latreuō,* which essentially means "to serve." This word is similar to the Old Testament word, which also means "to work or to serve" *('ābad).* Both take on the meaning "to worship" as appropriate in the context. It appears that the New Testament *Epistles* favor this term in descriptions for relating to God. Service becomes a form of worship or better, a pattern of life lived in devotion to God is worship.[4]

What is especially worth noting for the church today is that there is little instruction on corporate gatherings (1 Cor. 11; 14; Acts 2; Heb. 10) by which believers can determine content or style. This is not to suggest that style is neutral but only that Scripture does not mandate a particular style or what exactly the content of a service should be.[5] However, many passages deal with the integrity and sincerity of one's heart toward God in order to be pleasing to him.

---

[4] Peterson, *Engaging with God,* 64–70.

[5] The now familiar maxim of Marshal McLuhan, "the medium is the message," minimally encourages discernment in the combination of style and content. See Marshal McLuhan, *Television and Society, the World in 21 Inches* (Washington, D.C.: National Public Radio, 1977).

Unlike the old covenant, where clear regulations guided the believers' approach to God, the new covenant provides tremendous freedom in form made possible through Christ Jesus, but this faith relationship is the extent of the agreement. While many argue that some passages like Philippians 2:5–11 and Colossians 1:15–20 (and some in 1 Peter and the Apocalypse) are quotations of hymns and strongly suggest the form our liturgy should take today, the evidence is not strong. Even more importantly, the Scriptures do not say *how* such hymns should be included in worship or more broadly how worship should be expressed. With the inauguration of the new covenant by Christ Jesus himself, one inescapably concludes that the new covenant demands no specific external forms or style. There is greater freedom in expressions of worship.

The reason for this tremendous freedom may be that, in the development of salvation history that comes with Christ Jesus and an intensifying focus on the missionary task, the church can more easily move into every "tribe, tongue, people, and nation" (Rev. 14:6). Thus, without vacating the heart attitude of unadulterated worship, the one true God can be freely worshiped in any cultural context.

Two significant, theological implications rush to the forefront of worship issues with the redemptive-historical shift in the new covenant. First, Jesus is the one who lays the worship cornerstone into place by openly revealing to what the Old Testament writers pointed, namely, that he himself is the focal point of worship; or, said differently, the measure of authentic worship rests on whether Jesus Christ is magnified. Second, freedom in worship style comes with Christ Jesus and the inauguration of the new covenant. It is unwise to trundle into worship what the New Testament does not mandate.

An important concept, rooted in the magisterial Reformation and later developed by the Puritans, called the "regulative principle," specifies that anything that is not included in the Bible is forbidden in worship. Such matters as reading of Scripture (1 Tim. 4:13; 1 Thess. 5:27), singing (Eph. 5:19; Col. 3:15), corporate prayer (Acts 2:42; 1 Tim. 2:1), giving (2 Cor. 9:11–15; Phil. 4:18), etc., can be included. Those things not specifically mentioned in the Bible are forbidden.

It is doubtful, however, that the regulative principle can sustain the weight of the myriad of worship issues without collapsing into its own subjectivity (of interpretation) or becoming unduly legalistic.[6] The reason is that, by mandating a particular style or liturgy, the debate shifts to a focus on external excellence and personal tastes or preferences. While some in the worship debates contest that too much of the contemporary music is subjective (i.e., I feel, we want, I hope, etc.), and it may be, even a cursory reading of the Psalter reveals much of the same. If left only with the subjective, it would be insufficient. As in the Psalter, an objective dimension of biblical truth concerning the character and nature of God with his acts in history is needed. Jesus and his finished work at the Cross fill the heart with awe, wonder, hope, and strength.

If there is an area of strong direction with respect to the gathering of God's people in the New Testament, it is in "loving your neighbor." Additionally, sensitivity existed *for the edification of the entire body,* even the God-directed activities (i.e., prayer). The church in corporate gathering shares in the Holy Spirit; thus, how the body interacts with each other is an important and vital part of worship.[7] This is why relationships are even more important than the form or style the worship service takes. The priority rests on moral excellence, not technical excellence. Without diminishing the importance of amoral excellence (for

---

[6] Two helpful discussions can be found in Edmund P. Clowney, "Presbyterian Worship," in *Worship: Adoration and Action,* ed. D. A. Carson (Grand Rapids: Baker, 1993), 112–18; and John M. Frame, *Worship in Spirit and Truth* (Phillipsburg, N.J.: Presbyterian and Reformed, 1996), 38–43.

[7] For a good discussion on the importance of the gathering church ministering to each other as a key part of worship, see David Peterson, *Engaging with God: A Biblical Theology of Worship* (Leicester, England: Apollos, 1992), 194–227.

songs poorly played or sung can distract from worship), this emphasis on loving Christlike relationships as Paul encourages in Philippians 2:5–8, which Herb Bateman develops and applies in the introduction, paves the way for unity. In fact, one cannot rightly enter a dialogue with God if proper concern for another's best is not there (i.e., putting another's interest ahead of one's own).

We Gather to Worship God with All of Our Being

It would be too easy to merely ascribe worth to God in focusing on his nature or works cognitively, and thereby fall short of biblical worship. Just as God calls his people to love him *with all of their being,* so also worship entails coming to God holistically. Paul urges in Colossians 3:23, "Whatever you do, do your work heartily" (lit. from the soul); or, as the psalmist writes, "serve" (NASB) or "worship" (NIV) the Lord "with gladness; come before him with joyful singing." This is significant because worship involves the affections of the heart. Authentic worship engages both the heart and the mind.

The apostles sought to help the church (the "ones called out") live out their identity as the people of God. This truth about God's people living out their identity carries no small implications for what takes place when the people of God gather. The church is about God and his work. He created his people for *his* glory (Isa. 43:7). He elects his people for *his* glory (Jer. 13:9–11). God's infinite passion for his own glory is the foundation for his people concerning worship.

When all is said and done (and too often more is said than done when it comes to worship), authentic worship originates with God and is all about him. He establishes the structures and forms as he deems appropriate for a particular time and calls his people to respond to him with all of their being. These are the forgotten first things.

Restoring these forsaken first things allows for an appropriate biblical foundation. Out of the above concerns, some theological conclusions can be drawn that will help shape a practice of worship that unites:

- The most important aspect of worship is the focus: God.
- God has left a testimony about who he is and how he acts that provides a framework of truth on which to give people hope, confidence, faith, and joy.
- Worshipers must worship God with all of their hearts, mind, soul, and strength.
- Authentic worship engages the heart and the mind.
- The new covenant accords tremendous freedom in style and form of style while preserving the centrality of Jesus Christ in all and above all.
- Moral excellence (i.e., loving God and one's neighbor) is more important than technical or programmatic excellence.
- True joy and satisfaction in God is a by-product of genuine worship.
- Worship is an end in itself.

Two Shaping Questions About Worship

The above insights provided a direction for worship at Fox Valley Church. However, thornier questions surfaced that hindered developing a practice of worship that unites. It would be impossible to address all the challenges, but answers to two shaping questions provided a way forward.

Why Is Worship Essential for the Believer?

At first blush, this seems to be an odd question. But hopefully the reader will shortly see that the answer provides a strong shaping force in developing worship in the church. C. S. Lewis proffers insight into this question when he writes,

> But the most obvious fact about praise—whether of God or anything—strangely escaped me. I thought of it in

terms of compliment, approval, or the giving of honour. I had never noticed that all enjoyment spontaneously overflows into praise unless (sometimes even if) shyness or the fear of boring others is deliberately brought in to check it . . . I had not noticed either that just as men spontaneously praise whatever they value, so they spontaneously urge us to join them in praising it: "Isn't she lovely? Wasn't it glorious? Don't you think that magnificent?" The psalmists in telling everyone to praise God are doing what all men do when they speak of what they care about. I think we delight to praise what we enjoy because the praise not merely expresses but completes the enjoyment; it is its appointed consummation. It is not out of compliment that lovers keep on telling one another how beautiful they are; the delight is incomplete until it is expressed.[8]

In other words, worship is essential for believers because it completes or consummates their joy and satisfaction in God. So, when the people of God gather in the name of Christ Jesus, expressing their enjoyment provides completion. Therefore, *the service should provide opportunity for all the people to do this with music that engages the heart and the head.* A strong participatory element allows people to express their hearts to God. Of course, this can take a variety of forms. But, as pointed out in the introduction, music strikes at the core of who we are as a people. Because of this, it provides an important vehicle in engaging the soul. The Bible is replete with examples of the importance of music in worship.

God delights in the praise of his people. It is right to ascribe worth to God; it glorifies God and he delights in it. Additionally, expressing praise and adoration to God is good for the believer. The ultimate joy, satisfaction, and contentment of God's

---

[8] C. S. Lewis, *Reflections on the Psalms* (New York and London: Harcourt Brace Jovanovich, 1958), 93–95.

people are all rooted in the genuine worship of God. Worshiping God is essential for that full, complete satisfaction in him. Though God desires worship from us, this must not be confused with *duty*. An illustration from John Piper concerning his wedding anniversary may help. He writes,

> Mine is on December 21. Suppose on this day I bring home a dozen long-stemmed red roses for Noel. When she meets me at the door I hold out the roses, and she says, "O Johnny, they're beautiful, thank you," and gives me a big hug. Then suppose I hold up my hand and say matter-of-factly, "Don't mention it; it's my duty." What happens? Is not the exercise of duty a noble thing? Do not we honor those we dutifully serve? Not much. Not if there's no heart in it. Dutiful roses are a contradiction in terms. If I am not moved by a spontaneous affection for her as a person, the roses do not honor her. In fact they belittle her. They are a very thin covering for the fact that she does not have the worth or beauty in my eyes to kindle affection. All I can muster is a calculated expression of marital duty.[9]

This illustration highlights the importance of the attitude of the heart in worship. Too often, because of the importance and intensity of the subject, it slides into an obligation or duty—something believers must do rather than driven by a glad heart fixed on Christ Jesus. So, as believers seek to complete the delight they find in God as he has revealed himself, praise must emerge out of the affections for him as a person and not out of duty.

What Role Does Music or Art Play in a Worship Service?

This question often produces other questions, such as the following: Doesn't God require the best? Aren't the traditional

---

[9] John Piper, *Desiring God,* 2d ed. (Sisters, Ore.: Multnomah, 1996), 83.

hymns better compositionally than contemporary music? Isn't the contemporary music too repetitive and self-centered? The style of music (high art church music, traditional church music, folk music, and popular church music) presses the issue since all persons are aesthetic beings. Admittedly, it is difficult to fit all church music into these few categories. Further, some music tends to move from one category to another. Nevertheless, for the sake of this discussion, these terms will be used, though recognizing their limitations.

As aesthetic beings, this then forces the question about the role of art (especially music) in the liturgy. Many think of liturgy as applying to more formal structured churches, though I use the broader sense of the term, namely, that all churches have some form or structure to their worship service. Artistic expression has been accorded varying degrees of expression in the church liturgy. Some insight can be gleaned from Nicholas Wolterstorff when he writes,

> It is habitual for musicians trained within our institution of high art to approach the music of the liturgy by insisting that it be good music, and to justify that insistence by saying that God wants us to present our very best to Him—all the while judging *good* music not by reference to the purposes of the liturgy but by reference to the purpose of aesthetic contemplation. . . . Of course the church is not against art. It never has been and never will be. In principle the liturgy could take place without any arts being present. . . . Liturgy without art is something the church has almost always avoided. Not grudgingly, because art was forced upon it. Rather the Christian liturgy has itself called forth and continues to call forth a stupendous quality of art. But unless distortion creeps in, art in the liturgy is *at the service of the liturgy*.[10]

---

[10] Nicholas Wolterstorff, *Art in Action* (Grand Rapids: Eerdmans, 1980), 184.

Wolterstorff's notion of art being used *to serve* the liturgy protects the emphasis on God and him being worshiped, rather than on the particular art form or any mix in between. No doubt, high art people often bristle at this suggestion for fear of losing quality. The main rationale for considering the *functional art* idea is that the people are gathered for a purpose other than aesthetic contemplation. Second, the art should clarify the communication of the service and not hinder; thus, clarity is at a premium. Third, functional art "implies enabling the actions to be performed without tending to distract persons from the performance of the action of the art. When the music is so powerful, so striking, so novel, or so difficult to sing—or so bad in quality!—that the attention of the people tends to be drawn to itself, then it is no longer a humble servant of the liturgy."[11]

Once art is seen as a vehicle to augment or facilitate the liturgy, it follows that for many congregations there will be a need for simplicity (clarity, freedom from inappropriate complexity, absence of show) as noted earlier, though not simplistic (trying to condense everything to singleness or be excessively reductionistic). Another reason for simplicity becoming an issue is because, for a service to maintain a focus on God, the music must not draw attention to itself. The music should be good (not trite) and generally satisfying (congregationally relevant). This last thought, because of its vagueness, will cause some to want more explanation. That is difficult because this is where the aesthetic elements enter the equation, and, assuming a distinction between admirable and enjoyable beauty,[12] one's taste or trained sensibilities commends a particular piece as good or satisfying.

In the worship music debates, I find it quite helpful to acknowledge these differences, and as believers who maintain a corpus of truth, we must insist on admirable beauty, even if it

---

[11] Ibid., 185.

[12] The concepts of enjoyable beauty (the subjective aspect of beauty) and admirable beauty (the objective aspect of beauty) are developed by Mortimer J. Adler, *Six Great Ideas* (New York: Macmillan, 1981), 111–31.

is extremely difficult to determine *even among the experts.* That said, Adler writes, "the more admirable or beautiful an object is in itself, the more enjoyable it must be *universally*—to all human beings at all times and places and under all circumstances or nurture and culture. What is objectively beautiful because of its admirable intrinsic excellence or perfection must also be subjectively beautiful, enjoyable or pleasing to all who behold or contemplate it."[13] God is supremely beautiful and thus the basis of objective beauty. As discussed earlier, however, the quality of *what* is not a driving force for music in worship. Beyond this there is a need for the music to be appropriate (fittingness) to the lyrics and to its place in the service (i.e., communion, call to worship, etc.).

A related issue concerning the use of music is how a church determines a particular style to be used. The shaping force here is an attempt to contextualize the music for a particular congregation. This is significant because it assumes movement in the music as the congregation undergoes change or as the immediate surrounding culture changes.

For example, a church on the edge of Hyde Park on Chicago's south side drawing significant numbers of people from the academic environment of the University of Chicago most likely would choose a different selection of music than a church in Hyde Park with those totally apart from the university community. One is not better from a *functional* standpoint because the music is to serve the liturgy; instead, it is merely *different* because of purpose and the need to be appropriate to the context. Furthermore, congregations can develop musically over time and thus should seek to cultivate musical sensibilities. A congregation rhythmically weak can grow in this area; or, a congregation can cultivate its taste for varying kinds of music over time. A church should aim to grow in progressively developing its musical abilities and sensibilities over a period of time

---

[13] Ibid.

at the same time as its self-understanding (of the change) is reformed. If this is not accomplished simultaneously, conflicts will develop and any attempt to advance will likely fail.

The style of music that serves the people of *our* congregation is generally found in a mix of Traditional Church and Popular Church Music.[14] The ratio was established by the discerning leadership of the church with the goal of helping people engage in worship with the head and the heart. Such criteria as theological soundness, compositional integrity, singability, textual integrity, understandability, and cultural relevance help us to choose appropriate music.

For instance, we developed some probing questions for singability: Does the song have an easily learned melody and do the words fit in the time of the melody? Does the song have a simple structure or a rememberable pattern? Does the song have a common chord progression? Does the song have rhythmic complexity that renders it too difficult for congregational singing (i.e., difficult time signatures or a complex syncopated rhythm)?

We also sought to cultivate an appreciation for the great music of the past, as well as develop in our appreciation of different genres. Often the better hymns have provided a deeper theology of substance, while the stronger popular church music has been more engaging to our present congregation. Another aspect of the popular church music that has served us well is that in some of the simplicity it has afforded more time to reflect and meditate on what is being sung. The combination of this music has strengthened our worship in the exaltation of Christ Jesus with the head and the heart.

Another concern for the music in worship is the amount and variety *of special music* versus *congregational music.* Whereas by *special music* I mean any music that is performed by one or more people for the congregation and is used as needed (i.e.,

---

[14] These were the labels used by Donald P. Hustad in *Jubilate II* (Carol Stream, Ill.: Hope, 1993). They are adopted for convenience. However, there are difficulties with any such terms.

prelude, postlude, offertory, Lord's Supper, etc.) in the service, *congregational music* refers to corporate song worship.

It seems wisest to allow the bulk of the time allotted for music to be used in a participatory or congregational manner. Congregational music allows the whole person to be actively involved, whereas special music tends toward passivity and performance. "Since worship is the 'work of the people,' it is hardly debatable that the central—and only indispensable—music of the church is congregational song. Singing in worship is not reserved for priests or for trained artists; singing is for believers."[15] Music sung by the believer often engages the soul. Perhaps as noted by some, neglect of this in favor of spectatorist worship is one of the "besetting sins" of the twentieth century.[16] Indeed, the congregation has assembled for the very specific purpose of worshiping God.

Special music has an important place as well. It can provide a better variety of genres with different quality music by the gifted and trained people than would be possible in the congregational. This time of special music may allow greater cognitive response with accompanying emotions by the intensified, directed focus of the congregation and may also help the worshipers better apprehend the transcendent aspects of their faith.[17] With an emphasis being on personal involvement in the service and the time constraints of the service, the special music should probably be limited. Because special music seeks to focus the attention of the congregation, it requires a certain amount of variety. In addition, one can immediately recognize that there is a place for an ensemble of musical instruments, though it (as with all service components) must fit in the overall plan expressed. The point to be made, however, is that the ones bringing the special music need to guard their hearts against pride because of the focused attention on quality.

---

[15] Ibid., 448.

[16] Ibid.

[17] Ibid., 422–23.

Answering these two shaping questions directs the worship discussion in appropriate areas of expression. In response to the questions, some theological conclusions can be drawn that will again help shape a practice of worship that unites:

- Worship is essential for human beings, and they will have a diminished sense of joy and satisfaction until their love and devotion toward God is expressed to him.
- As one finds delight in God, he or she will *want* to express it, and in that sense worship will not first and foremost be a duty.
- If our worship shifts to "giving to God," it may mean a subtle but dangerous shift to focusing on *quality* and not the relational dimension of delighting in him. Quality is not the determining issue to satisfaction in worship and the very reason why objective excellence is not emphasized in the New Testament.
- The arts serve the liturgy; thus they take on a functional role in worship.

Conclusion

At the heart of biblical worship is God, who is most honored when his people find in him all of their joy and live in loving unity with each other. Jesus unequivocally prayed that believers would be in complete unity (John 17:21–23). The Bible is filled with ironies, but perhaps the greatest of ironies in the church today is that the very area that should be drawing the people of God together is, in fact, dividing them. Too often worship has been compromised. This chapter, if it is anything, is a call to the people of God to worship God in spirit and in truth *in loving harmony.* With the tremendous range of freedom granted in our redemptive-historical context of the new covenant, some have surmised that our worship should explode as the people of God come together to pay homage to the only true and living God. This freedom and concomitant flexibility provides generous room for any church body to come together in unity. Of course, the heart of the people must be fixed on living out the love that is poured out through the Holy Spirit (Rom. 5:5).

The specific expressions of worship must be appropriately contextualized for each congregation. In order to do this, at least three areas must be held in tension as a church seeks to develop a practice of worship: theology (i.e., the primacy of God as he has revealed himself in the Bible); ecclesiology (i.e., specifically, the biblical identity, purpose, and calling of the church); and anthropology (i.e., specifically, the nature of people and how they relate to God). Worship style is important and should aim to unite and edify a congregation (because of sensitivity to edification of the entire body). The leaders must be careful that the larger theological framework is not lost when attempting to be adaptive and innovative. As leadership goes forward, so goes the body. May God's appointed spiritual leaders of the saints lead with vigor under the sure vision, biblical revelation of Christ Jesus. It is their job to lead and loving leadership is a must. An irenic spirit should always be maintained.

As is often the case after stormy weather, a refreshing, gentle breeze started to blow. At Fox Valley Church, we are growing with respect to worship. The church has grown numerically since those early discussions, but more importantly we have grown in love and respect for each other. Those who walked through the process grew in appreciation for differing styles of worship; we always sought to champion unity in Jesus Christ. In striving for a God-centeredness (first commandment) in worship, while avoiding idolatry (second commandment) of man-centeredness (one idol among many found in the church today), we frequently taste of the goodness of God. We regularly aim to drink at the well of Living Water and eat at the table of the true Bread. I will, however, leave the latter discussion to Robert Webber, who develops the concept of regularly eating at the table in part three of our book, "Symbols: Images of Our Worship," which follows immediately after the discussion of the Bible and baptism as symbols of our worship.

PART THREE

SYMBOLS
Images of Our Worship

CHAPTER EIGHT

Scripture in Worship

An Indispensable Symbol of Covenant

Timothy J. Ralston

In a recent survey, 1033 American pastors described their highest ministry competencies as "scriptural knowledge (85%), teaching (83%), and preaching (81%)."[1] If the Bible is so important to the church, things should be good.

In the average pew, however, the parishoners' confidence seems misplaced. Most Christians can't recite at least five of the Ten Commandments, can't name the four Gospels, don't know that Jesus preached the Sermon on the Mount, and think "God helps those who help themselves" is a Bible verse.[2] The researcher concludes that "Lay members are abysmally ignorant of the basics of the Bible . . . no amount of Bible-based preaching, scriptural teaching or small-group meetings moves the congregation to a higher plane of Bible knowledge. . . . Obviously the Bible is not a high priority in the lives of most people."[3]

---

[1] George Barna, *Today's Pastors: A Revealing Look at What Pastors Are Saying About Themselves, Their Peers, and the Pressures They Face* (Ventura, Calif.: Regal, 1993), 70–71.

[2] Ibid., 48–49.

[3] Ibid., 48.

The Bible no longer seems important in our corporate worship either. Christian gatherings were once filled with the recitation of the Word of God. This tradition continues in some denominations, but the average evangelical worshiper won't hear much of the Scriptures in a service of worship. The Bible has slowly disappeared from the menu used to attract the Sunday morning crowd, being displaced by extended singing and a long sermon. The trend has influenced the sermon, which is less concerned with understanding the text than with presenting a biblical concept, sometimes offering just a self-help platitude. The commitment to Scripture reading receives lip service. It even spills over into our spirituality, where our perspectives reflect the nonbiblical practices of our worship, illustrating the profound effect of the *lex orandi lex credendi* principle.[4]

The downward momentum has been empowered by worship gurus who place the blame for our spiritual malaise in these "old-fashioned," Word-centered worship practices. Judged dull and unattractive, the cure is radical: abandon the "traditional" principles for more meaningful, contemporary alternatives. Assuming the New Testament contains no explicit service order for corporate worship, modern worship leaders are taught freedom to follow the principle of expedience. Whatever attracts is desirable. If it connects with the emotions, it's appropriate for corporate worship.

Scripture's teaching as to its own prominent place within the worshiping community of faith argues against these trends. For both Old and New Testaments, one consistent pillar of true worship has been the Word of God, a symbol of the Lord's

---

[4] This is common shorthand for the ancient theological principle summarized by Prosper of Aquitaine *(Indiculus), ut legem credendi lex statuat supplicandi*, meaning that, while worship practices display the church's belief, they also form the beliefs themselves. For a full discussion, see Kevin W. Irwin, *Context and Text: Method in Liturgical Theology* (Collegeville, Minn.: Liturgical, 1994), 4–6.

relationship and an expression of our allegiance. The challenge for the modern Christian church at worship is twofold: to understand the biblical teaching on the covenant symbolism of the Scriptures within worship and then to explore how God's people today can restore this dynamic sign of his covenant when we gather for his glory.

The Word as Symbol in the Scriptures

Early Years: The Word Assumed

One of the great themes of the Bible is covenant, an explicit statement of relationship and of mutual obligations. It's used to describe the relationship between God and human beings based on God's sovereign work and reflecting all he is. Biblical writers agree that we can only know God and relate to him through his covenant. Consequently, the concept of covenant lies at the heart of acceptable worship.

The Bible's various words for worship expresses the human side of this relationship. Some speak of the worshiper's approach as an inferior to superior: the Hebrew "come" (*bô*), "approach" (*nāgash*), and "draw near" (*qārab*). Others describe the worshiper's attitude as one consumed by willing submission: the Hebrew "fear" (*yārē'*), "bow down" (*hishtaḥăwâ*), and "do homage" (*śagad*); and the Greek "bow down" (*proskuneō*) and "honor by formal act" (*sebomai*). Still others describe the worshiper's vocation as an obedient servant: the Hebrew "service" (*ᶜăbōdâ*), "fulfill responsibility to an important personage" (*šārēt*), and "seek the will of a superior" (*dāraš*); and the Greek "service" (*latreia*) and "public acts for another" (*leitourgeō*).

Taken together these terms paint a vivid portrait. True worship begins with a proper self-evaluation before God, emerges in complete submission to God, and fulfills only the express actions of God. The assumption and conclusion of the language is inescapable: God only accepts acts of worship from those whom he calls his own and who are faithful to his covenant, the Word he has given them.[5]

Seen through this lens, there is no dichotomy between individual and corporate worship. Whether one acts alone or in community, biblical worship forms a statement of the worshiper's (re)orientation to the covenant with God, (re)stating commitment to the covenant through submission, and volunteering to do whatever the covenant requires through service. Sin, however, regardless of its form, represents a failure to maintain one's integrity in this covenant relationship. It is rebellion against the covenant. It contradicts and disqualifies anything the worshiper might say. Without confession and repentance, the worshiper is a hypocrite before God, or worse a liar to God. Individual and corporate worship differ only in degree—how many others are impacted (that is, whose worship is disqualified) by the worshiper's duplicity when offering worship on their behalf within a group.

Covenant existence and human integrity are the foundation for all acceptable worship. Consequently, from the beginning all records of worship, whether erecting altars or performing circumcision, always express a response of submission, obedience, and trust in God's verbal statement of relationship, his Word. When God shows he accepts the offering, worshipers receive assurance of their integrity before him in the covenant he has made with them. From the offerings of Cain and Abel through the sacrifices of Noah and the Patriarchs, worship is described in the Levitical language of the Sinai covenant. For example, the descriptions of sacrifice distinguish between clean and unclean animals, denote offerings from the firstlings of

---

[5] Such terms as the Hebrew *kābôd* and the Greek *doxazō* ("glorify") are sometimes included here. These terms, however, also describe the relationship of inanimate creation to God (e.g., Ps. 19:1). If worship assumes willing submission under a covenantal relationship, a willful act, then these terms, while they can describe the effect of worship offered with integrity, are not sufficient to define the totality of the conscious divine-human interaction described as "worship."

the flock and of its "fat," describe the product as a sweet savor, and carefully note God's regard for the offering. The uncanny resemblance of worship under an oral covenant to worship under the written covenant suggests the indispensable presence of God's Word, whether oral or written, to true worship.

Sinai: The Word as Symbol

A critical transition occurred when Israel left Egypt. At Sinai the covenant was no longer to be transmitted merely as an oral statement. Now it was given a written form. In addition, a portion of the written form became a visual symbol of the entire relationship and the worship that followed from it.

The transformation can be observed in Exodus 24. The order of events is significant. First, Moses offered an oral summary of God's covenant to which the people agreed (Exod. 24:3). Then he prepared a written summary, the "Book of the Covenant" (v. 4a). He read this to the people and they gave their assent again (v. 7). Now that both parties to the covenant had expressed their agreement, God proposed creating two stone tablets for his Law (v. 12). He provided detailed instructions concerning the tabernacle, the building that would symbolize his covenant rule and the center of all worship offered to him under that covenant (chaps. 25–31). With these details arranged, God gave Moses the two tablets written on both sides "with the finger of God" (31:18; cf. 32:16) on which were recorded the "Ten Words," a representative summary of the entire covenant recorded by Moses in a more detailed form elsewhere (34:27–28).

Scholars suggest that God's actions conformed to the custom of the time. After a covenant was made in the ancient Near East, both parties received an identical copy of the covenant document, one copy for each party to be placed in their respective religious sanctuaries. Hence, this underlies the need for two tablets, one each for Yhwh and for Israel. Since Yhwh and Israel shared the same sanctuary (tabernacle), both copies would be placed there, specifically in the ark of covenant (Exod. 25:16; cf. Deut. 10:2), in addition to the larger written statement of the law prepared by Moses (Deut. 31:9).[6] He commanded the preparation and preservation of his Word, the "Book of the Covenant." More significantly, he also was responsible for its physical symbol as the two tablets for which God assumed responsibility (Exod. 24:12; 31:18; 32:15–16). Therefore, God himself is responsible for the physical representation of his Word as a visual symbol for his people in their worship.

Moses was raised in the household of Pharaoh and, therefore, knew the ancient Near East treaty practice and understood this symbolism. Therefore, when Moses saw how the people had already broken the covenant by creating the golden calves (Exod. 32:1–10) and, despite arguing for God's mercy on Israel when God informed him of their apostasy (vv. 7–14), he shattered the stone tablets at the mountain's base to show Israel that their disloyal behavior had broken the covenant (v. 19). God, however, had already promised that he would not reject the nation (v. 14). Therefore, after a period of repentance, a second set of stone tablets re-created the covenant symbol (vv. 1, 4, 28). Israel would be reminded that this covenant remained in force at the center of their existence and of their acts of worship.

The centrality of the Word to Israel's life and worship was reemphasized by Moses as one of his last directives. He commanded Joshua to convene a covenant renewal ceremony (Deut. 27:1–8), which Joshua performed (Josh. 8:30–35). Following the relational symbolism of the tablets and the written document, a summary of God's covenant was written on the whitewashed stones atop Mounts Ebal and Gerazim, while the whole Law itself was read to the people standing in the valley between them.

---

[6] Meredith Kline, *The Treaty of the Great King* (Grand Rapids: Eerdmans, 1963), 19. See also K. A. Kitchen, *Ancient Orient and Old Testament* (Downers Grove, Ill.: InterVarsity, 1966), 97; and idem, *The Bible in Its World* (Downers Grove, Ill.: InterVarsity, 1977), 82.

In the Tabernacle and Temple

Sunday school descriptions of Old Testament worship usually emphasize Israel's sacrifices as if these were its primary focus. Israel's worship, however, "did not center in the sacrificial system, but in certain great annual feasts."[7] At Passover, Firstfruits, and Booths, all Israelite males were required to "present themselves before the Lord" (Exod. 23:14–17), an expression of national covenant renewal (34:10–17, 18–24). In addition, every seven years (following the Jubilee schedule in which all debts were remitted and slaves freed), the entire community was called together at the central sanctuary for the Feast of Booths. At this event they were to "read this law in front of all Israel in their hearing . . . that they may hear and learn and fear the LORD your God, and be careful to observe all the words of this law" (Deut. 31:11–12; cf. 9–13).

This public proclamation of God's covenant was the climax of each seven-year cycle symbolizing God's universal ownership of the nation, further emphasizing their renewed commitment to the role as God's covenant people. During Israel's early years, however, when the tabernacle was pitched at Shiloh, the records describe only a single, annual autumn festival (cf. Judg. 21:19; 1 Sam. 1:3, 21) at which the public reading of the Book of the Covenant was considered one of the central elements of the nation's religious life, prompting one scholar to conclude that, "This, and not sacrifice, was the heart of the cultic life of the tribal league."[8]

---

[7] John Bright, *A History of Israel*, 3d ed. (Philadelphia: Westminster, 1981), 171.

[8] Ibid. Allen P. Ross, "Worship in Israel" (class notes, Dallas Theological Seminary, 1987), concurs that "This public reading of Deuteronomy [probably] had become a fixed part of the fall festival. When the congregation gathered to worship God, they expected to hear from God, and hearing from God's word was the most direct way (see also Joshua 8:30–35, especially vv. 34 and 35)."

Joshua offered Israel the clearest summary of the centrality of God's Law to Israel's covenant life and worship: "This book of the law shall not depart from your mouth" (Josh. 1:8). You couldn't attend a festival or offer an acceptable sacrifice unless you had lived according to the covenant. God's requirements had no redeeming social value *per se*, but the Law's detail infused every act with *anamnemesis*, a conscious reminder of his covenant. Every act contained a pregnant reminder of God's care and control with the potential to nourish covenant fidelity. Life itself became a holy vocation, a spiritual discipline. Each decision assumed sacramental proportions, both qualifying and preparing the true worshiper. Hence, Webber concludes that "Jewish worship has always had scripture at the center of its worship."[9]

The Word Forgotten

Unfortunately, God's people slipped away into idolatry. Josiah's reform offers an important clue to the sequence (2 Kgs. 22–23; 2 Chron. 34:14ff.). Israel remembered to perform the sacrifices, but the major annual festival of Passover was no longer celebrated (2 Kgs. 23:22–23; 2 Chron. 35:18). Since, to the Jewish mind, Passover is the defining festival commemorating God's redemption of his people in fulfillment of his covenant, it seems likely that the lesser annual festivals suffered a similar neglect and the Israelites lost the critical opportunity to hear God's Word and renew the covenant as a community of faith.

Without the support of a society that knew God's requirement, covenant obedience came down to following accepted social standards defined by the spiritual integrity of individuals. But integrity without the supportive fabric of a godly community wears thin under the strain of ignorance. Without the proclamation of God's Law in community, God's people are reduced to measuring spiritual vitality by adherence to habit or by experiencing some predetermined emotion. Both yard-

---

[9] Robert E. Webber, *Worship Is a Verb* (Dallas: Word, 1985), 74–75.

sticks lead only to spiritual apathy and apostasy. With the redis-covery of the Law during the renovation of the temple and its restoration as a living document of covenant renewal within the community, spiritual recovery followed.

The prophets corroborate this picture. They repeatedly grieve how the loss of knowing God's requirements (Scripture) be-came a critical step in the corruption of worship, the decline of righteousness, and the downward spiral of God's people to destruction (Isa. 5:13; Jer. 4:22; Hos. 4:1, 6, 14; Neh. 9:16, 26, 29, 34). The failure of the priests and Levites, the worship lead-ers of Israel, to teach God's Word with honesty and integrity elicited God's severe condemnation (Mal. 2:1-9; cf. James 3:1). Apostasy takes root in the absence of God's Law in his people's life and worship. Conversely, covenant life and worship spring from the deep reservoirs formed by the presence of God's Word at the heart of his community and the community's submis-sion to its demands.

A similar pattern appears in the spiritual revival under Ezra (Neh. 8:5-8, 13ff.; 9:1-3). The national celebration began with a formal process of covenant renewal. A reading of the Hebrew text was followed by a translation (targum) into Aramaic for non-Hebrew-speaking Jews (Neh. 8:8).[10] Then, since a translation would make little sense unless it were explained, a summary of its meaning followed (v. 7), designed to provide "insight" on the manner of obedience in their current situation (v. 13). Ezra hoped to bridge the original biblical meaning with its current hearers' situation. The exiles may have celebrated the Feast of Booths earlier with its associated gathering and sacrifices (Ezra 3:1-6), but the text notes that they had not celebrated the full requirement of creating and living in temporary shelters since Joshua's time (Neh. 8:17). One wonders how much else had been regularly sacrificed by the temple officials in the name of expediency or efficiency.

---

[10] Cf. Abraham E. Millgram, *Jewish Worship* (Philadelphia: Jewish Publication Society of America, 1981), 182.

From their response, Torah reading had not been practiced or it had been read in such a way that its significance had long eluded the people. So it's easy to understand their grief and repentance when they discovered their failure in the very month and feast commanded by the Law.[11] The coincidence of time, obvious ignorance, and corresponding lack of obedience was more than they could bear. They offered a complete recommitment to the covenant stipulations of Deuteronomy (10:1–39). Again the Law (and their recovery of the very festival in which it was to be read) became a symbol of covenant renewal, a conscious appreciation of the God who, acting in the shadows, had accomplished a second Exodus.

Maybe these situations from the Old Testament explain why contemporary worship often complains of malaise, its participants searching for deeper spirituality, or even struggling with defects in basic theology, because the reading of the Word is treated lightly or even neglected. Worship wars erupt over incidental matters of aesthetic style (music), while the more fundamental issues of covenant truth, integrity, and community are ignored. These symptoms should drive every community of God's people to examine the way in which they experience the substance of God's Covenant Word, the Scriptures, in their corporate experience.

For the Synagogue

For pious Israelites living outside Palestine, the Law was the center of their religious life. They had lost the temple and its altar for too many years. Little hope remained for a remedy to address the sins and transgressions that violated the covenant. A new path developed: study the Law to understand its application in this new, nontheocratic context. The mind-set of stu-

---

[11] The passage portrays the event as providential. If Ezra was well trained in the Law and its instruction (Ezra 7:6), then he likely anticipated this coincidence, another biblical example of inductive (discovery) learning.

dents of God's covenant shifted. Formerly they might have understood the Law as God's means to expose their inadequacy, and they performed acts of sacrificial contrition and commitment. Now they approached the Law as God's means to express their righteousness. They studied to define the limits beyond which it was broken, creating the Mishna or "fence around the law."

The working assumption was to extend and apply the standard of Levitical life and devotion to all Jews in order to fulfill the covenant requirement for a people separate from ("Pharisees") those who did not seek after God *(am ha-aretz)*. Without the need for contrition and with the devotion demanded of Law study, the people grew to believe that Torah study was as if one sacrificed. Communities of pious Jews gathered to inquire of the Lord through prayer (Ezek. 14:1), hear the exposition of the Torah by the prophets (33:30ff.), and even receive prophetic oracles (8:1). The synagogue was born and the Word in Israel's worship shifted from a seasonal experience of covenant renewal to a weekly experience of dynamic piety.

To form a synagogue required a quorum of only ten Jewish males. Assuming the presence of wives and children, a small synagogue served at least forty persons and numerous small synagogues could coexist within a relatively small area. One Jewish source estimates that there were more than four hundred synagogues in Jerusalem alone at the time of Jesus Christ.[12]

Synagogue worship is characterized by multiple readings from the Scripture—the Law, the Prophets, and the Writings.[13] The primary elements of a typical synagogue service were the *Shema,* followed by prayer, reading from the Torah (in Hebrew), reading from the prophets (in Hebrew), and concluded with

---

[12] Millgram, *Jewish Worship,* 83. This estimate is supported by the synagogues in modern Jewish enclaves (cf. Paul Holmes, "Brotherly Enmity: No Love Lost Between Afghanistan's 'Last Two Jews,'" *Reuters* [Kabul, 2 December 2001]; accessed 22 February 2002; see http://www.isjm.org/press.htm).

[13] *Megillah* 4:1–5.

the blessing. A translator (targumist) followed each reading with an explanatory translation of the Hebrew text (targum).[14] Both readers and translators were to operate in relatively small units, such as a single verse (sentence), apparently to preserve the integrity of the translation. To ensure the text's flow of argument for the hearer, each reader covered at least three verses. To prevent reader fatigue (and subsequent misreading or mispronunciation of the Scripture), the typical morning Sabbath service required at least seven readers and an afternoon Sabbath service only three (since the afternoon service contained only one reading from the Torah and none from the Prophets).[15]

Finally, if a capable individual was present, he might be asked to offer an edifying discourse. (For some Jews, such as the philosopher Philo, this discourse was considered the most significant part of the entire service!)[16] Jesus took advantage of this opportunity (Matt. 4:23; 9:35; 13:54; Mark 1:21–22; 3:1; 6:2; 10:1; Luke 4:14–28, 44; 6:6; 13:10, 15–21), as did the apostle Paul during his travels (Acts 8:4; 9:20; 13:15). The Mishna portrays synagogue worship as an imitation of Jerusalem's temple worship. It shows that the Torah had assumed a more regular role in temple rituals. In addition, it describes how the Torah was read annually at every Jewish festival following the Old Testament pattern[17] and selected portions from the Torah read by the high priest on each Day of Atonement.[18]

---

[14] *Megillah* 4:4, 6, 10. The New Testament writers confirm the weekly synagogue practice (Acts 13:15; 15:21; 2 Cor. 3:14).

[15] *Megillah* 3:6; 4:1. Emil Schurer, *A History of the Jewish People,* trans. S. Taylor and P. Christie (New York: Charles Scribner's Sons, 1896), 4:80.

[16] See Schurer, 4:76, n. 113.

[17] *Megillah* 3:5–6.

[18] *Yoma* 7:1–3. This offers the context in John's Gospel for Jesus' teaching activity during his visits to the temple at this festival, from the middle (John 7:14) through the last day (v. 37; then 8:2) in which he announces the coming Spirit.

But "reading" means different things to different people. A hungry heart reads to understand. A bored student fans pages. A self-centered reader ignores any challenges. Jesus assumed that to "read" the Scriptures was also to understand and respond. He excoriated his contemporaries for not reading to understand God's heart and obey according to the spirit of covenant integrity (John 8:47). James, the Lord's brother and prominent leader of the early church, similarly expressed his incredulity that one might claim to have "heard" the Law, yet failed to obey (James 1:22–25).

For the Church

After Jesus' ascension, the first disciples kept vigil in Jerusalem until the Spirit's coming at the Feast of Firstfruits (Acts 2:1–4). They attended the temple's worship and festivals (cf. Acts 20:16) and shared the synagogue liturgy as mirrored in Paul's command for the public reading of Scripture, exhortation, and teaching (1 Tim. 4:13). The readings came from the Old Testament and apostolic correspondence classified as Scripture (2 Peter 3:16) including Paul letters (1 Thess. 5:27; Col. 4:16). The exhortations proclaimed Christ's community standards, while the teachings suggest the sermon, announcing the comfort from Christ's work (both also inferred from Old Testament eschatological expectations).[19] When combined with the "breaking of bread" commanded by Christ, the church's basic worship structure was complete.

The emphasis on the Word's necessity emerges as a consistent theme of the early Fathers. In the middle of the second century, Justin Martyr in Rome records that, when the Christians gathered on Sunday to celebrate their life in Christ, they listened to the Scriptures read to them for extended periods—

---

[19] Cf. Acts 13:15; Hebrews 13:22. Note the similar expression with sermonic overtones (1 Thess. 2:3; 1 Cor. 14:3).

"as long as time permits."[20] In the early third century, Hippolytus assumed that the first duty of Christians gathered for Christ's honor was "to hear the Word."[21]

But as aesthetic and ceremony increased, engagement with the Scriptures themselves decreased. By the last centuries of the first millennium, the services of the Eastern churches were growing so long with additional prayers and ceremonies that the Old Testament readings were often eliminated in the interest of time (whose effect still continues). The church lost touch with its synagogue heritage and the dynamic presence of the Word in worship, "probably the most important factor in the ultimate decline of the liturgy."[22] In time, however, just as the Enlightenment renewed Europe's interest in ancient learning, the Protestant Reformation restored a vital focus on the Scriptures in worship. In the following centuries, Protestants endured cycles of apathy and renewal, each one marked by neglect and then recovery of the Word in public worship.

From the New Testament forward, the most significant symbol of the Word is the Savior himself. He is the Logos, the Word of God incarnate (John 1:1, 18). His life, death, and resurrection are necessary for the inauguration of the new covenant. God the Father has made God the Son the archetypal symbol of the covenant. Like the twin tablets of the Law deposited in the tabernacle for both God and his people, the ascended Christ demonstrates to the watching universe the covenant's existence and God's faithfulness in it. Jesus sustains its participants and validates its promises. He is the lens through which every acceptable offering of worship comes to the Father.

Without submission to the Lord Jesus Christ, there can be no

---

[20] Justin Martyr, *1 Apology* 67. He describes a basic service: Scripture reading, sermon, congregational prayers, kiss of peace, Eucharist.

[21] Hippolytus, *The Treatise on the Apostolic Tradition*, 2d ed. (London: SPCK, 1968), 15. In fact, he requires every new believer to sit under the Scriptures for three years prior to baptism (17).

[22] E. H. Van Olst, *The Bible in the Liturgy* (Grand Rapids: Eerdmans, 1991), 88.

relationship with the Father and no participation in the covenant. Without the Lord's presence through the person of God the Holy Spirit in the hearts of his submitted people, a service of worship finds no acceptance with God. Worship must not become enraptured with the worshiper's ambitions or experience. It must move beyond mere deism or even theism in its statements about God and praises to God. It must not be content with sentimentalism that overemphasizes or misrepresents the fullness of his character. Overall it must see the uniqueness of Jesus Christ and focus on God through the covenant established in the Incarnate Word. In this way, worship that is anything less than Christocentric within the framework of Divine Triunity may be something, but it is certainly not "Christian."

Clearly, God's self-expression of relationship—his Word—is central to the worship of his people. It forms a symbol of God meeting with his people in covenant, of his dwelling among and within them. As the incarnation of his promises, it becomes a symbol of godly community and calls his people to live before him with the integrity necessary for their worship to be acceptable to him. Hence, its public reading and preaching within the worship exposes his demands, our inadequacy, and his grace. It calls for covenant renewal and lies at the heart of spiritual revival. Therefore, how can we offer acceptable worship, if his Word does not have a prominent place in our liturgy?

The Word as Symbol in Our Worship

Reverence for the Symbol

If we believe in the importance of the Bible as a tangible symbol of God's relationship with us, we ought to consider how we treat it. Robert Webber remembers.

> On one occasion, when I was nine years old, I happened to see my father wrapping his Bible in newspaper. "What

are you doing, Dad," I asked. "This is an old Bible that I am planning to bury in the back yard," he answered. "Because this is God's Word, it is important to always treat it with reverence. I've worn this Bible out and bought a new one. It would be irreverent to throw it in the trash, so I'm burying it."

My father had a point. The Bible is the record of God's living action and speech to us; therefore, it ought to be treated with the greatest reverence and respect. I have found this to be true, not only in my personal life, but also in my worship.[23]

Most of us don't treat our copy of the Bible with such deference. Let's admit it. Well-worn Bibles show our commitment to Bible study and (we assume) our corresponding maturity. We're suspicious of a preacher whose Bible looks too new. He can't have much to say. My own copy is rather tattered. I toss it in my briefcase where it suffers the abuse of mixing with the abrasive tools of my vocation. I'll sometimes see the Bible used as a doorstop or a projector stand. It does say something about our values system. Ron Allen made the following remarks after a recent experience in Thailand:

I was amazed and impressed with a note I received in one of the churches where I preached during my visit. It read something like this: "Dear American or British guest, we are a very polite people. Doubtless you have learned about taking off your shoes on entering the church assembly room, and not to point your feet at others when you sit. But we are most concerned about how you treat the Bible during our service. Please do not lay your Bible on the floor. Please do not handle your Bible carelessly. Please do not toss your Bible onto

---

[23] Webber, *Worship Is a Verb*, 73–74.

a chair. Remember: What you have in your hands is the Bible, the Word of God."[24]

If we believe God's Word is an important part of our worship, the challenge is to let the Bible be seen and heard. We ought to see evidence of its priority where we gather. Sometimes we etch its words on cornerstones. As we enter the dedicated worship space (our auditorium or sanctuary), we may see its phrases survey us from strategic perches. A biblical text should greet us from the bulletin. Perhaps even the entire passage for the sermon itself appears within its folds. An open Bible should be part of our decor. Larger churches may even display its digitized images on huge screens as the preacher expounds its truths. Most of all, if we truly believe in the significance of God's Word to our worship, we should hold a copy of it in our hands and receive encouragement from the pulpit to follow along as we hear it proclaimed.

Working with the Word

Some object that the Scripture is already there—in the songs! True, some songs do contain portions of the Bible, but these small shards aren't sufficient to fulfill our obligation. They are too brief. Despite numerous repetitions, they only offer scriptural snippets of emotive imagery. Without more text to engage our minds, we are abandoned to the aesthetic of the music. No longer moved by our spiritual engagement with the text, we are reduced to addicts for the narcotic of sentiment.

When longer passages do appear, their use sometimes ignores biblical-theological context, leaving the words open to misapplication. But even here the Scripture, masquerading as lyric, is invisible to the singer. Sometimes this is due to lack of familiarity with the Bible. Sometimes it can be obscured by the

---

[24] R. Allen, "The Bible, the Bible Alone" (paper read at annual meeting of the Midwest Region, ETS, 2000), 2.

aesthetic of the music whose beauty overpowers or even contradicts the meaning of the Scripture.[25] Therefore, Scripture in song is a wonderful expression of creativity in our worship, but it's not good enough. It is insufficient as the sole expression of our commitment to the covenant in worship. We need to read the Bible, too, not just because of its significance but because people don't.

> For most people sitting in the church on a given morning, the pastor knows that his Scripture readings and references will be the only ones to which they will be exposed during the week. Only 4 out of every 10 adults will read any portion of the Bible outside the church during the week. . . . Those people who do read will commit about one hour to Bible reading during the week.[26]

So how do we increase the amount of Scripture reading in our worship? Why not add a call to worship (the statement that summons the community to gather) or invocation (the prayer that opens and dedicates the service) drawn from the Scriptures? The Psalms (even whole psalms) are fertile texts. Then, of course, we can read the biblical text that forms the basis of the sermon. If that passage is too small, then read its context as well.

But if we limit our weekly reading to the sermon text, we

---

[25] For example, a biblical text asking for God's self-revelation or the worshiper's purification is accompanied by such a soothing melody that the singer believes the experience will be pleasurable, almost sensual. See, for example, "Purify My Heart" (Jeff Nelson, Maranatha! Music and Heartservice Music [admin. Music Services], 1993) and "Holiness Is What I Long For" (Scott Underwood, Mercy/Vineyard Publishing [admin. Music Services], 1994). Biblically the purification of God's follower is always a painful experience, and the attitude displayed by such music in worship can produce a misinterpretation of the Bible's teaching on sanctification.

[26] Barna, *Today's Pastors,* 48.

leave most of the Bible untouched. Both Jews and Christians saw they needed a more systematic method for public reading, if they were to hear the whole counsel of God. The "lectionary" was created, bringing together readings from two or more biblical genre for each gathering. Today, many churches use the Common Lectionary (CL) or the Revised Common Lectionary (RCL), although denominations often have their own special reading cycles.[27] Most service books will contain a list of such readings for each Sunday of the year. Some churches develop their own reading cycles. Some follow the themes of the annual Jewish festivals—complex, but very profitable![28] Perhaps the easiest and most effective way for most churches is at another convenient time in the service to read at least one other passage, either from Old Testament narrative, Old Testament poetry, Old Testament Prophets, Gospels, or Epistles, which will support the text and subject of the morning's sermon.

No matter how the Scripture is incorporated, all Scripture reading within a worship gathering occurs in one of two ways, either from those already present as leaders of the service (leader recitation) or as a corporate activity by those who have gathered to worship (congregational recitation).

Leader Recitation

Leader recitation is the oldest form of hearing God's Word. It occurs anytime someone reads the Bible to someone else.

---

[27] Even Seventh-Day Adventists have experimented with constructing a lectionary. See Donald Rhoads, ed., *The Greenwood Lectionary* (1996; distributed by D. Rhodes, 1000 W. Williams Rd., Bloomington, IN 47401). Despite the best intentions, lectionaries can present problems. Their compilers may truncate passages or omit "problem passages." Thematic links between a single day's passages can be obscure, forcing worship planners to have to exegete the lectionary desirner's thinking in order to be faithful to the reading schedule.
[28] Note Craig P. Scott, "Significance of the Old Testament Feasts to Contemporary Church Worship" (D.Min. dissertation, Dallas Theological Seminary, 1996).

The idea of leader-centered Bible reading is as old as God's promises. Before the Word was written, the ancient stories of those who received God's covenants were shared and passed down faithfully. Each new generation heard about God's spoken promises from their elders. Once the covenant and the redemptive history were provided in written form, the covenant record was read carefully by individuals selected and prepared for the purpose. The congregation listened. Sometimes they responded in some affirming way, such as the cultic "shout" (as indicated in Lev. 9:24; 1 Kgs. 8:39; 1 Chron. 18:36; 2 Chron. 7:3; Neh. 8:6; Ps. 2:11) or just a simple "amen," to express agreement with what they heard. But the congregation did not participate in the reading of the Word itself.

The reading of God's Word is always reader centered and audience focused. One reads a text in order to understand it. Every reader focuses on helping his audience understand what he reads, whether that audience is the reader himself or someone else to whom he reads. The conscientious reader seeks to instill in his audience an understanding of the passage that is at least as full as his own. The reader's understanding may not be complete, but he assumes that his appreciation of the text's coherence provides a foundation upon which the Holy Spirit may build further understanding and obedience in the listener.

The act of reading Scripture is audience focused. On the other hand, if the reader hopes to communicate without confusion, then the reader must know how to read well. Therefore, the issues in leader-centered Bible reading are preparation and interpretation. Regardless of who reads, the act of reading is actually a congregational activity.

In order for a reading to be participative, it must be understood. To be understood, it must be heard. Therefore, each reader must speak loudly enough to be heard by everyone in the audience. Even a microphone assumes good voice control that requires a firm stance, good posture, a clear voice tone, and appropriate voice projection. Then, if it is to be understood, each word must be heard distinctly and the word groups (phrases and sentences) uttered with inflections that help the listener grasp the word's meaning and the text's flow of thought, regardless of the genre. Diction, phrasing, and pacing become important. Although today anyone can own, read, and appreciate the Scriptures in private, leading us in its public reading and understanding should not be thoughtlessly delegated (as we often do) as if it were one of the lesser acts of worship. Reading God's Word as an act of corporate worship demands more—a dedication such that congregations throughout church history often limited this task to individuals trained in its disciplines.[29]

Leader-centered Scripture reading appears in one of three forms. The most common form occurs when we hear the Word read by someone who is already functioning as a leader of our worship. It may be the preacher who reads his sermon passage, the chairperson of the service, the music leader, or even one of the musicians. A less common form occurs when we hear the Scripture read by someone specially appointed by the church to this function, someone who isn't involved in the worship or pastoral leadership, who makes this their contribution to our worship. The least common, but highest form of this discipline, is "Readers' Theatre." Two or more individuals take responsibility for the reading. They carefully divide the text passage between them in order to emphasize its aspects, rhetorical elements, shifting points of view, or narrative dialogue.

But whenever one reads the Scripture to the congregation, it should be obvious that it's the Bible we're hearing. Readers should stand erect, holding the Bible high enough so that the congregation can hear and see that this is God's Word. A pulpit is nothing more than a fancy place to hold the Bible (and whatever other materials the leader or preacher might need)

---

[29] For example, in the synagogue (Millgram, *Jewish Worship*, 183–84), in the post-apostolic church (*2 Clement* 19:1), and in Protestant tradition. Question 156 of *The Larger Catechism* of *The Westminster Confession of Faith* (1648) stipulates that "all are not to be permitted to read the word publicly to the congregation."

between uses. A well-designed pulpit should rise no higher than one's elbow. This allows for strong gestures, which usually occur from waist height upward and presents more of the speaker to the audience, thereby increasing credibility with the audience. If we leave the Bible on the pulpit while we read, the audience cannot see the Word as we read and our downward pointed faces crimp our larynx and jaws, working against good delivery.

The physical relationship between the reader and listeners also impacts its perception. When the Scripture is read from the front behind a large pulpit or from a position above the listener, one hears authority. When the reader stands in the middle of the congregation (as often occurs with the gospel lection in many churches), the Word becomes a symbol of the Word's incarnation in Christ and the listeners' unity before God in Christ. A message of comfort is best heard when one is relaxed, perhaps sitting in quietness. But sitting can also suggest passivity and tempt the hearer to ignore a challenge. So there are times when God's people should stand to hear the message, express their respect for God's covenant, and engage with its requirements.

Of course, the easiest way to enhance reading is to add special effects: sounds that offer background audio "color" or special lighting that sets the mood or focuses attention. But these enhancements come at a price. Superficially, these effects can deteriorate to the level of media gimmicks that impress us with an experience at the price of impact with the truth. But worse, we risk diminishing our listeners' ability to engage their imagination, the arousal of our mental capacity to "see." The impact of truth depends directly upon one's ability to engage the emotions through the images of the imagination, assisted through a speaker's use of concrete language, images, and examples. Similarly a listener's imagination becomes less engaged as the level of external supports increases. When we provide numerous external stimuli, impact suffers.

On the other hand, sometimes the significance of the Word

can be enhanced if the reader chooses to recite the assigned text from memory. While it may seem contradictory, memorization enhances the text's importance. First, memorization requires work. This effort communicates value and importance, particularly now when easy information access and processors reduce the concept of memory to mere digital hardware. Second, memorization liberates the reader from the constraints of the printed page. You are free to tell the story with all of your faculties—face, eyes, hands, body, even feet! You become more than a reader. When Scripture comes to us from memory, its reader becomes the storyteller of the divine, reviving the most ancient way of sharing God's Word. The circle of history has closed.

Leader-focused reading can also be enhanced if there is an obvious connection between the reader and the passage in the mind of the audience. The congregation can identify the reader as one for whom the reading has a special significance. For example, what if a lawyer relatively well known to the congregation was to read "A certain lawyer . . ." (Luke 10:25–37 KJV)? Or an expectant mother recited the Magnificat (1:46–55)? Or someone who had recently lost a loved one were to read the story of Lazarus (John 11:17–44) or the promise of resurrection (1 Cor. 15)? Whenever the person of the reader embodies the characters or the issues in the Scripture reading, the text takes on a contemporary life before the eyes of the listeners. The Word comes alive.[30]

Congregational Recitation

Unlike leader recitation, congregational recitation focuses on the people assembled for worship. They do the work of

---

[30] For a more complete discussion of leader recitation, see Reg Grant and John Reed, *Telling Stories to Touch the Heart* (Wheaton: Victor, 1990), 11–26. Practical support is also available through *The Network of Biblical Storytellers* (NOBS), a national organization committed to the memorization and public recitation of Scripture.

reading. It's the ultimate act of liturgy ("participative" worship),[31] and reading together in concert fosters the sense of community, corporate (family) responsibility, and solidarity under the covenant as we worship.

In direct recitation, the entire congregation reads the passage in unison. (Over longer passages the exercise often produces a chant-like rhythm.) In antiphonal recitation, the reading is performed between sections of the congregation (intracongregation alternation), often verse-by-verse as the simplest form. In responsorial recitation, the congregation listens to a solo reader and makes a set response after each set of verses recited by the leader. The response can be taken directly from the Scripture passage itself (following the example provided in such passages as Deut. 27:12–26; Pss. 136:1–26; 118:1–4). The response can come from outside the text, such as a simple "amen" or "alleluia." It can even take the form of a cantor with the congregation repeating each line. The African-American practice of "call and response" illustrates the subtleties of this practice within an extemporaneous worship environment. Finally, in responsive recitation, a reader and the congregation alternate reading the passage, usually in equal segments. This format for Scripture readings often appears among the resources in evangelical hymnals. Verse-by-verse alternation of reading between leader and congregation is a common practice in many congregations.

Why don't we do more congregational reading? Repeated surveys say the number one fear of most people is public speaking. Reading together generates the same kind of fear because we're afraid of making a mistake and having everyone

---

[31] Christians use the term *liturgy* just as its Greek etymology suggests, to mean a service of worship in which all the congregation shares an active role. Liturgy applies "to all forms of worship of a participatory nature" (James F. White, *Introduction to Christian Worship* [Nashville: Abingdon, 1980], 23–24); cf. Donald Wilson Stake, *The ABCs of Worship: A Concise Dictionary* (Louisville: Westminster John Knox, 1992), 114; R. Meyer and H. Strathmann, "λειτουργέω," in *TDNT*, 4:219–31.

notice it. Starting too early, too late, or being heard above everyone else will be humiliating. Enjoyable corporate reading assumes a congregation's sense of competence at the task. Competence begins with effective leadership. Good reading leaders approach their task with an air of expectation and excitement. It models a living engagement with the Bible. A reader who displays boredom communicates irrelevance—and if a group senses irrelevance, watch motivation disappear. It is the leader's task to make the reading live!

Such leaders offer clear direction to the congregation. While their own reading emphasizes meaning, they also set an example of the cadence for the reading and how to phrase the text. Congregational reading requires a cadence. It almost sounds chantlike (which should tell you why Christians chanted the Bible for so many centuries). This sense of chant isn't bad if it moves clearly with a sense of expectation and power. In fact, it can be exciting! The congregation will hear the leader's cadence and follow it as long as it is sustained. But if the reading slowly sinks in pitch, decreases speed, and resembles "molasses in January," congregational reading will be rejected. Therefore, the leader must sustain this energy throughout the reading in order to animate the congregation's reply.

Whether we like it or not, acoustics are important to good public reading. People must be able to hear their voices blend together. They must get a sense of being part of something bigger. Modern worship spaces are often built around the sound system, rather than the congregation. In the dead air created by carpets and acoustic tile, it's hard to hear anyone around you. Your voice stands out to your own ears, even if not to anyone else's. Vocal expression of any form becomes a personal risk. Unless you're very secure with yourself, speaking and singing become muted. Good congregational reading, like good congregational singing, assumes that the congregation's sounds can rise, mix in the air, and then descend to their ears with a renewed richness. While this takes only two seconds in a well-designed worship space, the effect is dynamic for the experience of the Word, encouraging God's people to experience their corporate identity in its reading together.

The Word and the Preacher

When the Word is central to worship, the preacher cannot ignore it, if the Word expresses God's covenant. Besides the explicit statements of unchanging relationship, its stories give encouragement from earlier participants. Its wise dictums provide ethical guidance. Its Epistles distill the theology. Its Psalms speak to the emotional lows and highs of the pilgrim soul. If the Word is central to worship, the sermon must find the only legitimate foundation in the words on its pages. Building thereon, the sermon unpacks God's promises and exposes his expectations from the covenant he has given. Therefore, the heart of preaching within the gathering for covenant renewal is biblical exposition—not a lecture on what the Word *meant* within its historical-grammatical context (although this is fundamental to understanding it) but the application of what the Word *means* for its hearers within the new, complex situations in which they find themselves struggling to express their obedience.

Listeners ought to find the text of the Scripture before them throughout the sermon. When reading was a more difficult skill and books a luxury, extensive lections of the Bible preceded the sermon. The preacher made copious references to the reading, held in place by minds for whom memory was the warp of knowledge. With the coming of movable type, individuals could have a copy of the text before them and the preacher could range far before returning to each listener's open text. As translations proliferated, congregations struggled with the differences between their texts and the projection screen emerged as the way to unify the congregation's experience with the Bible. Now the preacher can be sure that everyone follows without confusion, maintaining the dynamic conversation with the eyes of the congregation without the distraction created each time their eyes drop to read the Bible in their hands. A modern Ebal and Gerazim, the people stand before the preacher and the covenant, relearning how to honor God by their respectful obedience to his Word.

While the modern method increases our sense of community and the dynamic of preaching, it also suggests caution. Providing the entire sermon text does not challenge the listeners to find the text and follow the sermon's logic in their own Bibles. The existential experience with the Word preached demands no personal validation in study, such as Paul commended in the Bereans (Acts 17:10–11). When the screen goes dark and the service ends, the people are not empowered to affirm the truth they have heard. It is the property of the preacher and his PowerPoint. While the Word may be prominent in the sanctuary, its symbol is missing from the hands and minds of the people. What was once central to the community's worship is now classified as something else, and the people themselves come to view the text as secondary to their life in Christ. Perhaps in a quest for the ease of corporate experience created by homogeneity, we have unwittingly contributed to the growing biblical illiteracy among contemporary worshipers.[32]

Conclusion

Can we go too far in reverencing the Word? Of course we can! Consider Yitzhak Levy, Zebolan Simanto, and twenty-eight other Jewish families. They lived together in Kabul, Afghanistan, and worshiped in one of the two synagogues in their apartment complex. When the Taliban came to power, the Jews gradually left. But these two men stayed. Why? The Interior Ministry had seized a Torah scroll. Each man demanded its return to him. Jealousy erupted in blows and betrayal, until two years later their reverence for a symbol had left two old

---

[32] Barna, *Today's Pastors*, 48–49.

men, the "Last Two Jews" in Afghanistan, to pray alone in separate synagogues in a crumbling apartment building.[33]

We want to revere God's Word, not idolize it. Just as we
revere the living Word in our hearts as the center of our witness and community, so also let the written Word be present,
not just its image but also its reality. It's too easy to have a
symbol but no reality.

In worship, God reaffirms his covenant and his people respond with renewal. His covenant has been recorded for his
people in the Scriptures. Whenever the words of the covenant
are present, whether verbally or in a symbolic form that reminds us of it, his promises and expectations are revealed. When
his people respond in acts of remembrance, the circle of covenant renewal is complete.

---

[33] Holmes, "Brotherly Enmity."

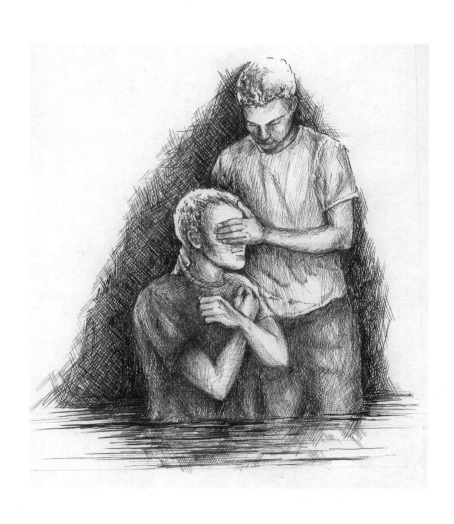

CHAPTER NINE

Baptism Spirituality

Robert E. Webber

One of the most memorable events of my spiritual history occurred when I was twelve. We lived in Montgomeryville, Pennsylvania, where my dad was the pastor of the Montgomeryville Baptist Church. This very old church, which dated back to the eighteenth century, was surrounded by a huge graveyard celebrating the lives of many people, including a number of Native Americans who once lived there.

One afternoon, as I was drinking a coke and munching on some cookies in the kitchen, my dad pulled up a chair, looked me in the eye, and said, "Robert, don't you think it's time for you to be baptized?" I really had not given the subject any thought. But my dad's inquiry along with subsequent conversations ultimately led me to stand with my father in the waters of baptism preparing to take the plunge of my life into the death and resurrection of Jesus.

During the baptism, I was taken by surprise when my father looked me in the eye and asked, "Robert, do you reject the devil and all his works?" I was only twelve! I hardly knew "all the works" of the devil. But I said, "I do." Then he asked, "Do you receive Jesus as your Savior?" Again I said, "I do." I was then baptized in the name of the Father and the Son and the Holy Spirit. Today, many years later, I am much more aware of the "works of the devil" and am still working out on a daily basis what it means to renounce the devil and all his works and to receive Jesus Christ as my Lord and Savior. This pattern of renunciation and affirmation, which connects us with the death and resurrection of Jesus, is the pattern of baptismal spirituality. This is the pattern I want to explore in its biblical roots, its historical development, and contemporary relevance. But first, I wish to make a few comments about the absence of baptismal spirituality in our evangelical heritage.

Absence of Baptism Spirituality

In many of our evangelical denominations, fellowships, and local churches, the issue of baptism revolves around infant versus adult baptism. While this is a matter of some importance, it is not the heart of the New Testament teaching on baptism. The major New Testament focus on baptism has to do with baptismal spirituality, a living into and a living out of our baptism into the death and resurrection of Jesus.

Many of our evangelical churches continue to practice baptism, but baptismal spirituality *has suffered a terrible reductionism*, a dumbing down, to use a term made famous by Marva Dawn.[1] We have failed to maintain the New Testament language of conversion with its inextricable link with baptism. We have separated baptism from conversion, making the two stand alone as distinct and separate expressions of faith. Conversion has become the primary language of salvation, while baptism has become relegated to an act of obedience, the first action taken by the new Christian. Baptismal language, which in the New Testament is the language of *continuous* existential identity with Christ, has been relegated to an event of the past having no meaning for our present and immediate spirituality. Consequently, evangelical spirituality suffers from the absence of the present power of baptism to shape our moment by moment

---

[1] Marva J. Dawn, *Reaching Out Without Dumbing Down: A Theology of Worship for the Turn-of-the-Century Culture* (Grand Rapids: Eerdmans, 1995).

identity with Jesus Christ and the ultimate pattern of spirituality, continuous death to the powers of evil, and continuous resurrection to the fruits of the Holy Spirit.[2]

Baptism is absent from our worship. For example, when I wrote my first book on worship, *Worship Old and New,*[3] I included a chapter on baptism. In a prepublication review by an evangelical leader, he raised the question about the propriety of having a chapter on baptism in a worship book. "What" he asked, "does baptism have to do with worship?" Not fully assured of the answer, I withdrew the chapter, but in the second edition, now more sure than ever that baptism has everything to do with our worship and with spirituality, I included an extended discussion on baptism in the book. My sense is that many evangelicals still question the place of baptism in worship and spirituality except as a testimony to faith and as a proclamation of obedience.

Because baptism is absent from our worship, it is also *absent from our piety.* The average evangelical Christian remembers baptism as an event of the past, an event recorded on a certificate and stored someplace in an attic suitcase. There seems to be little knowledge that baptism is linked with communion, inseparable with Christmas and Epiphany, the very image of lent, and the substance of our personal experience of Easter and Pentecost. The very rhythm of daily prayer, of Sunday worship, and the salvation events celebrated during the Christian year is the rhythm of baptism. But this is not known and not practiced as our fundamental piety and spirituality.

Because baptism *no longer shapes our piety, it has become absent in the crucial way it can form the communal embodiment of God's kingdom in the local church.* Evangelicals who have forgotten baptismal spirituality do not realize that they have lost what

---

[2] The idea of the "Absence of Baptism" has been borrowed from Alexander Schmemann, *Of Water and the Spirit* (Scarsdale, N.Y.: St. Vladimir's Seminary Press, 1974), 8–9.

[3] Robert E. Webber, *Worship Old and New* (Grand Rapids: Zondervan, 1982).

expresses their "distinction from the world." Baptism informs our values, our ethics, our philosophy of life, and our communal distinctions as an alternative culture to the culture of secularism, violence, permissiveness, and rebellion against God.

My goal in this chapter is to suggest how to return baptism to its proper place in the evangelical worship of the church and in the individual piety of all who have been baptized into the death and resurrection of baptismal spirituality in the New Testament of Jesus Christ.

Baptismal Spirituality in the New Testament

Two noted evangelical authors, one from the Baptist tradition and the other from an Anglican tradition, recently joined in a scholarly effort to determine what the texts of the New Testament say about baptism, texts that deal not with the mode of baptism but with the *meaning* of baptism. In their text, *The Water That Divides,* Bridge and Phypers agree that the New Testament teaches the following:

1. Baptism is a sign and means of repentance (Acts 2:38).
2. Baptism and the seal of the Spirit occur concurrently (2 Cor. 1:22; Eph. 1:1; 4:30).
3. Baptism demonstrates that salvation is all of grace (Titus 3:4–5).
4. Baptism is a participation in the death and resurrection of Christ (Rom. 6:4; Col. 2:12).
5. Baptism is our entry into the church (2 Cor. 12:13).
6. Baptism is oriented toward the eschaton (Titus 3:5–7).[4]

By all accounts Christians are agreed that the central image of baptism is found in Paul's letter to the Romans, especially

---

[4] Donald Bridge and David Phypers, *The Water That Divides* (Downers Grove, Ill.: International, 1977), 15–24.

chapter 6.[5] Paul's image is clearly that of having been baptized "into his death" (v. 3) and "united with him into his resurrection" (v. 5). This union is unequivocally stated: "The death he died, he died to sin once for all; but the life he lives, he lives to God" (v. 10). The obvious result of our baptism is to "count yourselves dead to sin but alive to God" (v. 11) and to no longer allow "sin to reign in your mortal body, so that you obey its evil desires" (v. 12). We are no longer to offer our bodies as "instruments of wickedness," but now that we are in Jesus Christ, we are to live our lives as "instruments of righteousness" (v. 13). Because we are now slaves to God, the benefit of our new state leads us "to holiness" and "eternal life." This is the gift that we have in Jesus Christ (vv. 22–23).

Paul's statements are clearly the language of continuous spirituality, not the language of a onetime event recorded on a certificate and hung on the wall. This life-encompassing goal of baptism is repeated again and again by Paul's exhortations to the spiritual life in the communities to which his letters were directed.

This same theme is directed to the community in Galatia. They misunderstood grace and sought to be pleasing to God through the works of the law. Paul's answer was to remind them of their baptismal instruction. Because they have been united in Christ, they are called to be free (5:13). An identity with Christ is a freedom to no longer walk in the "sinful nature" but to walk "by the Spirit" (vv. 16–18).

For the Galatians to walk in their sinful nature is to deny what they have become dead to in their identification with Jesus through baptism. They are called to be dead to "sexual immorality, impurity and debauchery," to "idolatry and witchcraft; hatred, discord, jealousy, fits of rage, selfish ambition, dissensions, factions and envy; drunkenness, orgies, and the like" (vv. 19–21). To live this way is to deny their baptismal identity, to blaspheme

---

[5] Michael Root and Risto Saarinen, *Baptism and the Unity of the Church* (Grand Rapids: Eerdmans, 1998), 12.

it, and to live under the condemnation of law. Freedom in Christ is never to be used "to indulge the sinful nature" but to live by "the fruit of the Spirit." The resurrected life, which is our baptismal identity, is "love, joy, peace, patience, kindness, goodness, faithfulness, gentleness and self-control" (vv. 22–23). In baptism and our identity with Jesus Christ, we have been called to crucify "the sinful nature with its passions and desires" (v. 24) and "not become weary in doing good" (6:9).

This same message is delivered to the believers in Colossae. Paul elevates the baptismal imagery when he tells the Colossian Christians, "You have been raised with Christ" (3:1). "Put to death," Paul exhorts, "whatever belongs to your earthly nature" (v. 5). There was a time, Paul states, that "you used to walk in these ways, in the life you once lived" (v. 7). But now, because you are baptized into Christ, you have "put on the new self, which is being renewed in knowledge in the image of its Creator" (v. 10). In the remainder of the letter to the Colossians, Paul sets forth the spiritual identity of those who have been identified with Christ through baptism. They are to clothe themselves with "compassion, kindness, humility, gentleness and patience" (v. 12). They are to forgive one another, forgive as Christ forgave, live by the virtue of love, let the peace of Christ rule in their hearts, be thankful, admonish each other with wisdom, sing psalms, hymns, and spiritual songs with gratitude, submit to each other, devote themselves to prayer, treat others wisely, and keep conversations full of grace.

What Paul is describing in these passages is our baptismal identity with Jesus Christ. To be baptized into Christ is to bring the old way of life to death and to birth a new way of life, a life of baptismal spirituality.

Baptismal Spirituality in the Ancient Church

This unity between baptism into Jesus' death and resurrection is clearly sustained and taught in the early literature of the church.

The Didache

The *Didache,* known as the teaching of the twelve disciples of Jesus (not written by the twelve but expressing their teaching) and available in Palestine within the first century, clearly links baptism and spirituality. Chapter 7, which contains the first noncanonical instruction regarding baptism, states:

> Now about baptism: This is how to baptize. Give public instruction on all these points, and then "baptize" in running water, "in the name of the Father, and the Son and of the Holy Spirit."[6]

The statement, "Give public instruction on all these points," refers back to the teaching of the first six chapters, which has been identified by Christian scholarship as instruction that is to occur before baptism. The instruction is in the "two ways," the way of death and the way of life. The two ways have to do with baptismal spirituality. These new Christians are being taught the Christian life. They are being instructed in their new identity. To be baptized into Jesus means to put off an old way of life and to put on a new way of life. *The instruction* is extensive, but the following brief passages from the *Didache* provide a flavor for the baptismal spirituality of the primitive Christian community. First, the writer sets forth the two ways:

> The Lord's Teaching to the Heathen by the Twelve Apostles: There are two ways, one of life and one of death; and between the two ways there is a great difference. Now, this is the *way of life;* "First, you must love God Who made you, and second, your neighbor as yourself." And whatever you want people to refrain from doing to you, you must not do to them.[7]

---

[6] See Cyril Richardson, ed., *Didache,* in *Early Christian Fathers,* LCC (Philadelphia: Westminster, 1953), 1:1774.

[7] Ibid., 171.

The way of life is then set forth extensively, followed by instructions to avoid the way of death. Here is a brief sample from the lengthy instructions on what to avoid as a Christian:

The second commandment of the teaching: "Do not murder; do not commit adultery"; do not corrupt boys; do not fornicate; "do not steal"; do not practice magic; do not go in for sorcery; *do not murder a child by abortion or kill a newborn infant.* "Do not covet your neighbor's property; do not commit perjury; do not bear false witness"; do not slander; do not bear grudges. Do not be double-minded or double-tongued, for a double-tongue is "a deadly snare." Your words shall not be dishonest or hollow but substantiated by action. Do not be greedy or extortionate or hypocritical or malicious or arrogant. Do not plot against your neighbor. Do not hate anybody; but reprove some, pray for others, and still others love more than your own life.[8]

A similar approach is taken to baptism in the second century, as evidenced in the writings of Justin Martyr (A.D. 150). Justin is writing to the emperor Titus to inform him of how Christians live and to persuade him that Christians should not be persecuted because they exercised a positive emphasis on society. Justin informs Titus that Christians are only brought to the baptismal waters after "those who are persuaded and believe that the things we teach and say are true, and promise that they can live accordingly."[9] While Justin is not specific about baptismal instruction and what it means to "live accordingly," it is clear from third-century liturgy that the teaching of second-century baptismal spirituality stands in the tradition of New Testament teaching and the instructions of the Didache, especially through the study of the major document on baptismal spirituality written by Hippolytus in the beginning of the third century, *The Apostolic Tradition.*

---

[8] Ibid., 172.
[9] Gregory Dix and Henry Chadwick, eds., *The Apostolic Tradition* (Ridgefield, Conn.: Morehouse, 1992), 192.

The Apostolic Tradition

The Apostolic Tradition introduces us to the form and meaning of baptism in existence by the third century. It presupposes four theological convictions and sets forth the trajectory of baptismal spirituality in four stages, three passage rites, and a fourth continuous rite for Christian nourishment, the Eucharist.[10]

First, the four theological convictions of third-century baptismal spirituality set forth the biblical and theological content of baptismal spirituality. Baptism is first identified with the *Christus Victor* content of Christ's death and resurrection. His death is the death of death. He has conquered the power of physical death. Death no longer defines our future. It has no ultimate hold on us because Jesus has conquered death and, as the early liturgies of the church proclaimed, "opened the way to heaven."

Eternal life, not eternal death, is the destiny of those whose identity is found in Christ Jesus through conversion expressed in baptism. But even more, the victory of Christ over the powers means new life now in this world. His death defeats the pervasive powers of those things, which bring death to life now in the present. Those who are baptized into Christ are baptized into his victory over the lifestyle of the flesh. His victory over the binding power of the sinful nature becomes our victory as we live into our baptismal waters. Also, the newness to life brought by his resurrection is now the freedom into new life given to us by the power of the Spirit. We are now free to daily turn from sin and turn toward our new life in Christ because of our identity with his victory over evil.[11]

The second layer of baptismal spirituality is *ecclesia mater,* the church as our mother. Second-century writer Cyprian knew

---

[10] For a study of *Christus Victor* in the early church, see Gustav Aulen, *Christus Victor* (New York: Macmillan, 1996), esp. chaps. 2–4, 16–81.
[11] See Cyprian, "The Unity of the Catholic Church," in *Readings in Historical Thought,* ed. R. Ferm (New York: Holt, Rinehart and Winston, 1964), 5.

the mothering power of the church, writing, "From her womb we are born, by her milk we are nourished, by her spirit we are animated."[12] We are not left to fend for ourselves in a world where the powers, though contained, still rage and battle against us. We are not individuals struggling with the barrage of onslaughts against us. We are instead members of a community, the body of Christ. This body is the communion of the saints, both the earthly and heavenly body of Christ. Within this body we are nurtured by worship, by Scripture, by prayer, by the faith, and by the great company of the angelic hosts who guide us, protect us, and nourish us in our baptismal spirituality.[13]

The third theological support to our baptismal spirituality is the commitment of the church to the *process* of spirituality. We are spiritual because we are *in* Christ, but our baptism into Christ is not a once-for-all act but a growing process, a formation of the spiritual life through stages of development and passage rites that symbolize the deepening of our baptismal relationship.[14]

Finally, there is an understanding of symbols having a *performative power.* Symbols are not empty, void of meaning, and essentially useless. Symbols perform. They speak, they act, they do. They express the energy of the Spirit, the transitions that take place in the journey into Jesus, a journey that never ends. While some symbols are performed only once, other symbols reaffirm the origins of our baptismal spirituality; still other symbols are repeated to nourish our souls, enliven our hearts, and quicken our wills.[15]

---

[12] See Carl E. Braaten, *Motherchurch: Ecclesiology and Ecumenism* (Minneapolis: Fortress, 1998).

[13] See Murphey Center for Liturgical Research, *Made Not Born: New Perspectives on Christian Initiation and the Catehumenate* (Notre Dame, Ind.: University of Notre Dame Press, 1976).

[14] See Tom F. Driver, *The Magic of Ritual: Our Need for Liberating Rites That Transform Our Lives and Our Communities* (San Francisco: Harper, 1991).

[15] For the ancient development and modern translation of this process, see Robert Webber, *Journey to Jesus: The Worship, Evangelism, and Nurture Mission of the Church* (Nashville: Abingdon, 2001).

Four Stages and Passage Rites of Baptism Spirituality

We turn now to the four stages and passage rites of baptismal spirituality in the third century. The first stage is that of the *seeker,* the one who has not yet chosen to be identified with Christ in baptism. The seeker is a pagan. The seeker is lost. But the seeker, by definition, has made some connection with a believer, generally by the choice of a believer who communicates Christ and the new way of life. When the seeker makes an initial commitment to identify with Christ, the seeker proceeds through the first passage rite, the rite of welcome. This rite contains powerful performative symbols. First, the seeker renounces all false worship. The seeker is signed with the cross, an invisible tattoo placed on the seeker's head to signify the seeker's identity with Jesus. Then the seeker symbolically walks into the community of faith to express his or her place within the church. The journey into Jesus has begun.

The second stage is that of the *hearer.* The hearer listens to the Word and is discipled by God's speech. In the early church, this was a three-year process of instruction that took place both within Sunday worship and in small group meetings throughout the week. The hearers stayed in worship for the Scripture readings and sermon. They were then dismissed to reflect on the Word in a room apart as the remainder of the community stayed together to pray, pass the peace of Christ, and celebrate the Eucharist. During this time they were taught Scripture, taught how to pray, and taught how to live the Christian life. At the end of the three-year period, if they had grown sufficiently in the Christian faith and in the virtues, they went through the second passage rite, the enrollment of names. This performative symbol affirmed once again their choice to identify with Jesus in baptism. At the invitation of the minister, they wrote their names in a book (like a covenant) to express their belongingness to Jesus and their commitment to follow him in baptismal spirituality.

They then entered into the third stage of their baptismal process where they became known as *kneelers.* Now they were spiritually formed and prepared especially for spiritual warfare. The theme of their training was Ephesians 6:12, "We wrestle not against flesh and blood but against principalities and powers." Herein is the tension of baptismal spirituality. Herein lies an intense readiness to identify with Christ Jesus' death and resurrection through the pattern of death to sin and resurrection to new life *in* Christ.

The third passage rite is baptism. In the early church, the primary day for baptism was on Easter Sunday because this day more than any other day of the Christian year was the day of baptismal identity. After a long night of Scripture readings that swept through salvation history, the kneeler was brought to the baptismal waters where the rich symbolism of immersion fulfilled the image of Romans 6. Plunged into the water, they were immersed into the death of Jesus so that they may continually live in the water of death. But, brought forth from the water, they were raised with Christ to the new resurrected life; and now for the first time in their spiritual journey into Christ, they prayed with the faithful, passed the peace of Christ, and received the Eucharist.

The fourth stage of baptismal spirituality continued throughout the seven weeks of Easter. During this time, they were called the *faithful*. They assembled to hear the meaning of the Eucharist, to discern and put to use their gifts, and to be encouraged to do works of love and service to others. The final rite of their journey into baptismal spirituality was the continuous rite of the Eucharist. For in this rite their faith was continually confirmed, and their baptism was continuously nourished through the food of Christ, the bread and wine.

This then is baptismal spirituality—a process that marks our identification with Jesus' death and resurrection and a continuous never-ending life lived out of our baptism—a life of perpetual existential death to sin and a life of continuous resurrection into the life of the Spirit.[16]

---

[16] See Thomas Aquinas, *On Baptism,* in *Readings in the History of Christian Thought,* ed. R. Ferm (New York: Holt, Rinehart and Winston, 1964), 440.

Baptism Among the Reformers

The baptismal spirituality of the early church did not survive into the medieval era. Adult baptism and the process of stages of development and passage rites gave way to the post-Constantinian turn toward infant baptism. Baptism eventually lost its connection to spirituality and became identified with salvation as early as Augustine in the early part of the fourth century. Augustine wrote that the church is the "medium for Christian salvation and that the baptism of Christ is only profitable in it."[17] Hence, baptismal regeneration was born.

Baptismal regeneration was maintained throughout the medieval era. For example, Thomas Aquinas wrote:

> Since baptism is a spiritual generation, the baptized are forthwith suited for spiritual actions—the reception of the other sacraments, for example, and other things of the sort—and forthwith there is due to them the place harmonious to the spiritual life, which is eternal beatitude. Hence we say that "Baptism opens the gate of heaven."[18]

While Luther maintained infant baptism, he disassociated it with regeneration. However, he saw infant baptism as a divine imprint and recovered baptismal spirituality as a living into the death and resurrection. Luther indicates this pattern of baptismal spirituality in the following words:

> For as long as we live we are continually doing that which baptism signifies, that is, we die and rise again. . . . You may indeed wander away from the sign for a time, but

---

[17] See Thomas Aquinas, *On the Truth of the Catholic Faith*, in Ibid., 469.

[18] by A. T. W. Steinhauser, Frederick C. Ahrens, and Adbel Ross Wentz, trans., "Babylonian Captivity," in *Luther's Works* (Philadelphia: Muhlenberg, 1966), 53.

the sign is not therefore useless . . . that which baptism signifies should swallow up your whole life, body and soul, and give it forth again at the last day, clad in the robe of glory and immortality. We are therefore never without the sign of baptism nor without the thing it signifies.[19]

Calvin also understood the nature of baptismal spirituality. While referring to Romans 6:3 in the *Institutes of Christian Living,* Calvin wrote:

> *Christ by baptism has made us partakers of his death, ingrafting us into it.* And as the twig derives substance and nourishment from the root to which it is attached, so those who receive baptism with true faith truly feel the efficacy of Christ's death in the mortification of their flesh, and the efficacy of his resurrection in the quickening of the Spirit. On this he founds his exhortation, that if we are Christians we should be dead unto sin, and alive unto righteousness.[20]

The Anabaptists differed from Luther and Calvin in that they restored adult baptism. For Anabaptists, the spirituality of baptism was expressed in the term *pledge* taken from their central baptismal verse in 1 Peter 3:21. "This water symbolizes baptism that now saves you also—not the removal of dirt from the body but the *pledge* of a good conscience toward God." In Anabaptist thought, baptismal spirituality took a special *turn toward communal living.* It was not only a *pledge to turn from sin and to turn toward God* as an individual; it was also and most especially a pledge to turn toward God within the community

---

[19] John Calvin, *Institutes of Christian Religion,* 2 vols., LCC, ed. John T. McNeil (Philadelphia: Westminster, 1960), 2:515.

[20] See Robert Freidman, *The Theology of Anabaptists* (Scottsdale, Pa.: Herald, 1973), 137.

of God's people on earth. They taught a *visible ecclesiology and a visible communal spirituality entered into through baptism.*[21]

Baptism Spirituality in the Modern Era

During the modern era, the official statements on baptism continue to express baptismal spirituality in one way or another. Here are several examples:

1. The Methodist Tradition: "We pray that *this child,* now to be baptized in this water, may die to sin and be raised to new life in Christ."[22]
2. The Baptist Tradition: "In baptism we are united with Christ through faith, dying with him unto sin and rising with him unto newness of life."[23]
3. The United Tradition: "Grant that, being united with Christ in his death and resurrection, they may die unto sin and live unto righteousness."[24]
4. An Ecumenical Baptismal Liturgy: "So as to live in the liberty of the sons and daughters of God, to be a faithful follower of Jesus Christ and to produce the fruits of the Holy Spirit, do you renounce being ruled by the desires of this world, the snare of pride, the love of money and the power of violence?"[25]
5. A typical evangelical congregation: "Do you renounce evil and promise to live as Christ taught?"

Despite these official and unofficial statements regarding baptismal spirituality, it is safe to say that the idea of baptismal

---

[21] See Max Thurian and Geoffrey Wainwright, eds., *Baptism and Eucharist: Ecumenical Convergence in Celebration* (Geneva: World Council of Churches, 1983), 61.

[22] Ibid., 67.

[23] Ibid., 77.

[24] Ibid., 94.

[25] Ibid., 94–96.

spirituality is absent from the thinking of most Protestant Christians and especially from the evangelical community. Why? An analysis of this reality must be made before we attempt to revive baptismal spirituality. I can only approach the loss of baptismal spirituality in its broadest terms. A detailed study of this issue requires a doctoral thesis and a detailed study of the cultural and theological factors involved in its demise.

First, the epistemological shift into the authority of reason made its impact on baptismal spirituality. In the early church and again in the Reformation era, baptism was not only into Jesus but also into a community committed to live out the way of Jesus in the world. Their approach to Christianity was communal. Baptism was into the community of Jesus, the people who lived a new and different way. Baptism accented the countercultural nature, not just of an isolated individual but of a community of committed people.

In the Enlightenment, the epistemological question of "how do we know" shifted from knowledge through the community to knowledge gained outside the community. Knowledge now came through the individual, through reason, and through experience.

The rationalists, following Descartes, believed in the authority of reason, the autonomy of the individual, and the ability to arrive at truth through the scientific method. This philosophy elevated the individual's ability to arrive at truth through the use of the intellect and *to do so alone*. The impact of rationalism on baptism was the loss of baptism's communal dimension and the loss of mystery. Individualism resulted in a reinterpretation of baptism as *my act of obedience*. Also, rationalism resulted in *the loss of the mystery* of participation in the death and resurrection of Jesus.

The experientialists, following the Romantic movement and their reaction against rationalism, located knowing in experience and intuition. *The impact of the Romantic* emphasis of knowing through experience was especially visible in the rise of revivalism. *The impact of revivalism on baptism was to separate baptism from conversion. Baptism, now no longer inextricably linked with conversion, became a witness to conversion.* Converts were told to be baptized as a public confession of *their* conversion, to invite their unchurched friends to come to *their* baptism, in the waters, and to be baptized as an act of public profession of faith.

In sum, the epistemology of the modern era, with its emphasis on individualism and reason, resulted in baptism as "*my* act of obedience" and "*my* testimony and witness to faith" in Jesus. The baptismal spirituality, though retained in the teaching of the various churches, was lost and no longer informed the spiritual life of the great bulk of Christians.

A second reason why baptismal spirituality was lost in the modern era is related to modernity's failure to view the world holistically. The modern cosmological revolution resulted in the Newtonian world machine. The world and its functioning were seen as a clock. The world was made up of many distinct parts, and it was thought that some day through reason and science these various parts could be understood. The impact of the scientific worldview was the separation of various disciplines into various segregated parts. The world was seen in distinct parts that could be separated from other parts and studied in isolation from the whole. These parts were lined up like the alphabet and viewed without any inner connection. This worldview impacted Christianity so it was no longer seen as whole. The disciplines of faith were separated from each other so that a person could study baptism apart from ecclesiology, ethics, and the Christian life.

Consequently, in modern seminaries and in churches, the issue of baptismal spirituality gave way to the great debate of adult versus infant baptism. The real meaning of baptism has thus been lost for most Protestant churches of the modern world. In sum, baptism has been disconnected from Christian spirituality and has now lost its meaning for most Protestant Christians. The question, then, for the twenty-first century is this: How do we recover the biblical and historical meaning of baptism? How do we restore baptismal spirituality in our churches collectively and among our people individually?

Recovering Baptismal Spirituality
for the Twenty-First Century

It has already become clear that the twenty-first century will be distinctly different than the twentieth. It is common among many evangelicals, especially the young, to speak of living in a postmodern world and of seeking to think through what it means to be an evangelical in the postmodern world.

Those who think and speak this way are becoming increasingly critical of the evangelical enmeshment with modernity, especially in the twentieth century. These same people are seeking to deconstruct the evangelical reliance on reason and science and move evangelicalism into a new or, should I say, an older way of thinking. Many younger evangelical thinkers are asking us to return to our roots in John Wesley, in the Reformation leaders, and in the Fathers of the early church. The concern is to recover the Christianity that flourished *before* the onslaught of modern rationalism, individualism, and science.

Current movements in science, philosophy, and communication theory support the criticisms of modernity and the return to an earlier time. Science has shifted away from the mechanistic worldview of the Newtonian world machine into a much more interrelated and complex understanding of the universe. Since 1950, we have passed more deeply into the complexity of the universe through the theories of Einstienian relativity, quantum physics, and now fractal geometry and the chaos theory. The world is no longer seen as a simple machine with identifiable parts but as a highly complex organism characterized by a web of interrelationships.

The impact of the scientific revolution is turning us away from the old linear concept of the alphabet lined up in sequence to a view of all the letters of the alphabet intertwined with each other yet making some kind of holistic sense. This view of the world is impacting our understanding of the various aspects of faith. They do not stand alone as individual entities but are intertwined and interdependent. This scientific understanding is a positive setting in which to recover the interrelatedness of our faith. The holistic view of faith encourages us to see the relationships between dimensions of faith. In this instance, relationship between baptism, ecclesiology, ethics, lifestyle, and the broader concerns of spirituality become clearer.

Second, the changes taking place in modern philosophy, with its emphasis on the analytical and arriving at truth to an empirical emphasis on philosophy as wisdom and lifestyle, have shifted our attention to mystery and to a new search for wisdom and direction in life. These shifts in philosophy raise new interest in baptism as a mystery. The mystery of entering into Christ, of participating in his death and resurrection as a pattern of life, is now much easier to embrace. The retreat of rationalism and the recovery of mystery open the doors to baptismal spirituality once again.

The shift in communication theory has also created a fertile ground for the recovery of baptismal spirituality. Communication has shifted from its attachment to print forms of communication to recover the more ancient understanding of cultural communications. Cultural communications emphasize how communities pass down their convictions. Commitment to a community means a commitment to its values and perceptions, which are learned not so much through cognitive instruction but through participation in the community. Baptismal spirituality is not just individual spirituality but participation in the alternative life of the church. Baptismal spirituality is learned by doing what the community does, by being formed and shaped through a communal ethic and spirituality.

Furthermore, the recognition that we live in a post-Constantinian world has led many scholars and church leaders to return to premodern times. Our postmodern and post-Christian society holds greater affinity with the first three centuries than any other time in the history of the church. Then and now, the church is faced with the power of evil in society, with astrology and the occult, with a high degree of sexual permissiveness and abortion, with a loss of values and the ascendancy of paganism. The early Christians did not live in a Christian world. Today, we do not live in a Christian world.

In the face of this cultural situation, Christians are returning to the theological convictions that undergird baptismal spirituality. There is a resurgence of the *Christus Victor* theme in the face of the rising awareness to the powers of evil. There is a recovery of the church as mother theme in the new emphasis in the church as community. There is a new awareness that conversion is a process. Even if a person is converted instantly, the battle to keep a convert in the church necessitates a process of spiritual formation through which the new believers' faith and character are deepened and strengthened. Also, the new emphasis on the performative power of symbols point to the need to have symbols to mine, to unearth as memorable turning events in the life of faith. All these shifts indicate that the time is ripe for the recovery of baptismal spirituality.

A Future for Baptismal Spirituality

If baptismal spirituality is going to be recovered in our individual and communal spiritual life, there are several things we need to do. First, we need to listen to the text of our current culture and critique the way modernity has altered the understanding of the faith and especially the view of baptism. We need to question the popular notion of baptism as an act of obedience in response to our conversion. We need to see that baptism is not merely a onetime event that serves as a witness to our faith, or a testimony to others to join us in our faith.

Second, we need to read the New Testament and its emphasis on baptism in a new way. We must see that Romans 6 and its emphasis on baptism as entrance into the pattern of death and resurrection in Jesus is a hermeneutical key to reading much of the New Testament. All passages that exhort us to turn away from sin and turn to the new life in Christ are baptismal instructions. They call us to the baptized life. They call us to a baptismal identity, to the new community of faith and entrance into the Jesus way. This means to put off the sin that so easily attracts us and to put on the fruits of the Spirit, which is the calling we have to live in the resurrection.

Finally, we should consider adapting the third-century journey into Jesus with its four stages, three passage rites, and the continuous rite of the Eucharist as our pattern for assimilating new believers into the church. This approach to baptism will ground us in our baptismal covenant and empower us to adapt a pattern of spiritual behavior that continually follows the pattern of death to sin and resurrection to the Spirit.

Our modern method of evangelizing people into Christ and sending them to the church of their choice must be reversed. We must evangelize people into the church *and* Christ even as we evangelize people through conversion *and* baptism, and baptism *and* spirituality. These areas of ministry are not separate as we thought them to be in the modern world—they are interrelated and whole.

In a postmodern world, we need to treat people whole and help them see the interrelationship between their baptism and all that they think, say, and do as Christians. This kind of baptismal spirituality is a key to the renewal of the individual, to the reinvigoration of the local church, and to the relevance of the whole church to our postmodern world.

Conclusion

The early church taught that baptism is an outward sign of an inward grace. This outward sign is not something to be done and discarded but a sign in which we are to live daily. To live in your baptism is to live in the pattern of the death and resurrection of Jesus Christ. It is a moment by moment, day by day, week by week, year by year identity with Jesus. It is not an intellectual idea, not a mere moral imperative, but rather a real authentic life of living, dying, and rising with Jesus at the very center of life. This is baptismal spirituality.

CHAPTER TEN

Eucharist Spirituality

Robert E. Webber

I grew up in a pastor's home where the Bible was highly regarded. The Scriptures were not only treated as true but as literally true in all its parts and images. My father, a fundamentalist, was proud to say that he received the Word of God as it was written. I, like my father, also had no trouble reading the Bible as factual truth. But I do remember an occasion in which my father and I were discussing Scripture and what my father had to say seemed inconsistent.

My father was a dispensational premillennialist who was unswervingly committed to interpreting the book of Revelation and all its images in a literal way. Once, when we were discussing the Battle of Armageddon, my father mentioned that Scripture says there will be so much blood it will reach to the horses' bridle. Having grown up on a farm, my dad figured that the blood in the valley would be approximately five feet and several inches deep. I found myself being somewhat skeptical about the literal nature of his interpretation and wondered openly if this could be a metaphor for "lots of blood."

I posed this as a possible interpretation to my father and received from him a rather lengthy lecture on the value of literal hermeneutics. Anything else, I was assured, would lead into the slippery slope of liberalism. Soon, I was told, all Scripture, even the historicity of Jesus, would be held in doubt.

During this conversation with my father, I recalled a recent sermon on John 6 in which the statement "unless you eat the flesh of the Son of Man and drink his blood, you have no life in you" (6:53) was dismissed as not literal. I asked, "Why do you take the depth of the Armageddon blood to be literal but take eating and drinking the body and blood of Christ to be a metaphor?" I don't remember the answer, but it must not have been adequate because I have never forgotten this discussion, and what seemed to me in my youthful mind to be a contradiction in my dad's hermeneutics.

My purpose in this chapter is to explore table worship and show this act of eating the flesh and drinking the blood as a crucial dimension of spirituality. My hermeneutic looks briefly at the Eucharist in Scripture, its development in history, and contemporary reflections on the Eucharist as we think, in a communal way, toward the matter of a Eucharistic spirituality.

Eucharist Spirituality in Scripture and the Early Church

Matters pertaining to the Lord's Table are complex and have resulted in a number of different inquiries. Debates have been raised over whether the Lord's Supper is a Passover Feast or a fellowship meal. Christians argue about the meaning of "Do this in remembrance of me," "The new covenant in my blood," "As often as you drink it," "You proclaim the death of the Lord," "Until he comes," "Is not the cup of thanksgiving for which we give thanks a participation in the blood of Christ? Is not the bread that we break a participation in the body of Christ?" and "Because there is one loaf, we, who are many, are one body, for we all partake of the one loaf."

These issues cover a gamut of exegetical issues, matters pertaining to biblical and historical theology, and questions dealing with worship, spirituality, and the practice of church. Any attempt to deal with all these matters would require a greater inquiry than the extent of this paper allows. Consequently, I will choose to focus on one question related to bread and wine, namely, the relationship between the presence of God at bread and wine and what bearing this has on the topic of this chapter, Eucharistic spirituality.

We begin with a brief survey of the terms used in the New Testament to refer to table worship and spirituality. Here we search for the images or pictures of bread and wine that emerge from the New Testament. First, the expression "Lord's Supper" found in 1 Corinthians 11 is interpreted by Paul himself in verse 26, "For whenever you eat this bread and drink this cup, you proclaim the Lord's death until he comes." Clearly, the common interpretation of this passage in the experience of the community of faith is that the Lord's Supper remembers Jesus' death and anticipates his Second Coming. Like all of worship and spirituality, the Lord's Supper is rooted in the church's memory (anamnesis) and the church's hope (Prolepsis).

A second New Testament image appears in Luke 24 in the story of Cleopas and his companion on the road to Emmaeus. The image "Breaking of the Bread" clearly deals with the matter of worship and spirituality. It occurs on Sunday, "The first day of the week" (24:1). The two central foci of worship are the explanation of the Word ("beginning with Moses and all the Prophets, he explained to them what was said in all the Scriptures concerning himself," v. 27) and the presence of Christ at the table ("when he was at the table with them, he took bread, gave thanks, broke it and began to give it to them," v. 30).

These two actions were surrounded by the act of gathering ("two of them were going to a village called Emmaus," v. 13) and the act of going forth ("they got up and returned at once to Jerusalem," v. 33). The spiritual impact of this story is found in the images of Scripture "burning within" as he talked with them on the road and "opened the Scriptures" (v. 32), in the personal insight gained by the breaking of the bread, "then their eyes were opened and they recognized him" (v. 31), and upon arriving in the Upper Room they declared "how Jesus was recognized by them when he broke the bread" (v. 35).

This experience of the risen Christ led the disciples to spiritual action, for immediately after the experience, they rose up and went out to tell others, saying, "It is true! The Lord has risen and has appeared to Simon" (v. 34). In this story, we see how Easter faith led to Easter witness. Clearly, this passage has been accepted throughout history as a spiritual experience of an encounter with the living and resurrected Christ. The power of the breaking of the bread has led people beyond their experience of dislocation into a new experience of relocation in God. Breaking of the bread has resulted in an encounter with the risen Christ and a renewed spirituality.

The third image of table worship is found in 1 Corinthians 10:16, "Is not the cup of thanksgiving for which we give thanks a participation in the blood of Christ? And is not the bread that we break a participation in the body of Christ?" The key word here is "participation in" *(koinonia)*,[1] sometimes translated as "communion." The emphasis is on relationship. The act of eating bread and drinking wine is an act of communication in which communion between God and each individual of the congregations is established as well as a relationship with each other.

The fourth term, Eucharist, is also found in a worship context. In 1 Corinthians 14, Paul is warning the Corinthian people about their use of tongues. "If you are praising God with your spirit, how can one who finds himself among those who do not understand say 'Amen' to your thanksgiving (Eucharist), since he does not know what you are saying? You may be giving thanks (Eucharist) well enough, but the other man is not edified" (14:16–17).[2] Here again the focus of table worship is on what God has done through Christ Jesus. Our responsibility, in this case, is to be thankful.

---

[1] See J. Hainz, "κοινωνός, οῦ, ὁ *koinōnos*," in *EDNT* (Grand Rapids: Eerdmans, 1991), 2:303–5.

[2] See H. Patsch, "εὐχαριστία, ας, ἡ *eucharistia*," in *EDNT* (Grand Rapids: Eerdmans, 1991), 2:88.

This brief survey of the images and pictures of New Testament table worship lead us to the following insight: Table worship has to do with the very center of the gospel message and of our response to it. Table worship says and enacts the metanarrative of the Christian faith. It sweeps from Creation to the Fall, to God's involvement in history through the story of Israel and the story of Jesus in whom God was incarnate to save the world, and ends with the consummation of all things in the new heavens and the new earth.

Nowhere in our worship is the story of God's redeeming love so eloquently expressed, so dramatically enacted, and so graciously applied. Everything one needs to know about God and God's redeeming love and re-creating power can be experienced and understood at the table. Here, in this act of eating and drinking, we are engaged in a language of mystery that goes far beyond our capacity to understand. Here we use the language of narrative to tell the story of God's redeeming involvement in history to restore and rescue the world. Here we are involved in the language of symbol to visualize and make tangible, indeed to ingest the story and to take Jesus into our stomachs and into our lives, to eat his body and to drink his blood so that we may actually and really participate in union with God the Creator and Redeemer of all that is visible and invisible.

Presence at Bread and Wine:
Scripture and the Early Church

Now we must ask: What does it mean to say, There is a presence of Jesus at bread and wine? This matter can only be expressed by looking at the larger question of the presence of God in biblical thought. The question we must ask is this: *Is God's presence connected to a real tangible reality or is it a spiritualized presence like an idea or concept?* In a work as limited in scope as this, I can only point in the direction of an answer to this question and suggest a way to think about the presence of God.

In brief, I will suggest that God's presence is everywhere within the created order, even though the paradox of God as wholly other is to be affirmed. God, who is transcendent, is above and beyond the creation; yet God, who is imminent, inheres within the entire created order.

This paradox underlies the notion that God who is everywhere *shows up with intensity in particular localities.* This conviction or belief shows up in the Old Testament, New Testament, the early church, and evangelical churches today.

Old Testament

In the Old Testament, prior to the Exodus, Israel believed God to dwell on Mount Sinai. When the nation was asked, "Where does God dwell?" the answer was on Mount Sinai, for there God met Moses in the burning bush (Exod. 3–4). But when God brought the children of Israel up out of the land of Egypt, God chose to become present in the tabernacle and to meet Moses and the people of Israel at the Tent of Meeting (33:7–23). Here Moses was promised, "My presence will go with you" (v. 14).[3]

God's presence was not a mere "spiritualized" concept but a real and tangible tent, where "the glory of the LORD filled the tabernacle" (40:35), a real presence that led the way into the future (vv. 36–38). This presence, the very glory of the Lord, was used to lead the Israelites into the Promised Land (Josh. 3:3) and into winning battles with the enemy (6:4). Through the visible and tangible sign of the tabernacle, Israel knew about the presence and power of God. For them, this was no illusion. The Creator God was everywhere and showed up in intensity at a particular place and time so that Israel knew without a doubt that God was present in all his glory and presence in, through, around, and under the tabernacle. The tabernacle itself was not God, but it was a real presence, not any empty symbol.

---

[3] Scripture quotations are from the *New International Version.*

New Testament

In the New Testament, God's glory and presence is manifest in a new way—in an actual embodied and physical presence of a man born of a woman in Bethlehem, a man with a real body, a real face, a man who walked among us, ate with us, talked to us, and shared our human existence. This man was Jesus of Nazareth, who, as Matthew testifies, is called "Immanuel"—which means, "God with us" (1:23), which Matthew drives home again at the conclusion of his work when the resurrected Son says to the church "I am with you" (28:20b).[4]

This man, Jesus, is God made flesh (John 1:14) and is, as Paul states, the very "image" of God. In the Incarnation, God was made tangible, visible, and earthed, and was made of the same stuff of creation. The early heresy of Gnosticism rejected the notion that material was good—implying that God could not become material or encounter us through the material. Gnostics, therefore, hold a docetic view of Jesus and do not believe that God has become enfleshed with Jesus. Jesus "seems to be real," but in reality he is a ghost, an appearance, a phantom. John countered the Gnostics by affirming the physicality of Jesus. The apostle wrote, "That which was from the beginning, which we have heard, which we have seen with our eyes, which we have looked at and our hands have touched—this we proclaim concerning the Word of life" (1 John 1:1).

The Early Church

During the second century, the battle with the Gnostics, which had been growing for more than 150 years, culminated in a huge debate. From this debate emerged the rule of faith. This rule is a primary document between the Scriptures and the Apostles' Creed. The rule of faith affirmed the physical and

---

[4] See N. Walter, "Ἐμμανουήλ *Emmanuel*," in *EDNT* (1990; reprint, Grand Rapids: Eerdmans, 1994), 1:443.

earthly nature of Jesus and of the Christian faith. The universal creed of the church proclaimed that God is not a dualistic entity in an eternal war between spirit and material. Rather, God is one. He is the one "who made the heaven and the earth." Also, he was "made flesh for our salvation." The rule of faith affirms the physical and earthly reality of our salvation by proclaiming terms: "the birth of a virgin, the suffering, the resurrection from the dead, and the bodily reception into the heavens of the beloved, Christ Jesus our Lord, and his coming from the heavens in the glory of the Father to restore all things, and to raise up all flesh."[5]

The rule of faith was used in the early church as the primary hermeneutic of the gospel. People who claimed to be Christian but refused to confess the enfleshed reality of the Incarnation and denied that God created and furthermore communicated to his creation through Creation were regarded as heretics. This was no new and novel idea at the end of the second century. It derived from the physical nature of faith in the New Testament and from the Pauline and Johannine confrontation with the Gnostics who rejected the earthed nature of the Incarnation.

This incarnational hermeneutic was also used by Ignatius, Bishop of Antioch, in A.D. 110. Ignatius wrote seven letters to bishops to warn them against the heresy of Gnosticism. In his letter to the Smyrneans, he cautioned them "to pay attention to those who have wrong notions about the grace of Jesus Christ." Ignatius claims that heretics "have no concern for widows or orphans, for the oppressed, for those in prison or released, for the hungry or the thirsty. They hold aloof from the Eucharist and from services of prayer, because they refuse to admit that the Eucharist is the flesh of our saviour Jesus Christ." Ignatius continues his teaching by calling on the bishops and their flock to "pay attention to the prophets and above all to

---

[5] See Irenaeus, *Against Heresies*, in *Early Christian Fathers*, LCC, ed. Cyril Richardson (Philadelphia: Westminster, 1953), 360.

the gospel. There we get a clear picture of the passion and allows us see that the resurrection has really happened."[6] The denial of an earthed and material faith led to a Gnostic rejection that God actually became one of us earthbound material creatures in the Incarnation. Ultimately, the question of Eucharist spirituality is intertwined with one's views of creation, incarnation, and re-creation.

The Evangelical Church

I know of no evangelical who would deny that God created the world, or that the world of the material is intrinsically good because God created it, or that in the Incarnation God actually became his creation. Yet the implication of Creation and Incarnation are generally denied when it comes to Eucharistic spirituality.

Biblical Christianity is an earthed faith. Biblical faith is not an esoteric, spiritual conception of reality. It is not a Gnostic rejection of creation as evil. It is not a neo-Gnostic interpretation of material reality as an illusion of the real. It does not teach that the soul is imprisoned in an embodied existence traveling through one reincarnation after another until it is free to return to its divine origin. But many people who confess to be Christians and affirm a physical incarnation are really spiritual Gnostics when it comes to understanding the presence of Christ at bread and wine.

For example, I recently encountered a confessing Christian who proclaimed this antimaterial perspective to be her understanding of life. "My soul," she said, "is who I am. It and it alone lives forever." Then she said, "I may go through many reincarnations until my soul is free from its material casing." She went on to affirm that her soul probably had a previous embodied existence and would more than likely have several more before it was completely free. I wanted to say "nonsense . . . you're a heretic, Irene," but I restrained myself (something

---

[6] See Ignatius, *To the Smyrneans,* in *Early Christian Fathers,* in ibid., 114.

I wouldn't do in the classroom) and calmly stated, "If you are just a soul hopping from one embodied existence to another, then you are not you and, if your soul simply returns to a 'divine source,' then you have no eternal destiny. If you are everything, then you are nothing. God made you Irene. You are a unique you—body, soul, spirit. There has never been another you; there will never be another you. You have your physical identity, which you will carry throughout all eternity." I think she grasped what I was saying: "Your spiritual uniqueness is tied into who you are as a physical, material being. Your soul and body is united into one being named Irene."

In sum, the Old and New Testaments clearly teach and orthodox Christianity rightly attests that the true faith embraces the paradox that the God who is transcendent, invisible, and incomprehensible has not only created a visible and tangible world but has made himself an incarnate and visible participant in the very stuff of creation, an earthed and embodied person who became man "for us and our salvation." Thus, creation is a worthy vehicle through which an encounter with the divine actually and really occurs. This incarnational understanding of the unity of the material and immaterial is the hermeneutic for understanding the mystery that takes place at bread and wine. It is the key that opens for us the meaning of Eucharistic spirituality.

Eucharist Spirituality in the History of the Church

Throughout the history of the church, discussions regarding the presence of Christ at bread and wine are marked by *the attempt to explain what cannot be explained*. The most acceptable nonexplanation that affirms the reality of a physical presence is presented by Justin Martyr in his *First Apology* written to explain Christianity to the emperor Titus. Justin wrote:

> This food we call Eucharist, of which no one is allowed
> to partake except one who believes that the things we

teach are true, and has received the washing for forgiveness of sins and for rebirth, and who lives as Christ
handed down to us. For we do not receive these things
as common bread or common drink; but as Jesus Christ
our Saviour being incarnate, by God's word took flesh
and blood for our salvation, so also, we have been taught
that the food consecrated by the word of prayer which
comes from him, from which our flesh and blood are
nourished by transformation, is the flesh and blood of
the incarnate Jesus.[7]

Justin is making a comparison between the Incarnation and
the consecration. This parallel is clearly seen when the heart of
his statement is set forth in its literary form as I have done
below:

Not Common Bread or Drink

Incarnation	**Consecration**
As Jesus Christ our Savior	So also the food
Being incarnate by God's Word	Consecrated by word of prayer
Took flesh and blood	From which our flesh and blood
For our salvation	Are nourished by transformation

is
the flesh and blood of that incarnate
Jesus

When we read the left column, "As Jesus Christ our Savior
being incarnate by God's Word took flesh and blood for our
salvation," we find the heart of New Testament Christianity.
These words present the Incarnation, which had as its purpose
"our salvation." God became the Second Adam to reverse the

---

[7] Justin Martyr, *First Apology,* in *Early Christian Fathers,* in ibid., 114.

Fall, to restore humankind, and to rescue the entire created order. This is the gospel, the good news we preach, teach, and proclaim to the world. No evangelical will deny this message. To affirm it is to be evangelical. This message strikes at the very heart of the Christian faith and proclaims the news that is always good to hear.

Consider the second side of the statement, the portion developed under the "consecration," which is set alongside and parallel to the Incarnation. "So also . . . this food consecrated by the word of prayer . . . from which our flesh and blood are nourished by transformation." The emphasis here is on a Eucharistic spirituality. We are nourished through the consecrated food "by transformation" because it is the flesh and blood of "that incarnate Jesus." In other words, Eucharistic spirituality is the ingestion of Jesus Christ, an intake of God the Creator and incarnate one who, having redeemed creation, now encounters and enters into our flesh and blood through bread and wine. This is real presence.

The consecration is neither explained nor explained away. Like the Incarnation that affirms the union between the human and the divine, the consecration affirms the union to be true and real, but as a *mystery* that words and concepts cannot disclose. Perhaps that's where the church should have remained. But it didn't. Reason went to work to explain what can't be explained.

Roman Catholicism

By the fourth century, a major dispute erupted between Ambrose and Augustine. Ambrose claimed that bread and wine consecrated by the word of prayer actually became the real incarnate flesh and blood of Jesus. This view, which is called "realism," was based on Ambrose's interpretation of the nature miracles and the power of Jesus' words to effect change. Ambrose writes:

If a human blessing had the power to effect a change in nature, what are we to say of the divine consecration where the very words of the Lord and Saviour are in operation? For the sacrament that you receive is effected by the words of Christ. Now if the words of Elijah had the power to call down fire from heaven, will not the words of Christ have power to change the character [species] of the elements?[8]

But Augustine, in opposition to Ambrose, taught symbolic realism. His most famous statement regarding the "how" of Jesus' presence at the Eucharistic table is "That one thing is seen in them, but something else is understood."[9] But Augustine also wrote, "Christ was once sacrificed in his own person; and yet he is mystically [in Sacramento] sacrificed for the peoples, not only throughout the Easter Festival, but everyday."[10]

The Ambrosian explanation won the day by the thirteenth century in Roman Catholic teaching. In 1215, the Fourth Latern Council declared the "body and blood are truly contained in the sacrament of the Altar under the figures of bread and wine, the bread having been transubstantiated into His body and the wine into His blood by divine power, so that, to accomplish the mystery of our union, we may receive of Him what He has received of us."[11]

Thomas Aquinas, the great Catholic theologian of the thirteenth century, offered an even more specific interpretation of what happened as a result of the consecration. "The complete substance of the bread," he wrote, "is converted into the complete substance of Christ's body and the complete substance of

---

[8] See Henry Bettenson, ed., *The Later Christian Fathers*, LCC (London: Oxford University Press, 1970), 185.

[9] Ibid., 244.

[10] Ibid., 245.

[11] See John H. Leith, *Creeds of the Churches* (New York: Doubleday, 1963), 58.

the wine into the complete substance of Christ's blood."[12] Aquinas used the Aristotelian categories of substance and accident to explain the change. The "accident," which is the external form of bread and wine, does not change. It continues to look and taste like bread and wine, but its substance changes into the real body and blood. Aquinas's view remained as the dominant Catholic view until the documents of Vatican II written and promulgated by the church between 1963 and 1965.

Protestant Reformation

It wasn't until the Reformation that the Augustinian interpretation of Eucharistic spirituality returned via the writings of Luther and Calvin. Both Reformers are highly committed to a real presence of Christ at bread and wine, a presence that nourishes faith and transforms the believers.

Luther shifted the idea of God's presence to the Word. For Luther, God's presence is found in the words of God's promise expressed over bread and wine, especially in the words "given and shed for you for the remission of sins." In his *Small Catechism,* Luther writes:

> These words, together with the bodily eating and drinking, are the chief thing in the Sacrament; and forgiveness of sins. Who then receives this Sacrament worthily? Fasting and bodily preparation are indeed a good outward discipline; but he is truly worthy and well prepared who has faith in these words: "Given and shed for you, for the remission of sins." But he who believes not these words, or doubts, is unworthy and unprepared; for the words, "For you," require only believing hearts.[13]

---

[12] Thomas Aquinas, "On the Truth of the Catholic Faith," in *Readings in the History of Christian Thought,* ed. R. L. Ferm (New York: Holt, Rinehart and Winston, 1964), 471.

[13] Hugh T. Kerr, *A Compound of Luther's Theology* (Philadelphia: Westminster, 1966), 170–71.

Because Luther was a theologian of paradox, he did not emphasize the Word so as to deemphasize the presence. Instead, he affirmed both. He argued that the Word is in the words of institution, "This is my body." For Luther, these words are interpreted with integrity only when they are taken literally. Because of his commitment to the unity of the spiritual and material in the Incarnation, Luther affirmed the implication of the Incarnation for Eucharistic spirituality. Christ is truly present in our eating and drinking to nourish and transform our lives.

John Calvin joined Luther in rejecting the word *transubstantiation* and the notion that the mass is a sacrifice. But Calvin also rejected Luther's literalism for a spiritual understanding of the presence of Christ at bread and wine. A primary difference between Luther and Calvin was in the question of the relationship between the material and the spiritual. Luther, following the implication of the Incarnation, affirmed that the infinite could be united with the finite. But Calvin, although affirming the Incarnation, did not embrace the implication of the Incarnation for the union of divine with creation as in the bread and wine. Rejecting this unity, Calvin argued, "the finite cannot contain the infinite," and thus rejected the literal interpretation of "this is my body." Because of Calvin's philosophical commitment to the separation of the immaterial from the material, the only logical conclusion for him was to assert the figurative and spiritual nature of the presence. It was a sign, a pledge, and a testimony to God's saving grace. In the Geneva Liturgy of 1542, Calvin thus exhorts the worshipers:

> Let us receive this sacrament as a pledge that the virtue of his death and passion is imputed to us for righteousness just as if we had suffered it in our own person . . . let us present ourselves to him with ardent zeal, in order that he may make us capable of receiving him.[14]

---

[14] John Calvin, *Form of Church Prayers* (Geneva, 1542). See R.C.D. Jasper and G. L. Cuming, eds., *Prayers of the Eucharist: Early and Reformed*, 2d ed. (New York: Oxford University Press, 1980), 156.

In spite of Calvin's figurative or spiritual interpretation, he has a high view of Eucharistic spirituality. Feeding on bread and wine is not an empty act but one that deepens spirituality and our connection to Christ who lives in us. Calvin writes:

> Since he is given us unto life, we understand that without him in us we would be plainly dead. [In the supper] he makes all of us one in himself, to desire one soul, one heart; one tongue for us all . . . we shall think that we, as being poor, come to a kindly giver; as sick, to a physician; as sinner, to the author of righteousness; finally as dead, to him who gives us life.[15]

Among evangelicals, the Reformer Zwingli has been the most influential. Zwingli debated Luther at a conference in Marburg in October of 1529, where the two differed significantly. Luther continued to insist on the literal interpretation of the words "This is my body," while Zwingli argued that the text is best interpreted to read "This *signifies* my body." Zwingli found this view in his interpretation of John 6:63, "The spirit gives life, the flesh counts for nothing." Zwingli started from the philosophical separation of the material and the immaterial, while Luther started with the affirmation of the union between the material and immaterial, the physical and the spiritual.

The Zwinglian influence made its impact on the successors of the Reformation—the Pietists of the seventeenth century, the revivalists of the eighteenth century, the missionary movement of the nineteenth century, and the fundamentalists and evangelicals of the twentieth century, all of whom with few exceptions followed the Zwinglian interpretation that the bread and wine are "signifiers" of a past event that is now remembered intellectually.

---

[15] John Calvin, *Institutes of Christian Religion,* 2 vols., LCC, ed. J. T. McNeil (1559; English translation, Philadelphia: Westminster, 1960), 1:419–20.

In this way, the divine presence, which had been affirmed from the beginning of the church, was replaced with a human remembering. Eucharist spirituality was no longer understood as the work of God in the soul communicated through bread and wine but the work of the person who remembers. The act of communion, always regarded as a special presence, a real genuine encounter with the risen Christ who is ingested into the body and who by the power of the Spirit nourishes and transforms the Christian by God's initiative and indwelling, is of no more value for spiritual formation than what can be attained outside the central symbol of faith. One can now achieve spirituality through one's own efforts at prayer, Bible reading, or silent meditation. This approach to spirituality fit the Enlightenment split of the material and the physical and resulted in a spiritual Gnosticism that found material reality to be downright bothersome.

Modern liberals followed the philosophical split between the material and the spiritual to its logical conclusion and offered us a Jesus who was little more than a myth. Consequently, the liberals made a distinction between the Jesus of history and the Christ of faith. The evangelicals, using the same premise of the split between the material and the spiritual, demythologized baptism, the Eucharist, and other symbols but never gave up the central conviction that Jesus was the God-man. But, by the end of the twentieth century, the pragmatic evangelical gave up all symbolism as they adopted the symbols of corporate America to reach the boomer yuppies. This reductionism has resulted in a Christianity that is becoming dangerously Gnostic.

In conclusion, Eucharistic spirituality appears to be absent from evangelical worship. There seems to be a misunderstanding as to why we observe the Eucharist. What is its meaning, its use? Why bother with this ritual when I can intellectually recall the death of Jesus as I drive my car to work or as I fall asleep at night. Why do I need to eat bread and drink wine? There also seems to be a great deal of confusion about how to observe the Eucharist. Do we tack it on to the end of our service? Is it funeral-like or is it a celebration? Do we need to do anything

other than read 1 Corinthians 11:23–26 and say a prayer? Do
we even need to do that? Some agonize over these questions.
Others totally dismiss the questions and disregard the Eucharist as a mere intellectual remembrance.

Because of the confusion in the church, there is no personal
Eucharistic spirituality. The bread and wine are taken and eaten
in a somber atmosphere but generally forgotten. There is little
if any preparation to receive and seldom any reflection during
the week on the implication the reception bread and wine hold
for communion with God or with daily Christian living. So where
are we to go?

The Future of Eucharistic
Spirituality Among Evangelicals

What is the future of Eucharistic spirituality among evangelicals? The evangelical tradition has a long standing embrace
of the Cartesian split between the spiritual and the material, the
secular and the sacred. The evangelical tradition is steeped in
the factual and in the rational. Yet throughout evangelical history, there is a deep strain of piety, a hunger for spiritual experience, and the reality of faith. So where do we go? There are
three positive directions now influencing the younger evangelical, directions that may lead us toward a more thoughtful embrace of a postmodern expression of Eucharistic spirituality.

Science and Philosophy

The first is that in both science and philosophy we are no
longer shaped by the Cartesian dichotomies of matter versus
nonmatter or spiritual versus the physical. The new scientific
revolution has shifted us from the Newtonian world machine,
which separated everything into separate entities, to a new
understanding of the world as an interrelated web. The old
distinctions are no longer valid. The ancient Christian understanding of the Incarnation as the union of spirit with matter

and of its implications for a Eucharistic spirituality may be able to be born anew in a postmodern world shaped by the interrelationship of matter with nonmatter.

If Christians embrace the new science that has moved away from seeing the world in separate categories, they will be driven back to the theology of the early church, especially to the deep thought of Athanasius, Cyril of Alexandria, and the Cappadocian Fathers. These ancient thinkers forged out a classical theology of the Incarnation and of its implications for Eucharistic spirituality that rejected a dualistic understanding of life. It is inside this classical Christian thought that we evangelicals will find a nondualistic approach to faith. By embracing the unity of the material and immaterial, we may once again gain an incarnational affirmation of faith that affirms God's presence in the material.

Symbols Communicate

A second direction for our weary but hungry souls is to reaffirm the ancient perception that symbols speak and act. A symbol is not empty, void, and contentless. A symbol, it is now known, participates in the reality that it represents. Because God co-inheres in his creation, symbols are the vehicles through which God is actually and really communicated.

Rollo May argues that the loss of symbols constitutes one of our culture's chief difficulties. Because we have no symbols to identify and illustrate the meaning of life, we cannot transcend the crisis of life. Hunger, war, death, unemployment, disease, and the other horrors that confront us on a daily basis seem to be the sum and substance of life. Without signs or symbols in *this world* to show us another world or a means of coping with the trials and strains of this world, we have nowhere to turn but to despair and absurdity.

The symbol of bread and wine is no empty, useless symbol. It speaks. It acts. It performs. It leads us beyond the explainable and encounters us with the *mysterium tremendum*. This experience may happen without a visible sign, but more frequently happens to us through a sign that acts upon us. The symbol is the vehicle because divine action for it participates in the reality, which it represents. A symbol is a vehicle, not the final destination. The other side of the symbol is the person who must be open and vulnerable to the action of the Holy Spirit through the symbol.

When the believer is open to the presence of the Holy Spirit and comes to the symbol through which the Holy Spirit is working, a synergism of communication occurs. So it is with Eucharistic spirituality. Christ is really present at the symbol of bread and wine, and we, too, come to the bread and wine full of the Holy Spirit. In that moment a communion occurs with the transcendent God who became human for us to live among us, to die for us, and to be resurrected to live in us. A real exchange occurs. His life is given for us as a mystical dwelling within us as we eat and drink. When we ingest the bread and wine, we really and actually ingest the incarnate Jesus, who is united to God, and receive the benefit of his death and resurrection for us.

Theological Imagination

A third direction for our thinking toward a Eucharistic spirituality is found in the recovery of theological imagination. In the visible sign we find the action of God, but what we bring to the visible sign is an active and intentional imagination.

The Enlightenment, with its emphasis on reason, in effect killed the imagination. Everything became fact. In this instance the fact was bread and wine. That's it. It looks like bread and wine, smells like bread and wine, and tastes like bread and wine, so it can be nothing else. That's modernity.

But in postmodernity all of that has changed. We now know there is more to see than the naked eye can behold. Theological imagination says that's the body and blood of our Lord. In order to achieve theological imagination, two things must occur: conversion and communication. In conversion our vision of reality is transformed so that we see through born again eyes. We know the story of God's world from Creation to the Fall, to the rescue, to the new heavens and the new earth. In the sign of bread and wine, we see the really real. We know the world as it is through this new way of seeing. Imagination is the transfiguration of our lives and the world into God's vision of reality.

Imagination allows us to *approach* the bread and wine out of this faith—our personal faith and the faith of the community. We recognize with the writer of Hebrews that, "Faith is being sure of what we hope for and certain of what we do not see" (Heb. 11:1). We then *ingest* the bread and wine presented in visible sign and received in the imagination that goes beyond the factual knowing that Jesus is, "The bread of life" (John 6:35), and that we are called to "eat the flesh of the Son of Man and drink his blood," for unless we do, we "have no life" in us (v. 53); also, so we eat and drink knowing as Jesus taught, "My flesh is real food and my blood is real drink" (v. 55).

Having ingested Jesus, we are now called to *embody* Jesus' presence in the way we live, for Christ, and all of what that name means for the whole world, now dwells within us—we *embody* Jesus and his kingdom. We are now "alive with Christ" (Eph. 2:5) and thereby able to be conformed *in* Christ (Phil. 2:5–8). We are therefore now to live for righteousness (Rom. 6), live according to the new man (Col. 3), and to walk in the Spirit (Gal. 5). For Christ, the new man is really present within us. The spiritual energy of his flesh mingled with ours. The spiritual energy of his blood poured through our veins. We are alive by the power of the Spirit, for Jesus truly lives within us because of the dynamic and active presence of his saving person united with our humanity communicating to us a relationship with the divine, with whom he is united in his incarnation.

Conclusion

Now we must ask, What is Eucharistic spirituality? In brief it is an affirmation of the actual presence of Christ living within us through a union with our humanity and empowering us to live our lives in and through him. His uniting presence is continually made real through bread and wine. By bread and wine, our flesh and spirit are nourished, and we are continually transformed into the image of the one who dwells within. We receive him by faith, ingest him as real, and embody him in all our ways. It is a mystery concretely and really lived out as an embodied reality. This is, in brief, Eucharistic spirituality.

I conclude with words taken from St. Cyril of Jerusalem, written about A.D. 315:

> After this ye hear the chanter inviting you with a sacred melody to the communion of the Holy Mysteries, and saying, "O taste and see that the Lord is good." Trust not the judgment to thy bodily palate; no, but to faith unflattering; for they who taste are bidden to taste, not bread and wine, but the anti-typical Body and Blood of Christ.
>
> In approaching therefore, come not with thy wrists extended, or thy fingers spread; but make thy left hand a throne for the right, as for that which is to receive a King. And having hollowed thy palm, receive the Body of Christ, saying over it, "Amen."
>
> Then after thou hast partaken of the Body of Christ, draw near also to the Cup of His Blood; not stretching forth thine hands, but bending and saying with an air of worship and reverence, "Amen," hallow thyself by partaking also of the Blood of Christ. And while the moisture is still upon thy lips, touch it with thine hands, and hallow thine eyes and brow and the other organs of sense. Then wait for the prayer, and give thanks unto God, who hath accounted thee worthy of so great mysteries.[16]

By restoring this ancient approach to receiving the bread and wine, we will attain to Eucharist spirituality, the energy of Christ within us to form and shape us into his image.

---

[16] St. Cyril of Jerusalem, *Catechetical Lecturers,* 4th ed. (Oxford, London: J. H. Parker, 1872), 278–79.

CONCLUSION

CHAPTER ELEVEN

The Challenges of Multicultural Worship

Thomas M. Stallter

An exploration of cultural systems and their implications for the understanding and application of biblical truth is only beginning to become important to evangelicals. Though there are a number of informed evangelical scholars in the field of intercultural studies, the implications of their findings have not yet overhauled our missionary endeavors overseas and, far less, affected the ministry of local churches in North America. In spite of a great amount of cultural diversity all around us, North American Anglos are among the most culturally unaware of peoples. Our individualism, informality, and egalitarianism cause us to ignore differences between cultures that can be quite important to relevancy and accuracy in our worship and ministry. And yet, we are at a juncture in history that is ushering in the most multicultural situation the U.S. church has ever seen.

Not only is legal and illegal immigration at its highest since World War I, the U.S. is no longer the "melting pot" it was at that time.[1] Thirteen percent of the population in the U.S.

---

[1] "Legal Immigrants Admitted to the U.S. Since 1820," *World Book Encyclopedia* (Chicago: World Book, 1999).

uses a language other than English in the home, and more
and more immigrants are maintaining their cultural identity
and creating a new pluralism across America.[2] By 2005, the
Hispanic population in the U.S. will surpass the Black population, numbering 98 million by 2050, while Blacks will number 59 million. In 2056, the majority of the U.S. population
will no longer be Anglo-American. By 2075, Hispanics will
make up 30 percent of the total population and continue to
grow at a rate of over 9 million people per year. Asians and
Pacific Islanders will triple their present population in the
U.S. by 2045 and make up 12 percent of the total population
by 2075.[3] The urgency and opportunity of this situation, and
the disastrous results of ignoring it, have not yet stunned our
Anglo-American hearts. How will we who have been called to
take the gospel to all the world cope with the dimensions of
social and cultural difference for worship in twenty-first century, multicultural America?

Most middle-class Anglo-Americans do not know how to answer that question or do not realize the complexities of what it
means to succeed in multicultural worship in their local church.
The subtleties of cultural differences call for considerations we
have never had to deal with before. We lack the understanding
we need. It is new ground we are plowing and just where you
least expect it there are hidden rocks that block our progress.

In this chapter we want to look at the issues involved for worship involving more than one cultural group. We want to un-
cover the rocks by looking at the nature of hidden value systems
at work in the multicultural situation. The chapter is intended to
give the reader a different vantage point than his or her own
culture has provided and create an attitude of caution and care

---

[2] There is an estimated 125 ethnic communities that maintain their cultural
cohesion in the U.S. as noted by Patrick Johnstone, *Operation World* (Upper
Darby, Pa.: Interserve/USA, 1993), 563–66.

[3] Population Projections Program, Population Division, U.S. Census Bureau,
Washington, D.C. 20233.

as we set about meeting the challenge of multicultural worship in the U.S. during the twenty-first century.

The Subtlety of Cultural Differences

I was in an Anglo church once where a number of Japanese attended the services faithfully. They were wonderful people and were very well accepted by the rest of the congregation that, though a small number of other nationalities were present, was led by middle-class Anglo-Americans. There were intercultural aspects to the church services in the way of readings, drama, and music. There was even an ethnomusicologist among the leadership. The Anglos were well aware of the mixture of the group and sought to make everyone feel welcome. Everything seemed to be going well.

But one day the Japanese asked if they could have their own worship service and still be a part of the other functions of the church. This was shocking to the Anglos who saw their church as truly intercultural. Why did they want to separate for worship? The existing worship services were exceptional. Isn't the body of Christ one? Yes, but the fulfillment of the inner need to worship God takes different forms and expressions for those of different cultures, especially for first generation immigrants. The church remained a multicultural church but one with two congregations and regular combined celebrations. In this arrangement, authentic worship for both the Japanese and the Anglos was expressed and the Word of God was preached in a manner relevant within their respective cultural value systems.

This example is not intended to say that combined, multicultural worship is not possible. Stephen Rhodes gives the detailed example of the church that he pastors in Fairfax County, Virginia. The Culmore United Methodist Church is truly multicultural in its congregation and staff.[4] But there are

---

[4] Steven Rhodes, *Where the Nations Meet: The Church in a Multicultural World* (Downers Grove, Ill.: Intercultural, 1998), 11–14. See also Kathy Black, *Culturally Conscious Worship* (St. Louis: Chalice, 2000), 4–5.

considerations for this challenge in regard to worship that must be taken into account, as set forth in this chapter, if this experience is to be a success.

One major consideration is the fact that the subtle differences of other cultures or subcultures are often masked by our search for similarities as Westerners. We move among these cultures as if we were deaf and blind; we have no perception of the real differences at hand.[5] This is revealed by advice given to those going on a short-term missions trip. People come home from these trips saying things like, "love is the universal language," or "they are just like we are," or yet, "we are all the same in God's family."

These observations may go beyond differences in dress or greetings but they are still based on perceived similarities in behavior. We see that the host people are friendly and extend extraordinary hospitality. They smile and seem to enjoy our conversation. Even out in the bush they provide a great meal. They sing our translated church hymns. Mothers care for their children and fathers build houses so everything seems very much as it ought to be. We see similarities since we are not attuned to look for differences and we come away, saying, "People are basically the same all over the world."

These are observations of behavior, the most superficial level of culture. Edward Hall says it this way, "Culturally-based paradigms place obstacles in the path to understanding because culture equips each of us with built-in blinders, hidden and unstated assumptions that control our thoughts and block the unraveling of cultural processes."[6] The "what" and "why" behind the behavior are not readily discerned in a short stay in another culture where we are denied an understanding of the context. Not only does our own culture keep us from seeing these differences, but the silent waters of the other culture run

[5] William Howell, "Communication Seminar" (Unpub. notes, University of Minnesota, 1964).

[6] Edward Hall, *Beyond Culture* (New York: Doubleday, 1976), 220.

deep. Specific and developed skills are needed that will bring these differences to the surface.

The questions that need to be asked have to do with what is really happening, not only with what is apparent. What does it mean? Why does that behavior make sense to them? What function does the behavior have in their community and for the maintenance of their society? These are crucial questions. More foundational still is to ask, how do they see the world and how does that influence their behavior? These questions are no less significant for intentional multicultural ministry and worship among first generational immigrants.

Western Reluctance

It is difficult for Western Christians to imagine that there may be other dimensions of the worship of God that are outside their knowledge and experience, dimensions indeed beyond their cultural capacity to experience without help. This comes from two parts of a frame of reference lodged in the Western brain that are inseparable. First is Western man's limited scientific view of the world as he assumes it to be and therefore of the nature of reality itself. Second is his ethnocentric understanding of the Bible. By assumptions concerning the world and the nature of reality, we mean a sense of the way things are, and ought to be, that is outside of consciousness and therefore to which we cannot readily imagine any alternatives. As such, this view of the world remains unexamined.

Ethnocentrism grows out of these presuppositions. By ethnocentrism here we mean an inability to conceive of the Scriptures as possibly indicating something more, or other, than we have interpreted them to mean and applied them to effect in our own cultural setting. In other words, we often read our cultural values into the Scriptures based on underlying assumptions and we tend to insist on the results for all other Christians. It is hard for us to realize that to obey and worship God in another culture may mean doing very different things than we would do in our own culture.[7] There is a certain amount of uneasiness in learning that, in this sense, our culture has deeply influenced, if not defined for us, what is appropriate worship of God.

Cultural Vantage Points of Worship

The worship of God is greater than the minds and hearts of those of one culture just as the object of our worship exceeds man himself. The worship of God is a need for every man and woman. The *Imago Dei* is not bound by cultures. However, our expressions of authentic worship are products of our culture as biblical truth has come to us through that grid. Our enculturation has limited our perspective and therefore our response. By its control of us, our culture gives us a selective perception of the possibilities for the implications and applications of the biblical text. As a result, we see or accent only certain facets of God's grandeur, power, and loving-kindness in our worship.

Other eyes from other vantage points see other facets, facets to which we are blind because they are from angles impossible for us. They emphasize biblical truths that we treat as somewhat incidental if we notice them at all. This is natural and expected, given each person's cultural frame of reference. It is one reason why people from other value systems often worship God for reasons different from those of middle-class Anglo-Americans.[8] A second reason is the deep cultural differences in the genuine expression of respect, awe, love, humility, and thanks aroused by each group's intimate knowledge of God. We should take great interest in this first reason as an opportu-

---

[7] For cross-cultural ethics in particular, see Bernard Adeney, *Strange Virtues: Ethics in a Multicultural World* (Downers Grove, Ill.: InterVarsity, 1995).

[8] For examples of these differences, see Pedrito U. Maynard-Reid, *Diverse Worship: African-American, Caribbean, and Hispanic Perspectives* (Downers Grove, Ill.: InterVarsity, 2000).

nity for us to learn from each other. The second reason demands caution because of hidden and deeply held expectations. Worship is neither "in spirit" nor "in truth" if we fill it with forms and verbiage that come from a foreign context. It must be indigenous to its own cultural context to be meaningful to the people in each situation.

Though worship is to a great degree context specific, our understanding of the person and character of God, and therefore our worship, can be expanded as we learn what our culture has withheld from us. We can also grow in our respect for different forms of authentic worship. Every ethnic group needs to become aware of other vantage points and value systems that have elicited other kinds and forms of authentic worship.

Doing this can have three results. First, we will better understand those different from ourselves in worship. Second, we will gain insight into the difficulties of adjusting to changes in worship patterns across cultural boundaries, a stressful event that I refer to as "worship shock." And last, this awareness has the potential of enriching our worship, if we will let it modify our perceptions and soften our cultural boundaries. Paul-Gordon Chandler refers to Christianity expressed in other cultures as *"windows on God."* He says, "Christianity worldwide is a *divine mosaic*, with each piece being a different cultural expression of the Christian faith, and the whole portraying the beauty of God's character as perhaps nothing else can."[9] God loves the world, and we must learn to understand, respect, and welcome the cultural diversity of it.

To approach the topic of cultural expressions in the worship of God, we will have to look at some of the underlying issues of intercultural understanding. At the outset, two things must be said to set the stage. First of all, it must be clear that worship is indeed culturally defined and controlled, as surprising as that statement will be to most conservative evangelicals. Second,

---

[9] Paul-Gorden Chandler, *God's Global Mosaic: What We Can Learn from Christians Around the World* (Downers Grove, Ill.: InterVarsity, 2000), 17, 19.

our ethnocentrism has left us with a skeleton in the closet. We, as North Americans, have demonstrated in our taking Christianity to "all nations" that we think our ways of worship are the only ways to do it. There has been a general trespassing on other cultures by our well-intentioned missionary efforts at bringing the Good News to the lost and training disciples and leaders of the newly formed churches in those contexts. We have exported our culture with the gospel. From 1800 to 1950, churches on the mission field were shaped after the model of the expatriate sending churches, including forms of church government, evangelism, and, of course, worship. These were, as the Willowbank Report has it, "exported and unimaginatively introduced into the new mission-founded churches."[10]

It was natural for the new Christians to assume that these patterns were God's way, having received them along with the gospel from the missionaries God sent to them. These were the methods and forms that the missionary saw as the most biblical and most effective in his home country. We must be careful not to take the same attitude toward worship in the multicultural U.S., especially when dealing with first generational immigrants.

The Nature of Culture and Its Affect on Worship

To talk about the affect of culture on worship, we need a working definition and an idea of the purpose of culture. There are many definitions of culture. I want to suggest for our purpose here that culture is *a learned and shared, integrated system of values, beliefs, and assumptions for understanding, coping with, and relating to the world, which results in behavior that is characteristic of a group of people and a personal and social identity for the members of that group.*

---

[10] *The Willowbank Report*, report of the 1978 consultation on "Gospel and Culture," sponsored by the Lausanne Committee for World Evangelization and conducted in Willowbank, Somerset Bridge, Bermuda.

But why do cultures exist? Here we see God's hand on the concept of culture for human beings. Cultures are systems of solutions for coping with the common problems and needs for survival and relating to perceived reality. It was God's design, when he created man and woman, to set up certain rules for their social organization and their relationship to the world around them (Gen. 1:27–30; 2:8–17). These rules were for man's good. After the Fall, further rules were necessary for mankind to survive amid the effects of the curse (3:16–24). More complex social systems of solutions came into force as mankind grew in numbers and groups became separated by geography (4:16–22) and later languages (11:1–9), which appears to be God's preference for man (cf. 10:32). Since that time, man has been preoccupied with the search for solutions not only for survival but also for the enjoyment of life.

How to stay right with the supernatural has been a concern of man from the beginning and in all cultures. We see this throughout secular anthropology as well as in the Bible. It is one of the five social institutions found in all cultures, though it is given varying degrees of functional load for the maintenance of each society.[11] Even the denial of God or of his authority is in response to this problem. For that person the solution for staying right with the supernatural is to deny that he or it exists. It is this need and its solution that is expressed in the false religious beliefs in any culture as well as in the true worship of God in any culture. But commonness of need and even the true worship of God do not result in sameness of form and expression, if the cultural frame of reference is different.[12]

A myriad of factors separate one culture from another, and

---

[11] See Steven Grunlan and Marvin Mayers, *Cultural Anthropology: A Christian Perspective*, 2d ed. (Grand Rapids: Zondervan, 1988), 219–26; and David Filbeck, *Social Context and Proclamation* (Pasadena, Calif.: William Carey Library, 1985), 23–43.

[12] The implications for generational and social class differences in these pages is evident since these cases represent similar differences in cultural frames of reference.

these factors shape the characteristics and behavior of the people in each culture. This means that they necessarily affect the worship of God and a personal response to the person and works of God.[13] Though these factors are grouped and labeled differently by various cultural anthropologists, the terminology and research is beginning to congeal around some twenty to twenty-five major differences, each having hundreds of individual aspects. These major differences are on continua between extremes and can have various behavioral outcomes so that a culture cannot be labeled precisely but rather must be described. These various areas of difference can be grouped within the broad domains of values, beliefs, and assumptions about the nature of reality.

Values (what is good, appropriate, beneficial) and beliefs (what is true or possible) are closer to the surface and are more easily verbalized by the individual. Assumptions, however, are more subtle. For the most part they are unconsciously held and therefore unquestioned. These presuppositions concerning reality underlie the values and beliefs of a culture and make up their worldview. That worldview was absorbed from the person's surroundings at an early age and is shaped by various influences within a larger system that may have been dominated, for example, by Confucianism,[14] science and materialism,[15] or animism.[16] When by grace through faith God

---

[13] Kathy Black, *Handbook: Worship Across Cultures* (Nashville: Abingdon, 1998), studies distinctive worship behaviors for each of twenty-one groups in America.

[14] Tsu-Kung Chuang, "Shang-di: God from the Chinese Perspective," in *The Global God: Multicultural Evangelical Views of God,* ed. Aida B. Spencer and William D. Spenser (Grand Rapids: Baker, 1998), 189–206.

[15] Edward C. Stewart and Milton J. Bennett, *American Cultural Patterns: A Cross-Cultural Perspective* (Yarmouth, Maine: Intercultural, 1991).

[16] Tokunbo Adeyemo, "Unapproachable God: The High God of African Traditional Religion," in *The Global God: Multicultural Evangelical Views of God,* ed. A. B. Spencer and W. D. Spenser (Grand Rapids: Baker, 1998), 127–45; and idem, "The God Above Tradition Who Speaks to All Traditions: An African (Ghanaian) Perspective," in ibid., 146–65.

breaks into the life of an individual, he or she sees God through a certain cultural frame of reference. People cannot do otherwise.

It is hard to exaggerate the importance of culture for human existence. People are not aware of it, but they depend on their cultural system for their survival and as a map to find their way through each day. Their culture gives them a sense of personal and social identity. The system is not optional. People do not select one of many that might appeal to them, nor do they easily trade theirs for another except on the most superficial levels. Separation from one's culture causes a sense of personal disorientation, which we refer to as "culture shock."

Culture and God's Word in Worship

God reveals himself and the true nature of reality in his Word. People, however, are predisposed to see this truth through their cultural categories and to apply it to their lives within their cultural system. God always related to people within their cultural context in the Bible and that makes understanding that original culture important to interpretation today, but he does not ask men and women to change cultures in order to know him and worship him. It is important to understand, however, that people bring their culture with them into their relationship with God and to their understanding of the Bible. They do not realize it, but this causes them to read through eyes that are predetermined to see certain things, certain implications and applications.

As we have said, people tend to read their own cultural beliefs and values, and therefore their cultural applications, into the Scriptures. A culture that is more person oriented than task oriented and more collective than individualistic will tend to value generosity more than frugality and social obligation more than personal independence. For instance, they will see this emphasis in and have far less difficulty applying Philippians 2:5–8, which was discussed in the introduction of this book.

The same is true in forms of worship, as we will see in the comparisons appearing later. One wonders how much of this is God's intention in order that we might have a fuller, richer understanding of himself. Is it possible that he expects us to learn from each other?

A problem we face as we look at the relationship of revelation and culture is that understanding culture and how it works and insight into cultural differences has been limited to formal anthropological and missiological studies. This leads to a good deal of apprehension concerning the validity of the findings for Christian ministry. Terms such as "cultural relativity" and "dynamic equivalence" may bring fear or suspicion to evangelicals who have not studied in these fields, even when other evangelicals use the terms. It sounds like we may be sneaking into the fold with ideas of moral relativity or situational ethics. Yet the correct use of these concepts is essential for cross-cultural ministry and central to understanding worship on a global scale. These areas of understanding must be explained for evangelical Christianity to begin to appreciate cultural themes in ministry and worship other than their own.

In the instance of the term "cultural relativity," for example, it must be said that by a correct use of the concept, we mean the realization that any behavior finds its real meaning and purpose only within its own cultural context. The legitimate use of cultural relativity, then, is interpretive, not evaluative. It cannot tell you if a behavior is right or wrong, only what it means to the people who practice it. When it is used to evaluate the moral or ethical dimension of an activity, it is an abuse of the concept. It has no standard.

The Bible, on the other hand, when interpreted correctly, *is* evaluative. It does tell us if a behavior is right or wrong, beneficial or detrimental. It does not, however, intend to tell us what a particular behavior means to the people who practice it today. For example, it does not tell us why Christians from Asia see North American Christian homes for the elderly and retirement communities as a shameful flaw of American Christianity. Nor does it tell us why Christians from Africa question the morality of American Christians who do not have children or limit their "family" to only two. The meaning behind these behaviors is relative to the cultural values of U.S. middle-class Anglos. The same kinds of culture-driven values surround worship and can lead to misunderstanding.

Cultural Expressions of Worship

It is necessary to compare cultural contexts to see what they each bring to the evangelical act of authentic worship. For this we will need to call on the interpretive use of cultural relativity or we will be left with our own ethnocentrism for understanding what the various behaviors of other cultures in the act of worship mean. We will compare first generation immigrants or visitors from other cultures to the U.S. American, white, middle class and see what can be learned from the contrasts.

The Use of Silence

For the first comparison we will look at the use of silence. To the American, silence may mean various things. It may mean it is your turn to talk in a conversation. It may mean the other person in a discussion is clueless. It may be interpreted as anger during an argument. Lulls in a worship service may be interpreted as a poorly organized program or as something going wrong, perhaps with the sound system.

For a very context-oriented Asian group such as the Japanese, however, silence is of central importance, conveying respect and unity in their worship of God and harmony and empathy in their relations with each other in the body of Christ. This is in contrast to a hand-clapping, chorus-singing activity and verbally oriented Anglo-American group that would find the use of silence ineffective or even boring in the worship service and of little value in relationships at all. Japanese worship is more intuitive, while Anglo-American worship in general is more demonstrative. Anglo-American worship, however, is not nearly as demonstrative as Black-American or Hispanic-American worship.

We feel it is right to say that we can learn from each other, but even while admitting this, the U.S. American would feel bored in a Japanese worship service, while the Japanese would feel that Western worship is somewhat disrespectful and perhaps annoying. Silence can convey deep feelings of respect and honor for God as well as express dependency and obligation for an Asian person, a deep aspect of worship.[17] The North American evangelical might prefer choruses with raised and swaying hands as the heart of worship. Not that Asians do not sing. They do and very well. But they have a dimension to their worship missed by the Western Christian because this use of silence is not a value in Western culture. In the U.S., personal achievement rather than personal honor, equality rather than respect for royalty, and independence rather than social obligation give us a very different approach to corporate worship that does not call for silence and sets us apart from the Asian Christian.

Silence can mean more than no speech. Asians find, for example, the North American use of prayer as a "curtain closer" so worship teams can get in place and equipment made ready, an offensive and disrespectful activity. Silence before God, especially in prayer, expresses our infinite obligation to him in his greatness and requires the cessation of movement as well as of speech. The corporate aspect of the worship service can be equally different. A silent bow conveying respect and giving honor to the person next to the Japanese is difficult to replace with a noisy round of "greet your neighbor" from the informal

---

[17] Satoshi Ishii and Tom Bruneau, "Silence and Silences in Cross-Cultural Perspective: Japan and the United States," in *Intercultural Communication: A Reader*, 7th ed., ed. Larry A Samovar and Richard E. Porter (New York: Wadsworth, 1994), 246–51. Sheila Ramsey, "Interactions Between North Americans and Japanese," in *Basic Concepts of Intercultural Communication* (Yarmouth, Maine: Intercultural, 1998), 111–30.

Anglo-American worship time. Similarly, applauding special music is out of order for the traditional Japanese.

Silence is only one aspect of the high-context cultures of Asia. Erwin McDaniel mentions ten other aspects of nonverbal behavior and what they communicate in the way of group orientation, hierarchy, social balance, formality, humility, in-group orientation and affinity, social harmony, perseverance and sacrifice, collectivism, and empathy for the Japanese.[18] Most of these, if not all, affect personal and corporate worship directly.

Values on High and Low Context

We need to look at the values of high or low context in more detail regarding various cultures to see what the barriers are to understanding and learning from each other in the area of worship. A value on high context means most of the meaning is in people and their shared values. They depend on circumstances, situation, and nonverbal behavior for the main thrust of their communication. Verbal messages are indirect and add to the overall message but are undecipherable on their own. A value on low context means people depend on the verbal message in communication, and nonverbal context and behavior provide a limited analog background for the more binary, linear, and objective use of words.[19]

Most of the rest of the world is high context in their communication values, while mainly Western Europe and North America are low in their value on context. East Asian cultures seem to have the highest value on context in communication. Indian, African, Arab, and Latin American cultures are also

---

[18] E. McDaniel, "Nonverbal Communication: A Reflection of Cultural Themes," in *Intercultural Communication: A Reader,* 8th ed., ed. L. A. Samovar and R. E. Porter (Belmont, Calif.: Wadsworth, 1997), 257–65.

[19] Edward Hall first brought these concepts to public attention in his works *Beyond Culture* (New York: Anchor Books, 1989) and *The Silent Language* (New York: Anchor Books, 1990).

high, but may not be as formal in their expressions of the value as in Japan, Korea, Thailand, and Taiwan. One of the countries with the least dependence on context in communication is Germany with the United States not far behind.[20] It is evident that these two values, high context and low context, in communication and relations would affect forms of worship. Yet this is only one of many factors.

The following major contrasts between high-context and low-context people are adapted from Richard Porter and Larry Samovar, Edward Hall, and Bernie Harder.[21] First, verbal messages are extremely important in low-context cultures. Nearly all the information to be given is encoded in verbal symbols. It is not readily available from the objective or subjective environment since low-context cultures do not learn to perceive much information in this way. The result is a somewhat wordy communication.

Second, people in high-context cultures perceive people from low-context cultures, who rely on the verbal transmission of information, as less attractive and less credible. To the Japanese for example, "Language tends to be distrusted for establishing truth."[22] People from high-context cultures, on the other hand, are perceived as evasive, ambiguous, and uninformed by those of low-context cultures. This is because they cannot hear the main thrust of the communication.

---

[20] Edward Stewart and Milton Bennett, *American Cultural Patterns: A Cross-Cultural Perspective* (Yarmouth, Maine: Intercultural, 1991), 45–60, but esp. 153–61. See also Richard E. Porter and Larry A. Samovar, "An Introduction to Intercultural Communication," in *Intercultural Communication: A Reader,* 8th ed., ed. L. A Samovar and R. E. Porter (New York: Wadsworth, 1997), 24.

[21] Porter and Samovar, "An Introduction to Intercultural Communication," 5–26. Edward Hall, *Beyond Culture* (New York: Anchor Books, 1989). Bernie Harder, "Weaving Cultural Values on the Loom of Language," *Media Development* (March 1989): 25–28.

[22] Masao Kunihiro, "US-Japan Communications," in *Discord in the Pacific: Challenges to the Japanese-American Alliance,* ed. H. Rosovsky, (Washington, D.C.: Columbia, 1972), 97.

Third, people in high-context cultures are more adept at reading nonverbal behavior and the environment. They are more conscious of shared values, feelings, and attitudes in a more formal culture. In the fourth place, people in high-context cultures expect others to perceive a great deal of information from the context and therefore do not speak as much as people from low-context cultures. This style produces the tendency to distrust wordy communication. Last, in low-context cultures the *speaker* is more responsible for meaning (creating meaning in the receiver through the explicit transfer of information), while in high-context cultures the *receiver* is more responsible for meaning (reading the intended meaning from existing or created context). It is easy to see the confusion and misunderstanding this can bring to a combined worship service.

Individualism and Collectivism

Another comparison that illustrates the theme is the major polarization between cultures that are collective and those that are individualistic. Collective cultures are more people and event oriented as opposed to individualistic cultures, which tend toward task and time orientations. This is a major difference between Western and non-Western cultures. The United States is the most individualist of the forty countries studied by Geert Hofstede.[23] Some of the cultures strongest in collectivism are those found in Africa, Asia, and Latin America.

Collective people have a loyalty to the group that defines their behavior. Worship and prayer as a large group is very important to them. The value is not on numbers as an indicator of the success of the program but as a factor indicating the

---

[23] The terms *individualistic* and *collective* are used widely by cultural anthropologists. See Geert Hofstede, *Culture's Consequences* (Newbury Park, Calif.: Sage, 1984), 171–74. For time and event orientations and task and person orientations, see Sherwood G. Lingenfelter and Marvin K. Mayers, *Ministering Cross-Culturally* (Grand Rapids: Baker, 1986), 37–51 and 81–94, respectively.

success for inclusiveness. The group is needed and people are dependent on it. Small group fellowship for prayer, for example, is not as important, while people missing at the large event is a serious concern.

Individualistic cultures enjoy large groups, too, but for different reasons; and even though it is a large group, it is a large group of independent, self-reliant people. This is still called corporate worship since the people are all together in one room, but relationships are less dependent and more superficial. There are always some people missing from the meeting. This is considered normal in the medium-sized and larger churches. Small groups designated for prayer or Bible study become necessary to promote the feelings of social belonging and mutual care desperately needed by the larger, highly individualistic congregation. The effects on worship are evident. For the most part, the highly individualist people are not sharing the experience. They are simply doing it together in the same place.

Individualism makes people self-centered rather than focused on others. American Christians have to work at being God-centered in their lives since their whole culture is concerned with the self. This is an issue in worship, and a lot of effort is expended to help middle-class, Anglo-Americans focus on God for the duration of a worship service. There is a tendency to mix concern for self and focusing on God so that what people do in worship is not altogether based on who God is but is combined with how the individual is doing.

Individualism has a second characteristic that affects worship. It makes true humility and reverence more difficult to achieve. This is in contrast to many peoples around the world. Russian Christians, for example, never seem to lose their perspective in worship, never seem to lose their sense of awe for who God is and the mystery of his greatness.[24] It is little wonder that the Eastern Orthodox Church has taken and maintained the forms it has. Evangelicals may argue points of doctrine

---

[24] Chandler, *God's Global Mosaic*, 21–40.

and form with them, but we cannot argue against their reverence, humility, and awe in the worship of God.

Time and Event Orientations

When people are event oriented, as they are in most of the
countries of Africa[25] and South America,[26] the U.S. American
visitor notices the difference immediately. Though they may find
that change fascinating at first, church services that never start
or end at any predictable time eventually become a nuisance to
the North American. Collective values and event orientation often
go together since being with the other people is more important
than watching the clock. What is happening and with whom it is
happening is more important than when it starts or how long it
lasts. Worship can go on and on. Cutting the service off abruptly
because the clock says so is unsettling to say the least.

Time is a major concern, however, for the pastor or worship
leader in the West. It would be inconsiderate to ignore the
concerns of the congregation for their schedules. For some in
the West, because they are future and goal oriented and see
time in a linear fashion, what happens next and when it will get
started can be more important than what is happening now.
Non-Western people see this as disruptive and disrespectful for
worship.

Monochronic and Polychronic People

Another value orientation that goes along with these differences is the polarization between people who are monochronic

---

[25] Thomas M. Stallter, "An Orientation to Intercultural Ministry in the Central African Republic and Chad" (D.Miss. dissertation, Western Seminary,
Portland, Ore., 1993), 18, 176, 195–97.

[26] Felicity Houghton, "Some Reflections on the Meaning and Practice of
Worship from Inside South America," *Worship: Adoration and Action,* ed. D. A.
Carson (Grand Rapids: Baker, 1993), 158–68.

and those who are polychronic.[27] Monochronic people are generally from the West and prefer to do one thing at a time in an orderly fashion. Polychronic people from Latin America, the Middle East, Africa, Native American tribes, etc., feel no confusion with many things happening at the same time. A practical result would be that Africans, in an authentic situation, would not need to close the doors or have a nursery in order to have an effective worship time with the group. They are not frustrated by delays, sudden changes, or interruptions in the program and enjoy a certain spontaneity in the music and dancing.

Communication Styles

Styles of communication affect worship styles directly. As Stewart and Bennett show, some cultures are more referential in their style, such as the Germans, depending on technical information and logical reasoning. Some are more expressive in their style as are Russians. Some are more emotional as are the Latinos and Africans. Anglo-Americans are very persuasive and more direct in their style, using a referential style to support them as they seek to convince others of their point of view. Japanese are excellent in the use of a very indirect phatic style in communication to nurture relations.[28] Cultures use their dominant style of communication in worship. Other styles are not authentic to them and therefore seem foreign and are uncomfortable for them. This obviously affects the entire worship service in any particular cultural setting as people express themselves to God.

Other cultural values that affect worship concern tolerance

---

[27] See discussions on monochronic time and polychronic time by Hall, *Beyond Culture*, 17–24; and idem, *The Silent Language* (New York: Anchor Books, 1990).
[28] Information here is adapted from E. Stewart and M. Bennett, *American Cultural Patterns: A Cross-Cultural Perspective* (Yarmouth, Maine: Intercultural, 1991), 154.

for ambiguity as opposed to uncertainty avoidance,[29] dicho-
tomistic or holistic thinking styles, positive or negative feelings about exposing personal vulnerability,[30] values concerning
power distance and masculinity,[31] and feelings concerning formal, informal, or technical behavior as the societal norm.[32]
There is a good deal of secular research in these areas that
Christians can apply to differences in the act and attitude of
worship. Of these we want to address only behavior styles
here.

Behavior Styles

Cultures characterized by formal behavior have tradition-
ally prescribed ways of doing things. There are rules for behavior so that an individual can know in any circumstance
what is expected of him. In informal cultures, there are only
general expectations with a wide range of possibilities for
behavior that will be more or less acceptable. People cannot
state the rules as such in an informal society, and there is
some anxiety over the uncertainty of what to do or what one
has done in certain situations. Technical behavior is found in
written codes. Military life is a form of technical behavior as is
driving a car.

Worship is directly affected by the individual's dominant cultural behavior style. Christians from a Muslim cultural background, for example, whether they were Muslims or not, have
difficulty relating to the informal style of U.S. Americans. Asia
contains many formal cultures such as the Thai who find U.S.
American informality irreverent. Even animistic cultures from

---

[29] It is well established in literature that non-Western cultures have a greater
tolerance for ambiguity and even prefer it to logical structure and reasoning
in expressing themselves since that seems to distort reality. Hofstede, *Culture's
Consequences*, 110–47.

[30] See Lingenfelter and Mayers, *Ministering Cross-Culturally*, 53–67, 105–16.

[31] See Hofstede, *Culture's Consequences*, 65–105.

[32] See Hall, *The Silent Language*, 123.

around the "two-thirds world," such as in Malaysia[33] and Africa[34] are more formal and have prescribed ways of approaching God in worship and respecting others in the collective act. Some cultures actually tend toward technical behavior patterns. The Thai have a cultural rule book that the children have to study in early school years. The Germans take technical behavior in their culture more seriously than other formal cultures, appreciating exactitude in the way things ought to happen. They often do not find enough content and structure in the Anglo-American worship service.

Culture and Worship Shock

Cultures are made up of integrated systems of thousands of values, beliefs, and assumptions. The deepest of these are learned unconsciously in the cultural setting as a child grows up. Because of this, these deeper assumptions and beliefs do not make up what he or she defines the world to be like but rather the way the world is. Communication, what worship is made of, is affected by most of these as part of that system. The words, sounds, and forms of worship are selected and used according to each person's personal and culturally defined mental list of possible and most appropriate meanings or what we call their "personal perception set." Change is resisted when it is outside the possibilities or the appropriateness of this personal perception set. Being integrated as they are, changing a value for behavior in one area of the culture affects the system in other areas so that understanding the resistance to such change becomes rather complex. This can be seen in change regarding worship because it is a strongly culturally defined experience.

---

[33] Carl A. Reed, "Toward a Contextualized Worship Among the Dyaks of West Kalimantan, Indonesia" (Th.M. thesis, Grace Theological Seminary, 1990), 74–90.

[34] Stallter, "An Orientation to Intercultural Ministry," 123–62.

Authentic worship involves an individual's deepest experiences, the expression of which must be completely relevant to the cultural values that have shaped him or her or it does not have purpose. An obligatory change of behavior in this area of a person's life can be extremely unsettling, disturbing the appropriate way to approach God from his or her cultural frame of reference. The individual may not be able to identify all the reasons he or she feels such a resistance, making his or her response basically an emotional one and hard to verbalize. For this person worship has become dissonant and confusing. What is "normal," "natural," or "appropriate" no longer works and no longer makes sense to the people around him or her. Long-term frustration of expectations in worship can wear a people down and they may seem to become unreasonable to those around them. They may withdraw in an effort to escape the new values being thrust upon them. It is also possible that they would become aggressive, seeking to reassert their own values of worship.

For a person immersing himself in another culture, this is part of the larger experience of culture shock.[35] We often fail to recognize this "worship shock" in people of other ethnic groups when they come into our Anglo churches. Rather, we expect them to worship as we do or to adjust to our way of worship if we notice theirs is different. We rationalize that, after all, the worship of God among evangelical Christians in the world is universal. God is the same in every culture, as are the truths of his Word concerning which we worship him. However, the perception of God and his Word or in what is an appropriate response or worship style and feelings about that go as deep as culture itself.

---

[35] Adrian Furnham and Stephen Bochner, *Culture Shock: Psychological Reactions to Unfamiliar Environments* (London: Methuen, 1986). Marge Jones with E. Grant Jones, *Psychology of Missionary Adjustment* (Springfield, Miss.: Logion, 1995). Kelly O'Donnell and Michele O'Donnell, eds., *Helping Missionaries Grow: Readings in Mental Health and Missions* (Pasadena, Calif.: William Carey Library, 1988).

Why did the Japanese want their own worship service? A better question might be, how could they not want their own worship service? All but the most flexible people or those seriously attempting to adjust to another culture are driven by their need to be authentic in their enculturation, if they are to worship in spirit and truth. This can become a complex issue in a multicultural setting requiring a great deal of understanding and consideration. Insisting on one cultural worship style for someone from a different cultural background is to be insensitive to how God has formed each person in his or her own cultural setting.

The ethics of insisting that *others change to be like one's self* in the matter of worship are yet to be considered in future studies. One consideration that must come to the fore in the subject is that God values human cultures as adequate vehicles for his Word and work. Although they all have sin and inadequacies, God never deals with people outside their general cultural framework. If God works with people within their cultural systems, then we are bound to conclude that they are adequate vehicles for his praise and adoration as well. A second consideration is the fact of God's intention for each individual to have been enculturated in his or her specific situation. He forms each individual, and his or her cultural background is part of his plan for them.

Conclusion

The church began with a sermon by Peter to those of *"every nation under heaven"* (Acts 2:1–12). It was important to God that a number of cultures be represented. They would each take the news announced back to their own people. They did not have to learn a new language to understand the message. They each heard in their own tongue, and in a way that made sense to them. God respected the language barrier so they would understand what they heard even if they did not yet understand all the implications of that message.

Language is at the heart of culture. Communication is more than just vocabulary and grammar. People also think in their language in a way that fits their conceptual framework and personal perception set. The relationship of language to culture has been a major discussion in cultural anthropological circles, with some saying it shapes a culture, defining the categories people have available to them for thinking.[36] But, as important as it is, language is not enough. One cannot fully communicate with those of another culture without an understanding of their culture.

The miracle of God in Acts 2 is more than just a language miracle. It respects each person's culture. It provided for each person to get a clear understanding of Peter's message and then to go back to his or her respective national group and contextualize that message within his or her own cultural situation. Those who became believers in Jesus through this supernatural act of God undoubtedly began to worship him. Are we to suppose that they all worshiped him in the same manner?

If the message of Christ was intended for a culturally diverse group the first day it was preached, and if those cultural distinctions are maintained at the end (see Rev. 5:9–10; 7:9–10), then we can expect cultural diversity today and must show the same respect for it. We must begin to see a beauty in it and learn from each other what we may have missed on our own concerning the nature and works of God.

So what are the implications for multicultural worship? How we can design and maintain multicultural worship in the U.S. is another subject of lengthy study. I only want to say here that multicultural worship is possible, enjoyable, and a rich experience when the situation is right for it and leaders are sensitive to the cultural variables involved. It can be a strong message of God's love for the world (John 17:20–23). Unfortunately, it often ends

---

[36] See Benjamin Lee Whorf, "Science and Linguistics," in *Basic Concepts of Intercultural Communication,* ed. Milton Bennett (Yarmouth, Maine: Intercultural, 1998).

up disregarding the less dominant or less direct group, or in its radical form, disregards the host culture in favor of the diverse group, or at times disregards everyone's culture. In this last case, each group in the gathering can only relate to a few fragments of the worship service since the rest of it relates to other groups. Motives are also a concern. Mixed worship can never be based on romantic feelings or a need for self-fulfillment and success. Any attempt should not be without cultural awareness training for the whole church.

A bicultural or tricultural church with separate worship for each group can be more practical and relevant for all in many cases. With this, however, there must be times of common celebration and meals together that maintain the unity of the whole body amid the diversity of the cultures involved. This is important so that the world may know that God sent Jesus and that he loves them (John 17:20–23). Separate worship with common celebrations can maintain unity without forcing people to be like each other or to submit to irrelevancies, while still providing the opportunity to learn from each other.

For a truly multicultural church of more than three cultures, separate worship is nearly impossible and probably undesirable. These are churches that come about in extremely multicultural situations such as in Steven Rhodes's situation in Fairfax County. They are more easily grown than developed from existing mono-cultural churches. The people who attend may be attracted be-cause they know it is multicultural and they will be welcome. Some have nowhere else to go. Sometimes they choose the diverse set-ting because it more nearly matches the world they live in from day to day, a mixture of value systems. It is a world they have come to call their own. This effort is different from a romantic idea of a culturally mixed worship service. It is a real world solution. How deeply each cultural group feels that the organized worship ex-presses their deepest feelings and desires for God depends on the person and on the diversity and level of cultural sensitivity of church leadership. It may not be ideal for everyone present but the essen-tial element is Christ at the center.

As the body of Christ, we can celebrate our differences and learn from each other that which our own cultural vantage point has withheld from us. Conversion to Christ must not also mean conversion to the evangelist's culture. We can maintain our biblically scrutinized, cultural distinctions in worship without feelings of guilt or inferiority. In seeking unity, we must not ignore the legitimacy of Christianity within cultural systems other than our own. It is deeper than a discussion of liking one style more than another. It is not a matter of inflexibility, defensiveness, or the weaker brother. It is a matter of deep cultural values, of authenticity before God, of truly worshiping in spirit and truth. These are things we should seek to preserve for each other while promoting appreciation, respect, love, and unity in the body of Christ in creative ways. Preserving these *is* to love one another and reflect authentic worship.

Select Bibliography

Although not exhaustive, the following bibliography provides a list of books for those who wish to read or study further aspects of worship.

References for Church Libraries

Historical Surveys on Worship

Brown, Paul B. *In and for the World: Bringing the Contemporary into Christian Worship*. Minneapolis: Fortress, 1992.

Maxwell, William D. *A History of Christian Worship: An Outline of Its Development and Forms*. Grand Rapids: Baker, 1936.

White, James F. *A Brief History of Christian Worship*. Nashville: Abingdon, 1993.

———. *Christian Worship in North America, A Retrospective (1955–1995)*. Nashville: Abingdon, 1997.

———. *Christian Worship in Transition*. New York: Abingdon, 1976.

———. *Protestant Worship: Traditions in Transition*. Lousville: Westminster John Knox, 1989.

Wilkens, Michael J., and Terence Paige, eds. *Worship, Theology and Ministry of the Early Church: Essays in Honor of Ralph P. Martin. Journal for the Study of the New Testament* Supplement Series 87. Sheffield, England: Sheffield Academic, 1992.

General Works

Berkey, Jim, ed. *Leadership Handbooks of Practical Theology*, 3 vols. Grand Rapids: Baker, 1992. Vol. 3: *Word and Worship*.

Davis, J. G. *The New Westminster Dictionary of Liturgy and Worship*. Philadelphia: Westminster, 1986.

Stake, Donald Wilson. *The ABCs of Worship: A Concise Dictionary*. Louisville: Westminster John Knox, 1992.

Webber, Robert W. *The Complete Library of Christian Worship*, 7 vols. Nashville: Star Song, 1993.

White, James F. *Introduction to Christian Worship*. Nashville: Abingdon, 1990.

———. *Documents of Christian Worship: Descriptive and Interpretive*. Louisville: Westminster John Knox, 1992.

The Object of Our Worship

Biblical Studies

Hill, Andrew E. *Enter His Courts with Praise: Old Testament Worship for the New Testament Church*. Grand Rapids: Baker, 1993.

Lindsay, Dennis R. "What Is Truth? Ἀλήθεια in the Gospel of John." *ResQ* 35 (1993): 129–45.

Miller, Patrick D. *They Cried to the Lord: The Form and Theology of Biblical Prayer*. Minneapolis: Fortress, 1994.

Peterson, David. *Engaging with God: A Biblical Theology of Worship*. Grand Rapids: Eerdmans, 1992.

Stuart, Streeter S. "A New Testament Perspective on Worship." *EQ* 68 (1996): 209–21.

Vogels, Walter. "Review of the Life of Moses: The Yahwist as Historian in Exodus-Numbers, by John Van Seters." *Studies in Religion* 26.2 (1997): 227–28.

General Works

Carson, D. A., ed. *Worship: Adoration and Action*. Grand Rapids: Baker, 1993.

Dawn, Marva J. *Reaching Out Without Dumbing Down: A Theology of Worship for the Turn-of-the-Century Culture*. Grand Rapids: Eerdmans, 1995.

——. *A Royal "Waste" of Time: The Splendor of Worshiping God and Being Church for the World.* Grand Rapids: Eerdmans, 1999.

Frame, John M. *Worship in Spirit and Truth.* Phillipsburg, N.J.: Presbyterian and Reformed, 1996.

Green, Robin. *Intimate Mystery: Our Need to Worship.* Cambridge, Mass.: Cowley, 1988.

Hayford, Jack W. *Worship His Majesty.* Waco: Word, 1987.

Helyer, Larry R. *Yesterday, Today and Forever: The Continuing Relevance of the Old Testament.* Salem, Wis.: Sheffield, 1996.

Liesch, Barry. *People in the Presence of God: Models and Directions for Worship.* Grand Rapids: Zondervan, 1988.

Martin, Ralph P. *The Worship of God: Some Theological, Pastoral, and Practical Reflections.* Grand Rapids: Eerdmans, 1982.

McMinn, Don. *Entering His Presence: Experiencing the Joy of True Worship.* South Plainsfield, N.J.: Bridge, 1986.

Poythress, Vern S. *The Shadow of Christ in the Law of Moses.* Phillipsburg, N. J.: Presbyterian and Reformed, 1991.

Saliers, Don E. *Worship and Spirituality.* Philadelphia: Westminster, 1984.

——. *Worship as Theology: Foretaste of Glory Divine.* Nashville: Abingdon, 1994.

——. *Worship Comes to Its Senses.* Nashville: Abingdon, 1996.

Torrance, James B. *Worship, Community and the Triune God of Grace.* Downers Grove, Ill.: InterVarsity, 1996.

Wainwright, Geoffrey. *Doxology: The Praise of God in Worship, Doctrine and Life.* New York: Oxford University Press, 1980.

Webber, Robert E. *Worship Old and New.* Rev. ed. Grand Rapids: Zondervan, 1994.

Forms of Worship

Benedict, Daniel, and Craig Kennet Miller. *Contemporary Worship for the 21st Century: Worship or Evangelism?* Nashville: Discipleship Resources, 1994.

Harper, John. *The Forms and Orders of Western Liturgy from the Tenth to the Eighteenth Century: A Historical Introduction and Guide for Students and Musicians.* Oxford: Clarendon, 1991.

Webber, Robert E. *Planning Blended Worship: The Creative Mixture of Old and New*. Nashville: Abingdon, 1998.

Expressions of Our Worship

Historical Works

Greenburg, Robert. *How to Listen to and Understand Great Music*. San Francisco: San Francisco Conservatory of Music. Audio version, Great Courses on Tape series. Springfield, Va.: The Teaching Company, 2001.

Harper, John. *The Forms and Orders of Western Liturgy from the Tenth to the Eighteenth Century: A Historical Introduction and Guide for Students and Musicians*. Oxford: Clarendon, 1991.

Wilson-Dickson, Andrew. *The Story of Christian Music from Gregorian Chant to Black Gospel: An Illustrated Guide to All Major Traditions of Music in Worship*. Minneapolis: Augsburg Fortress, 1996.

Music in Worship

Adler, Mortimer J. *Six Great Ideas*. New York: Macmillan, 1981.

Begbie, Jeremy S. *Theology, Music and Time*. Cambridge, Mass.: Cambridge University Press, 2001.

Best, Harold M. *Music Through the Eyes of Faith*. San Francisco: HarperSanFrancisco, 1993.

Edwards, Jonathan. "Praise, One of the Chief Employments of Heaven." In *The Works of Jonathan Edwards*, 2 vols. Edinburgh: Banner of Truth, 1974. 2:913–17.

Foley, Edward. *Foundations of Christian Music: The Music of Pre-Constantinian Christianity*. Collegeville, Minn.: Liturgical, 1996.

Frame, John M. *Contemporary Worship Music: A Biblical Defense*. Phillipsburg, N.J.: Presbyterian and Reformed, 1997.

Hustad, Donald P. *Jubilate! Church Music in the Evangelical Tradition*. Carol Stream, Ill.: Hope, 1980.

——. *Jubilate II: Church Music in Worship and Renewal*. Carol Stream, Ill.: Hope, 1993.

Johansson, Calvin M. *Discipling Music Ministry: Twenty–First Century Directions*. Peabody, Mass.: Hendriksen, 1992.

Jones, Ivor. *Music–A Joy Forever*. Nashville: Abingdon, 1990.

Kendall, R. T. *Before the Throne*. Nashville: Broadman and Holman, 1993.

Liesch, Barry. *The New Worship: Straight Talk on Music and the Church*. Rev. ed. Grand Rapids: Baker, 2001.

Neufeld, Bernie, ed. *Music in Worship: A Mennonite Perspective*. Waterloo, Ontario: Herald, 1998.

Orr, N. Lee. *The Church Music Handbook for Pastors and Musicians*. Nashville: Abingdon, 1991.

Ortlund, Anne. *Up with Worship*. Rev. ed. Wheaton: Regal, 1982.

Piper, John. *Desiring God*. 2d ed. Sisters, Ore.: Multnomah, 1996.

Ryken, Leland. *The Liberated Imagination*. Wheaton: Harold Shaw, 1989.

Spencer, John Michael. *Protest and Praise: Sacred Music of Black Religion*. Minneapolis: Augsburg Fortress, 1990.

———. *Sing a New Song: Liberating Black Hymnody*. Minneapolis: Augsburg Fortress, 1994.

Watson, J. R. *The English Hymn: A Critical and Historical Study*. Oxford: Clarendon, 1997.

Westermeyer, Paul. *Te Deum: The Church and Music*. Minneapolis: Fortress, 1998.

Willis, John T. *Worship and the Hebrew Bible: Essays in Honour of John T. Willis*. Edited by M. P. Graham, R. R. Marrs, and S. L. McKenzie. Sheffield England: Sheffield Academic, 1999.

Wilson-Dickson, Andrew. *The Story of Christian Music from Gregorian Chant to Black Gospel: An Illustrated Guide to All Major Traditions of Music in Worship*. Minneapolis: Augsburg Fortress, 1996.

Wright, N. T. *For All God's Worth*. Grand Rapids: Eerdmans, 1997.

The Arts in Worhip

Edwards, Brian. *Shall We Dance? Dance and Drama in Worship*. Durham, England: Evangelical, 1984.

Lewis, C. S. *Reflections on the Psalms*. New York: Harcourt Brace Jovanovich, 1958.

Veith, Gene Edward, Jr. *State of the Arts*. Wheaton: Good News, 1991.

Wolterstorff, Nicholas. *Art in Action*. Grand Rapids: Eerdmans, 1980.

Symbols: Images of Our Worship

Scripture in Worship

Bartow, Charles L. *Effective Speech Communication in Leading Worship*. Nashville: Abingdon, 1988.

Grant, Reg, and John Reed. *Telling Stories to Touch the Heart*. Wheaton: Victor, 1990.

Macleod, Donald. *Word and Sacrament: A Preface to Preaching and Worship*. Englewood Cliffs, N.J.: Prentice-Hall, 1960.

Van Olst, E. J. *The Bible and Liturgy*. Translated by J. Vriend. Grand Rapids: Eerdmans, 1991.

Baptism Spirituality

Beasley, Murray, G. R. *Baptism in the New Testament*. Grand Rapids, Eerdmans, 1962.

Bridges, Donald, and David Phypers. *The Water that Divides: The Baptismal Debate*. Downers Grove, Ill.: InterVarsity, 1977.

Cullman, Oscar. *Baptism in the New Testament*. Philadelphia: Westminster, 1950.

Green, Michael. *Baptism: Its Purpose, Practice and Power*. Downers Grove, Ill.: InterVarsity, 1987.

Kavanagh, Adam. *The Shape of Baptism: The Rite of Christian Initiation*. New York: Pueblo, 1978.

Murphey Center for Liturgical Research. *Made Not Born: New Perspectives on Christian Initiation and the Catechumenate*. Notre Dame, Ind.: University of Notre Dame Press, 1976.

Schmemann, Alexander. *Of Water and the Spirit: A Liturgical Study of Baptism*. Scarsdale, N.Y.: St. Vladimir's Seminary Press, 1974.

Stookey, Laurence Hall. *Baptism: Christ's Acts with the Church*. Nashville: Abingdon, 1993.

Thurian, Max, and Geoffrey Wainwright, eds. *Baptism and Eucharist: Ecumenical Convergence in Celebration*. Geneva: World Council of Churches, 1983.

Wainwright, Geoffrey. *Christian Initiation*. Richmond: John Knox, 1969.

Webber, Robert. *Journey to Jesus: The Worship, Evangelism and Nurture Mission of the Church*. Nashville: Abingdon, 2001.

White, James F. *Sacraments as God's Self-Giving*. Nashville: Abingdon, 1983.

Willimon, William. *Remember Who You Are: Baptism, a Model for Christian Life*. Nashville: The Upper Room, 1972.

Eucharist Spirituality

Bodey, Richard Allen, and Robert Leslie Holmes, eds. *Come to the Banquet: Meditations for the Lord's Table*. Grand Rapids: Baker, 1998.

Borgen, Ole E. *John Wesley on the Sacraments: A Theology Study*. Nashville: Abingdon, 1972.

Bouger, Louis. *Eucharist: Theology and Spirituality of the Eucharistic Prayer*. Notre Dame, Ind.: University of Notre Dame Press, 1968.

Bridges, Donald, and David Phypers. *Communion: The Meal that Unites*. Wheaton: Harold Shaw, 1981.

Falardequ, Ernest R. *A Holy and Living Sacrifice: The Eucharist in Christian Perspective*. Collegeville, Minn.: Liturgical, 1996.

Just, Arthur R. *The Ongoing Feast: Table Fellowship and Eschatology at Emmaus*. Collegeville, Minn.: Liturgical, 1997.

Kreider, Eleanor. *Communion Shapes Character*. Scottsdale, Pa.: Herald, 1997.

Laverdiere, Eugene. *The Breaking of the Bread: The Development of the Eucharist According to the Acts of the Apostles*. Chicago: Liturgical Training Publications, 1998.

Macy, Gary. *The Banquet's Wisdom: A Short History of the Theologies of the Lord's Supper*. New York: Continuum, 1993.

Mazzo, Enrico. *The Celebration of the Eucharist: The Origin of the Rite and the Development of Its Interpretation*. Collegeville, Minn.: Liturgical, 1999.

O'Conner, James T. *The Hidden Manna: A Theology of the Eucharist*. San Francisco: Ignatius, 1998.

Reich, Photina. *Bread and Wine*. Translated by H. R. Kuehn. Chicago: Liturgy Training Publications, 1998.

Rordorf, Willy, et al. *The Eucharist of the Early Christians*. Collegeville, Minn.: Liturgical, 1978.

Schmemann, Alexander. *Eucharist: Sacrament of the Kingdom*. Scarsdale, N.Y.: St. Vladimir's Seminary Press, 1988.

Stookey, Laurence Hall. *Eucharist: Christ's Feast with the Church*. Nashville: Abingdon, 1993.

Thurian, Max, and Geoffrey Wainright, eds. *Baptism and Eucharist: Ecumenical Convergence in Celebration*. Geneva: World Council of Churches, 1983.

Watkins, Keith. *Celebrate with Thanksgiving: Patterns of Prayer at the Communion Table*. St. Louis: Chalice, 1991.

Webber, Robert, ed. *The Sacred Actions of Christian Worship*. Vol. 4, the Complete Library of Christian Worship. Peabody, Mass.: Hendrickson, 1994.

White, James F. *Sacraments as God's Self-Giving*. Nashville: Abingdon, 1983.

Multicultural Worship

Adeney, Bernard. *Strange Virtues: Ethics in a Multicultural World*. Downers Grove, Ill.: InterVarsity, 1995.

Bennett, Milton, ed. *Basic Concepts in Intercultural Communication*. Yarmouth, Maine: Intercultural, 1998.

Black, Kathy. *Culturally Conscious Worship*. St. Louis: Chalice, 2000.

———. *Worship Across Cultures: A Handbook*. Nashville: Abingdon, 1998.

Chandler, Paul-Gorden. *God's Global Mosaic: What We Can Learn from Christians Around the World*. Downers Grove, Ill.: InterVarsity, 2000.

Chuang, Tsu-Kung. "Shang-di: God from the Chinese Perspective." In *The Global God: Multicultural Evangelical Views of God*. Edited by A. B. Spencer and W. D. Spenser. Grand Rapids: Baker, 1998.

Corbitt, J. Nathan. *The Sound of the Harvest: Music's Mission in Church and Culture*. Grand Rapids: Baker, 1998.

Costen, Melva. *African American Christian Worship*. Nashville: Abingdon, 1993.

Furnham, Adrian, and Stephen Bochner. *Culture Shock: Psychological Reactions to Unfamiliar Environments*. London: Methuen, 1986.

Gonzalez, Justo L. ed. *Alabadle! Hispanic Worship*. Nasville: Abingdon, 1996.

Hall, Edward. *Beyond Culture*. New York: Doubleday, 1976, 1981.

———. *The Silent Language*. New York: Doubleday, 1959.

Harder, Bernie. "Weaving Cultural Values on the Loom of Language." *Media Development* (March 1989): 25–28.

Hofstede, Geert. *Culture's Consequences*. Newbury Park, Calif.: Sage, 1984.

Lingenfelter, Sherwood G., and Marvin K. Mayers. *Ministering Cross-Culturally*. Grand Rapids: Baker, 1986.

Maynard-Reid, Pedrito U. *Diverse Worship: African American, Caribbean and Hispanic Perspectives*. Downers Grove, Ill.: InterVarsity, 2000.

McDaniel, E. "Nonverbal Communication: a Reflection of Cultural Themes." In *Intercultural Communicaiton: A Reader*, 8th ed. Edited by L. A. Samovar and R. E. Porter. Belmont, Calif.: Wadsworth, 1997.

Pitts, Walter F. *The Old Ship of Zion: The Afro-Baptist Ritual in the African Diaspora*. New York: Oxford University Press, 1993.

Porter, Richard E., and Larry A. Samovar. "An Introduction to Intercultural Communication." In *Intercultural Communicaiton: A Reader*, 8th ed. Edited by L. A. Samovar and R. E. Porter. Belmont, Calif.: Wadsworth, 1997.

Rhodes, Stephen A. *Where the Nations Meet: The Church in a Multicultural World*. Downers Grove, Ill.: InterVarsity, 1998.

Stewart, Edward C., and Milton J. Bennett. *American Cultural Patterns: A Cross-Cultural Perspective*. Yarmouth, Maine: Intercultural, 1991.

Uzukwu, Elochukwu E. *Worship as Body Language: Introduction to Christian Worship: An African Orientation*. Collegeville, Minn.: Liturgical, 1997.

Walker, Wyatt Tee. *The Soul of Black Worship: A Trilogy: Preaching, Praying, Singing*. New York: Martin Luther King Fellowship, 1984.

Whorf, Benjamin Lee. "Science and Linguistics." In *Basic Concepts of Intercultural Communication*. Edited by M. Bennett. Yarmouth, Maine: Intercultural, 1998.

Scripture Index

Subject Index

Author Index